Promises, Promises

Marriage Litigation
in Scotland
1698–1830

LEAH LENEMAN

NMS ENTERPRISES LIMITED

Published by NMS Enterprises Limited
National Museums of Scotland
Chambers Street
Edinburgh EH1 1JF

ISBN 1-901663-52-3

British Library Cataloguing in Publication Data
A catalogue record of this book
is available from the British Library.

Design by NMS Enterprises Limited – Publishing.
Printed by Athenaeum Press Ltd, Tyne and Wear.

CONTENTS

AUTHOR'S NOTE   iv

ACKNOWLEDGEMENTS   v

INTRODUCTION   vii

CHAPTER 1   THE OVERALL PICTURE   1
Case Study 1   Stewart v. Barbour: A Marriage at Midnight   17
Case Study 2   Lowe v. Allardyce: Future Promise = Present Marriage   21

CHAPTER 2   MODES OF PROOF   26
Case Study 3   Murray v. Cranston: The Disowned Wife   45
Case Study 4   Currie v. Turnbull: The Meaningful Scrap   49

CHAPTER 3   CONTESTING A CASE   53
Case Study 5   Stewart v. Lindsay: The Equivocator   70
Case Study 6   Young v. Arrot: The Greatest Villain that ever was   74
Case Study 7   Aitken v. Topham: An Unexpected Twist   80

CHAPTER 4   MISTRESSES   85
Case Study 8   Aiken v. Bartholomew: A Girl over in Edinburgh   97
Case Study 9   Welsh v. Fraser: Call me Mrs   101

CHAPTER 5   NEITHER WIFE NOR MISTRESS   104
Case Study 10   McInnes v. More: A Narrow Escape   115
Case Study 11   Baird v. Campbell: Not for want of trying   118

CHAPTER 6   SEDUCTION   120
Case Study 12   Kennedy v. McDowall: An Incredible Influence   135

CHAPTER 7   RIVAL CLAIMS   141
Case Study 13   Campbell v. Cochran: The Dead Man with Two Wives   151

CHAPTER 8   DEAD BUT WED?   156
Case Study 14   Guy v. Osburn: Lost at Sea   172
Case Study 15   Campbell v. Campbell: Separate Lives   174
Case Study 16   McGregor v. Campbell: An Unequal Relationship   176

CHAPTER 9   SUBVERTING THE NATURAL ORDER   182
Case Study 17   Forbes v. Cochrane: Misalliance   200
Case Study 18   Allan v. Young: The Child Bride   203

CHAPTER 10   ABANDONED CASES   208

CHAPTER 11   UNCONTESTED CASES   215

CHAPTER 12   FREEDOM AND PUTTING TO SILENCE   225

CHAPTER 13   THE VERDICT   233

BIBLIOGRAPHY   240

AUTHOR'S NOTE

M UCH of this book is in the original words of the participants. In all quotations original spelling and punctuation have been retained, except when they impede understanding. Abbreviated words, including 'ye' for 'the', are given in full, and ampersands have been replaced by 'and'. Double ffs have been replaced by capital Fs. Underlinings have been rendered as italic.

Under Scottish law a wife retained her maiden name, whether married or not. Using surnames only after the first mention of the names makes it difficult for the reader to remember which is the man and which the woman, while using the man's surname and woman's first name gives the man a spurious superiority; first names are therefore used throughout.

All CC references in the footnotes are in the Scottish Record Office.

ACKNOWLEDGEMENTS

I GRATEFULLY acknowledge the generous financial support of the ESRC for the research. And I am grateful to the Department of Economic and Social History, University of Edinburgh, for backing and resources. Graeme Morton prepared the Figure in Chapter 1 for me.

I thank Alison Lindsay and all the staff at West Register House for their kindness and assistance. And I thank Professor Rab Houston for telling me about the Session Papers at the Signet Library, and the staff at the Signet Library for their helpfulness.

As always, my work has benefited enormously from the editorial hand of my partner, Graham Sutton, who shares my aversion to the institution of marriage. What the Commissary Court would have made of our 23 years together is another matter.

INTRODUCTION

THE human mating instinct is strong, but an important part of civilisation has been to regulate and channel it, so that families are raised within stable unions. Church and State have created sets of rules that distinguish a lawful union from an unlawful one. Sometimes their control over marriage was very strict, forcing couples to marry in certain circumstances and forbidding them to do so in others.[1] Elsewhere marriage was not actively policed, but there were nevertheless laws defining a valid marriage, and individuals could raise legal actions to validate a union. For example, a woman might claim that she, not the rival newcomer, was the rightful wife of a man, and that her children were legitimate and should inherit his property.

This book deals with such legal actions in Scotland between 1698 and 1830. (Litigation over the breakdown, rather than the establishment, of marriage, has been dealt with in a previous book, *Alienated Affections*.[2]) The records of disputed marriages open a window into the private and domestic worlds of men and women in the eighteenth and early nineteenth centuries. The fascination lies in the universality of emotions expressed within the specific framework of beliefs and social circumstances of that era.

Medieval canon law in western Europe saw the sacrament of marriage as being constituted simply by the free consent of the parties, with the ceremony merely the public affirmation of this. The Reformation no longer held marriage to be a sacrament but did not dispute the axiom that marriage was constituted by mutual consent. But since such consent could be perfectly valid if expressed only to one another, without witnesses, the rest of the community might not know if a couple were legally married or not, and indeed the couples themselves could disagree. Litigation was an inevitable result.[3]

The difference between a legally binding marriage and an illicit affair was obviously important, for, as R B Outhwaite puts it, marriage 'profoundly alters the status of the parties, especially women and any children they might bear; and it is nearly always accompanied by transfers of legal rights and, frequently, of property'. A feminist historian, Laura Gowing, writes: 'Marriage defined women's status, their economic lives, and their social contacts ... for women, the moment of marital choice could be the moment of deciding an identity.'[4]

The word 'choice' is an important one, for as Alan Macfarlane, in particular, has pointed out, over most of the world, both now and in past centuries, marriage has been considered far too important to be left to the individuals concerned. The notion of a man or woman choosing who and when to marry, or whether to marry at all, is a peculiarly western one.[5] Why, then, have individuals chosen to do so? Attraction and companionship are the obvious answers, but historians have sought others.

Some of the reasons adduced – for example, the requirement for children to support their parents in old age – have not been relevant in British society, and others, like women's biological urge to bear children and men's desire to pro-create an heir, never appear to have been dominant reasons in Britain.[6]

The chance to 'improve' oneself, either financially or socially, was certainly a consideration in the eighteenth century, and there were other pragmatic motives. John Gillis argues that in early-modern England most agricultural labourers would live in and therefore have to remain single until they saved enough to start their own households, but from the late eighteenth century onwards employers and overseers 'favoured marriage as a source of cheap, docile labour'. In the towns at this time, he believes, instead of marriage depending on attaining economic independence, men could hope to become their own masters only if they had a working wife as well. 'It was not only what a woman brought to the arrangement, but her labour and housekeeping that made the difference between survival and destitution.'[7]

However, the overwhelming reason for marriage was the desire for compan-ionship, affection and romantic love. Incredibly, the idea that this was a late development, propounded in the past by Lawrence Stone,[8] still has credence amongst some historians today. Gillis claims that 'in the seventeenth century, the idea that two people could find fulfilment in their mutual affection was so new as to be regarded as subversive,' and 'the idea of companionate marriage ... was not fully accepted, even among the middle classes, until the Victorian period.'[9] The evidence is all the other way. Macfarlane cites Shakespeare and Milton in the seventeenth century, and goes back to one of the earliest accounts of the marital relationship in the first encyclopedia to be translated into English, in about 1230, to show the importance placed on love as a basis for marriage.[10] Nor was this merely literary or prescriptive. Martin Ingram, studying litigation in the English ecclesiastical courts between about 1350 and 1640, found that 'something very close to our idea of "romantic love", with all its heartaches and inconstancies, emerges quite strongly from the pages of depositions in matrimonial suits.'[11]

Feminists have found it difficult to believe that companionate marriages existed in any earlier century because of the patriarchal character of the institution. The legal system ensured that men retained the upper hand, and biblical authority was constantly quoted. John Ovington, addressing his 1813 treatise to men, wrote that the husband and wife must be 'of one heart, and of one soul: and each must endeavour in all things to please the other', but went on:

> *Let not your dear partner be displeased at being reminded in an affectionate and friendly manner ... that she owes submission and reverence to her husband, as well as affection. This was particularly enjoined by the Almighty himself. Because the woman was first in the transgression, therefore it was said; 'Her desire shall be to her husband, and he shall rule over her.'*[12]

For modern readers it is hard to see much joy in such an unequal relationship, but we start from a different viewpoint. A woman brought up on the idea that her role in life was to be helpmeet to a superior being would see nothing inconsistent between that belief, falling in love, and enjoying a happy marriage. That would have been the case as recently as the 1960s, and even today the words of the marriage service reinforce the old patriarchal ideal. And, as Robert Shoemaker puts it, 'companionship was not incompatible with patriarchy'.[13]

Also, prescriptive literature seldom matches reality, or even the hopes and wishes of individual readers. Writers on both England and Scotland in the eighteenth and early nineteenth century have noted the importance of the 'ballad heroine', of popular songs with titles like 'I'll Be No Submissive Wife', and of folk songs about women who were prepared to take the initiative in courtship and who looked for romantic love in marriage.[14]

The evidence from Scotland bears out the belief that love was considered of paramount importance long before the end of the eighteenth century. The standard wording for a divorce suit stated that the husband or wife had alienated his or her affections from the spouse,[15] making it clear that mutual affection was the very basis of marriage. Similarly, in the first declarator of marriage case that appears in the registers of decreets, in 1698, the couple were said to have contracted and professed 'a sincere matrimoniall love and affection one towards another'.[16]

This is not to argue that nothing changed over the course of the 132-year period. Various observers noted how differently the sexes interacted in the early and late eighteenth century. John Ramsay of Ochtertyre recorded a 'wonderful change upon female manners, in consequence of playhouses, assemblies and concerts'.[17] But, whereas in the mid-eighteenth century men and women in Edinburgh had 'merry suppers' together, by the end of the century women would retire after dinner, leaving the men to their drink and masculine conversation. Thus, though women had become much better educated, with minds broadened by exposure to the outside world, they had fewer opportunities to converse with men.[18] This was all part of new ideas about masculine and feminine roles. As Shoemaker puts it, by the early nineteenth century, 'women benefited from a broader range of opportunities outside the home, but they were simultaneously constricted by the higher moral standards they were expected to uphold.'[19]

Love and marriage are all very well, but what defined a marriage in Scotland? The 'regular', and commonest, way of constituting a marriage was *in facie ecclesiae*, by having the banns proclaimed three times and then being married by the parish priest or minister in the presence of the congregation. But there were three 'irregular' yet equally valid ways.

The first was *per verba de praesenti*. A couple who were not within the prohibited degrees of kinship and had reached the requisite age – twelve for women and fourteen for men – could solemnly declare that they took each other as husband and wife, and thereby constitute a legally binding marriage. Parents' consent was not a requirement, nor was the presence of witnesses, though obviously the latter was a useful safeguard. In 1868 Lord Neave wrote a song entitled 'The Tourist's Matrimonial Guide Through Scotland', in which he summed up this form of irregular marriage thus:

> *This maxim itself might content ye,*
> *That marriage is made – by consent;*
> *Provided it's done* de praesenti,
> *And marriage is really what's meant.*
>
> *Suppose that young Jocky and Jenny*
> *Say, 'We two are husband and wife,'*
> *The witnesses needn't be many –*
> *They're instantly buckled for life.*[20]

The second 'irregular' method was *per verba de futuro subsequente copula*, a promise to marry in the future, followed by sexual intercourse.[21] (Rosalind Marshall has commented that some nineteenth-century historians misunderstood this form of marriage, sometimes known as 'handfasting', believing that it 'was a trial marriage which could be dissolved at will, but this was not so'.[22]) Lord Neave's verse went on as follows:

> *I ought now to tell the unwary,*
> *That into the noose they'll be led*
> *By giving a promise to marry,*
> *And acting as if they were wed.*[23]

The third method was generally known as 'habit and repute' and was described by a legal commentator as follows:

When a single man and woman cohabit together openly and constantly, as if they were husband and wife, and conduct themselves towards each other, for such a length of time, in the society and neighbourhood of which they are members, so as to produce a general belief that they are truly married persons, their lawful union in matrimony is held to be established by complete and harmonious proof of these facts, without any more direct and positive evidence.[24]

Or, more succinctly, by Lord Neave:

A third way of tying the tether,
  Which sometimes may happen to suit,
Is living a good while together,
  And getting a married repute.[25]

Ironically, it was the Reformation in Scotland that preserved those medieval forms of marriage after 1560. In Catholic Europe the law was altered at this time so that no valid marriage could be performed except in the presence of a priest, thereby placing power over marriage exclusively in the hands of the clergy. That clerical grip was profoundly repugnant to the Scottish reformers, who therefore rejected any such changes.[26] At this time England also continued to adhere to canon law.

In 1563 Edinburgh Commissary Court was created as the national consistory court, the only one that could pronounce on the legal validity of a marriage, though appeal was allowed to the Court of Session (Scotland's supreme civil court) and, after 1707, to the House of Lords. The action was known as a declarator of marriage, and there was also its converse, a declarator of freedom, to repudiate a claim of marriage. In practice, during the century after the Reformation the overwhelming majority of couples married regularly, though a few declarator of marriage actions were raised before the Commissary Court.[27] In 1661 a statute (consolidating statutes of the 1640s) was passed penalising those who married irregularly with fines ranging from 1000 pounds Scots for a nobleman to 100 merks for a person of low status. Judging by cases recorded in the register of the Scottish Privy Council, it seems likely that this legislation was instigated by the propertied classes to prevent heirs and heiresses marrying against their wishes.[28] While in post-Restoration London (roughly between 1670 and 1695) clandestine marriage 'reached epidemic proportions',[29] there was nothing comparable in Scotland during that period, with only a handful of cases surfacing in kirk session (parish court) records.

This all began to change in the eighteenth century, and with more irregular marriages, and an increasingly litigious people, Edinburgh Commissary Court found itself called upon to decide, in an enormous variety of situations, which relationships were to be validated and which were not.

Notes

1   See Anne-Lise Head-König, 'Forced marriages and forbidden marriages in Switzerland: state control of the formation of marriage in Catholic and Protestant cantons in the eighteenth and nineteenth centuries', *Continuity and Change* 8 (3), 1993, 441-65.

2   Leah Leneman, *Alienated Affections – The Scottish Experience of Divorce and Separation 1684–1830* (Edinburgh, 1998).

3   See Martin Ingram, 'Spousals Litigation in the English Ecclesiastical Courts c.1350–1640', in R B Outhwaite ed *Marriage and Society – Studies in the Social History of Marriage* (London, 1981), 35–57, and Lawrence Stone, *Uncertain Unions – Marriage in England 1660–1753* (Oxford, 1992).

4   Outhwaite ed, *Marriage and Society*, Introduction, 11. Laura Gowing, *Domestic Dangers – Women, Words and Sex in Early Modern London* (Oxford, 1996), 7.

5   Alan Macfarlane, *Marriage and Love in England – Modes of Reproduction 1300–1840* (Oxford, 1986), 11.

6   Ibid, 116, 148, 151–2, 258–9.

7   John R Gillis, *For Better, For Worse – British Marriages 1600 to the Present* (Oxford, 1985), 113, 174. Gillis's 'Britain' encompasses only England and Wales.

8   Lawrence Stone, *The Family, Sex and Marriage in England 1500–1800* (London, 1977).

9   Gillis, *For Better, For Worse*, 4, 14.

10 Macfarlane, *Marriage and Love in England*, 158–9.

11 Ingram, 'Spousals Litigation', 50.

12 'But it will depend in a great measure upon you, my dear Sir, to take care that it shall always be her *great pleasure*, to make you happy.' John Ovington, *The Duties, Advantages, Pleasures, and Sorrows, of the Marriage State* (London, 1813), 8, 10–11. Italics in original.

13 Robert Shoemaker, *Gender in English Society 1650–1850 – The Emergence of Separate Spheres?* (London, 1998), 308.

14 Ibid, 38; Deborah A Symonds, *Weep Not for Me – Women, Ballads, and Infanticide in Early Modern Scotland* (Pennsylvania, 1997), c.2; Rosalind K Marshall, *Virgins and Viragos – A History of Women in Scotland from 1080 to 1980* (London, 1983), 187.

15 Leneman, *Alienated Affections*, 7.

16 Scottish Record Office (SRO) CC8/5/1. Cook v. Johnstoun.

17 Quoted in Paul Langford, *A Polite and Commercial People – England 1727–1783* (Oxford, 1989), 109.

18 Symonds, *Weep Not for Me*, 220.

19 Shoemaker, *Gender in English Society*, 34.

20 'Claverhouse' (Meliora C Smith), *Irregular Border Marriages* (Edinburgh, 1934), 153.

21 The question of whether promise *con Copula* 'constitutes very marriage, without any farther proceeding' or whether it 'constitutes no more than an indissoluble precontract' was still being debated in the mid-nineteenth century – see Patrick Fraser, *Treatise on the Law of Scotland as applicable to The Personal and Domestic Relations* (Edinburgh, 1846), Vol I, 164–84. But even in the eighteenth century if a promise followed by intercourse was proved the couple were found to be married persons.

22 Marshall, *Virgins and Viragos*, 28.

23 'Claverhouse', *Irregular Border Marriages*, 153.

24 James Fergusson, *Treatise on the Present State of Consistorial Law in Scotland* (Edinburgh, 1829), 116.

25 'Claverhouse', *Irregular Border Marriages*, 155.

26 W D H Sellar, 'Marriage, divorce and the forbidden degrees: Canon law and Scots law', in W N Osborough ed, *Explorations in Law and History – Irish Legal History Society Discourses, 1988–1994* (Dublin, 1995), 154.

27 There is no way of calculating how many such actions were raised. Only one has survived in SRO.CC8/6/1, but process papers were not kept in any systematic way until

after 1684 when a register of decreets was started. (The first case after that date was not until 1698.) Three additional ones are mentioned in A D M Forte, 'Some Aspects of the Law of Marriage in Scotland: 1500–1700' in Elizabeth Craik, ed, *Marriage and Property – Women and Marital Customs in History* (Aberdeen, 1984), 107–9.

28 Rosalind Mitchison and Leah Leneman, *Girls in Trouble – Sexuality and Social Control in Rural Scotland 1660–1780* (Edinburgh, 1998), 55, and Leah Leneman and Rosalind Mitchison, *Sin in the City – Sexuality and Social Control in Urban Scotland 1660–1780* (Edinburgh, 1998), 128.

29 Jeremy Boulton, 'Clandestine marriages in London: an examination of a neglected urban variable', *Urban History* Vol 20, No 2 (Oct 1993), 208.

CHAPTER 1

THE OVERALL PICTURE

R EASONS for marrying were discussed in the Introduction, but why did couples marry irregularly rather than regularly? This chapter begins by looking at some motives, then describes the chronology of the phenomenon and the celebrators of irregular marriages. After that the focus switches to marriage litigation.

Irregular Marriage – Motives

Historians of irregular marriage in eighteenth-century England have pondered this question. Outhwaite writes: 'Every couple who chose to marry in irregular fashion, rather than to tread the canonically approved path, must have had their own personal reasons for doing so.' But the proportion of those marrying irregularly in eighteenth-century London and Edinburgh was so high there cannot have been all that many personal reasons. Jeremy Boulton described it as a fashion, without being able to explain why it became so popular and continued for so long. But fashion has always defied logical explanation (hence we call it a 'craze'). As has been suggested for Scotland in the heyday of irregular marriage, if one's friends and acquaintances were getting married in this way, then perhaps one simply followed suit.[1]

As Stone emphasises, while a fraudulent minority gave irregular marriage a bad name, most of those who contracted such marriages had no evil intent at all. Some just wanted a modest, quiet affair with no publicity. Those who kept their marriage secret might have had good reasons for doing so. Apprentices who would be in breach of their articles if they married before their apprenticeship was over, and college fellows who would have to resign their fellowships if news of their marriage became public, are two examples provided by Stone.[2]

However, one dominant motive, in Scotland as elsewhere, was parental opposition. Although parental consent was not a legal requirement for marriage, parents and other kin could still wield enormous power over the younger generation. This motive for marrying secretly has a long history: in his study of marriage litigation in England between 1350 and 1640 Ingram found many cases where the marriage was against the wishes of the defendant's family. Gillis writes that in the seventeenth century 'most who resorted to clandestine marriages seem to have been persons of normal marrying age who had encountered parental or parish resistance ….Whether rich or poor, young people often encountered parental opposition and thus were drawn to the alternative forms of marriage that thwarted patriarchal authority.'[3]

Gillis also thinks that though the conflict of generations had a very long history, the tensions were increasing in the early eighteenth century, 'particularly in those areas of mixed agriculture and domestic industry where the family had reconstituted itself as a productive unit'. A situation often encountered by Stone in his study of marriage litigation in early-modern England was 'where one of the partners – usually the man – had or professed to have expectations from a wealthy but cantankerous parent or relative. On the grounds that this benefactor would cut him out of his or her will if it became known that he had married without consent, he insisted that the marriage be kept secret until his aged benefactor should die.'[4]

Such a scenario will recur throughout this book. In some instances there clearly never was any such benefactor and the man made up the story to get the woman to have sex with him. In others the story was initially true, but by the time the benefactor died the man had gone cold on the woman. However, the tale could be genuine, as illustrated in cases where the young man was sent out of the country, the legal action against the woman being fought by his relatives. For example, when William Lauder, eldest son of Sir Andrew Lauder of Fountainhall, baronet, married a household servant, Helen Adam, in 1762, he was sent first to London and then to the East Indies. (She was able to prove her marriage.)[5] In a particularly vicious case George Young, eldest son of a doctor in Edinburgh, had married Margaret Cassa while studying at Leiden in the 1740s. When he returned home his father was so incensed he made certain that his son could not be found and wrote to Margaret (translated from French): 'Hope for nothing from me. My Eldest Son is disinherited, and banished for ever. Look for him in the Indies. He cannot help you.'[6]

Irregular Marriage – Chronology and Celebrators

Marriages constituted without any kind of ceremony or witnesses were obviously risky, and in the seventeenth century the majority of Scots may have been unaware that legally valid marriages could be constituted in alternative ways. Thus couples who might, given a choice, have preferred something more private, felt obliged to marry regularly. This began to change after the Revolution of 1688–9. The establishment of Presbyterianism ousted over two-thirds of Scottish Episcopal parish ministers from their posts, and hundreds of unemployed ministers flocked to Edinburgh, seeking other forms of income. Marriage by such ex-ministers was no more 'regular' than marriage without any minister at all, but it seemed so. Some kind of ceremony was enacted, the right sonorous phrases were uttered, witnesses were present, and a certificate was presented to the couple at the end of it. At the same time no banns were called, so no one could claim an impediment; no awkward questions were asked; and there was an element of privacy or friendly conspiracy incompatible with marriage in a parish church. Irregular marriage became increasingly popular (and in the 1690s the statutes against irregular marriage were amplified to include the banishment of ministers celebrating such marriages). This seems to have created a new market, or at any rate an increasing awareness (particularly amongst the urban populace) that an irregular marriage was perfectly legal. But what if one party claimed to be married and the other denied it? Kirk sessions (parish church courts) became increasingly involved in such disputes,[7] though for a legally binding decision they had to refer couples to Edinburgh Commissary Court.

Edinburgh was always the irregular marriage capital of Scotland, though from the 1730s onwards celebrators of those marriages were no longer Episcopal ministers. In that decade David Strang, a Presbyterian minister who had been thrown out of a northern parish for misconduct, held a near monopoly on the trade. Even excommunication and a spell in jail did not stop him, though toward the end he used an alias. After him no single celebrator predominated, though there were still some colourful characters, like David Paterson, a probationer minister caught *in flagrante*, who gave up the idea of a career in the ministry to earn a living celebrating irregular marriages. Although the Church fulminated against such reprobates, the existence of a specific band of irregular marriage celebrators was actually very useful for kirk sessions, as their handwriting would be recognised on certificates when parishioners presented them as proof of marriage.[8]

In England the heyday of irregular marriage was the first half of the eighteenth century when at least half, and possibly three-quarters, of Londoners married in that way (though few did so anywhere else in England). Hardwicke's Act put an end to this after 1753. In Scotland the peak period varied in different areas. From the 1720s in South Leith, adjacent to Edinburgh, irregular marriages outnumbered regular ones until the 1750s. In September 1731 North Leith kirk session noted that 'a very few of a Long time have been married in that Decent, regular, and publick manner, as the Laws of the Nation both Church and State do allow'. But the heyday of irregular marriages in the west of Scotland appears to have been some decades later. Over the whole of the eighteenth century, it was estimated, something like a third of marriages in Scotland were irregular.[9]

After 1753, when irregular marriage was prohibited in England and Wales, Scottish marriages were still recognised as legal, so some English couples fled to Scotland. For celebrators of irregular marriages, proximity to the border was obviously helpful, and business thrived, so that the very name Gretna Green became synonymous with eloping couples.[10] Whether the London craze for irregular marriage would have spread to other parts of the country, or whether it would have died down without the 1753 Act, cannot be known, and there continued to be ways of avoiding a public marriage in England, whether by special licence, if it could be afforded, or by so-called 'common law marriages' accepted by the community even if not valid legally.[11]

By the late eighteenth century in Scotland there was a phrase in common usage – a 'half-merk marriage'.[12] The actual cost varied enormously. In 1731 a couple paid the celebrator of their marriage five guineas, but the husband was the son of a baronet. In 1740 David Strang charged a couple eight shillings. In 1770 a celebrator 'did insist for half a Guinea for his pains but at last agreed to accept of seven shillings or seven shillings and sixpence'. And in 1775 a witness who had taken a couple 'to the house of one Herd ... who as the deponent had heard was one of the people who made half merk marriages' heard the man ask Herd 'what he would take for marrying them, does not recollect what sum Herd demanded but at last agreed for three shillings'.[13]

The great demand for irregular marriages (and the money to be made from them), coupled with kirk sessions' disapproval, led to a new scam in the second half of the eighteenth century whereby for a suitable bribe some Edinburgh session clerks provided couples with 'lines' stating that the banns had been proclaimed. By presenting such 'lines' to a minister the couple could obtain a 'regular' marriage and could therefore return to their rural parishes armed with a marriage certificate from a minister. In populous city parishes, with a high rate of mobility, ministers could not keep track of all their parishioners, and some innocently assumed that all the couples who came before them really did reside in the parish and the banns had actually been proclaimed. Some simply chose not to enquire closely. And others knew perfectly well that the 'lines' were a sham but demanded them in order to evade any penalties attached to celebrating irregular marriages. Most notorious of these was Joseph Robertson.

Robertson's name first appears in the records as having celebrated a marriage in 1777. He was at that time minister at the Gaelic chapel in Edinburgh where he officiated for many years. Later he was described as minister at Leith Wynd Chapel. By the 1790s he would marry individuals in private houses, though continuing always to demand a certificate of proclamation of banns first.[14] But in 1817 he was old and careless. Two servants of John Grant of Rothiemurchus turned up asking for marriage to two soldiers quartered in Edinburgh. They 'did not wish that Mr Grant should know that they were to be married' nor did the soldiers wish their commanding officer to learn of the intended marriages. The girls 'had heard of a Mr Joseph Robertson marrying a great many persons and they thought that he might marry them when other Ministers might refuse and they did not understand that any proclamation of Banns was necessary'. When the two couples arrived at Robertson's house he said that he would marry them if they got 'lines' from a session clerk. But by this time the authorities were less tolerant, and no session clerk could be found to provide this document, so he married them anyway. Unfortunately, after the marriage the soldiers demanded the 'lines', so Robertson's accomplice, an innkeeper called Pearson, forged them. After Grant of Rothiemurchus complained, Robertson and Pearson were brought to trial. It could not be proved that Robertson knew that the document had been forged, but the statute ordaining banishment for celebrators of irregular marriages was still on the books, and though the advocates debated 'whether it would be expedient to bring this old man to trial for what in a Clergyman of more respectability would perhaps have been passed over without notice', he was in fact banished, and a plea for mercy on account of his second wife, then pregnant with a fourth child, failed.[15]

Basically, the tolerance of celebrators of irregular marriages that prevailed in the mid-eighteenth century did not survive into the nineteenth. Fortunately, there were other ways of marrying irregularly yet obtaining written confirmation – particularly in the west of Scotland. Kirk sessions kept control of their parishes for considerably longer in the Glasgow area, and in Barony parish from the 1770s onwards when couples came before the session to acknowledge themselves married the session wrote out a declaration for them to sign; the session retained the document and recorded the marriage on that date.[16]

A secular means of registering an irregular marriage was to appear before a Justice of the Peace, admit that such a marriage had been entered into, pay the fine required under the seventeenth-century statutes, and thereby obtain documentary evidence of the fact. Many examples could be cited throughout the second half of the eighteenth century, and by the early nineteenth century one town was renowned for the willingness of its magistrates to do this. In 1820 a defender argued that 'Rutherglen marriages are proverbially ridiculous in that part of the Country as being nothing more in general than the effects of a drunken frolic,' but as the couple had appeared before a Rutherglen magistrate, acknowledged themselves married, and paid the requisite fine, the marriage was declared valid.[17] In 1827 a man was persuaded to accompany a woman 'to the Town of Rutherglen, and then and there to have what is called a Rutherglen marriage performed by acknowledgement in presence of Witnesses before one of the Magistrates and a Justice of Peace in the said Town, that they were married persons'.[18]

By the 1820s the Commissary Court became increasingly hostile to this corrupt procedure. In one action raised in 1824 it was found that Glasgow magistrates had a supply of printed forms with blanks left for names and dates, and the commissary (judge) who discovered this complained:

it would appear that upon statements manifestly collusive and fictitious a decree has been obtained from a Court which has no Consistorial Jurisdiction for the real purpose of constituting or declaring a marriage under the pretence of imposing an illusory fine, and that this practice has become so common that there is a printed form of procedure for it bearing one hundred merks as to be imposed in all cases and because it may be at least doubtful whether such alledged proceedings are not to be altogether rejected as inadmissible.[19]

5

But the procedure appears to have continued at least until the mid-nineteenth century when the Court of Session 'strongly discountenanced these proceedings, and recommended to the Lord Advocate to prosecute parties engaged in them, as having incurred the penalties directed against clandestine marriages.'[20]

Although Hardwicke's Marriage Act meant that after 1753 the law of marriage was fundamentally different in England and Scotland, the attitudes of the courts toward irregular marriages had diverged well before that time. The English distinguished between 'clandestine' marriage, in which a ceremony had taken place, and 'contract' marriage, in which the couple simply agreed to be married. English ecclesiastical courts were so hostile to contract marriages, regardless of the canon law in their favour, that such marriages (or, at any rate, litigation concerning them) disappeared by the 1730s. The Commissary Court evinced no hostility to such marriages, so naturally they – and the attendant litigation – continued.[21]

In the course of the late eighteenth century an increasingly sophisticated populace, particularly in Scotland's rapidly growing cities, tended to resort to litigation over a variety of issues and also became more aware of the possibilities inherent in Scotland's marriage law.

Marriage Litigation

Two types of cases – attempting to prove or disprove a marriage – came before the court. The first was a declarator of marriage. This usually included adherence, which would, in theory, force an individual to cohabit with, or alternatively (if a man) pay alimony to, the spouse. If brought by a woman such an action would often also demand legitimacy for the children. The second type of case was one for freedom and putting to silence, which would not only legally repudiate the 'marriage' but also prohibit the defender from publicly claiming to be married to the pursuer. (This type of action also existed in England while irregular marriage was still allowed, where it was known as jacitation.)[22]

The procedure for both types of cases was the same. The person raising the action (the pursuer) would hire a lawyer as his or her 'procurator' in court plus one or more agents to do the investigative and clerical work. The lawyers would draw up a 'libel',[23] with the facts supporting the pursuer's claim. This would be accompanied by a summons that would be delivered to the defender. If the action was contested the defence would present the alternative view of events. The pursuer, if he or she desired, could give in replies. On the basis of these documents the commissaries (judges) would decide if there was a case to answer and allow both parties a proof. Over time, and to avoid quibbles, before allowing a proof the commissaries came to demand a 'condescendence of relevant facts', in which the points to be proved would be set out systematically with a note of the witnesses who would be cited to prove them. Answers would be given in to the condescendence and then a revised condescendence and revised answers. At any stage of the proceedings either party had the right to appeal to the Court of Session and, after 1707, to the House of Lords, although in the early nineteenth century they would have to petition the Commissary Court before they could do this.

Written evidence might comprise a marriage certificate or letters or an acknowledgment of being married. A woman who claimed to have yielded to a man under promise of marriage, and who could not bring any proof of this, could demand that the man appear in court to be judicially examined under oath. In some instances a woman, whether pursuer or defender, might also be ordered to do this. At such times the individual's own testimony is heard, unfiltered through lawyers. But men could lie under oath – or at least convince themselves, and sometimes the court, of a version of events very different from the woman's. As a result there evolved a fallback position: if the woman had sex with the man believing herself married, but the court did not uphold that marriage, then she must have been seduced and could claim damages for seduction.

After considering all the evidence the commissaries would record their decision (which might, of course, be appealed against), followed later, if appropriate, with an award of aliment or damages or expenses. An additional amount was payable for 'extracting' the decreet (decree), which meant that every word in the process papers was transcribed into a volume. (After 1823 only the final decision was recorded in the volumes, so it became much cheaper – but much less use to the historian, who has to sift through process papers.) Extracting a decreet was costly and not a legal requirement, and therefore many cases were never recorded in this way. And, of course, cases were abandoned at all stages of the proceedings.[24] Process papers were kept somewhat more systematically after a register of extracted decreets was begun in 1684. Papers for cases that went to appeal were sometimes sent to the Court of Session or the House of Lords and not returned, but fortunately printed summaries have survived amongst the Session Papers at the Signet Library.

The first declarator of marriage case after the court began to keep a register of decreets was in 1698. Between that date and 1830 some 506 cases of marriage or freedom were initiated. Unavoidably, the last decade is an underestimate since many of the final cases were transferred to the Court of Session after the Commissary Court was wound up and do not appear in the records.

As can be seen in Figure 1 (page 22), the rise in declarator actions began in the 1730s, when irregular marriage first became the 'fashion'. This rise continued in the following decades, but in the 1770s (when figures for divorce cases shot up) there were actually fewer cases, and the peak came in the first decade of the nineteenth century, just as irregular marriage was going out of fashion. Thereafter numbers diminished slightly. This is an entirely different picture from that of divorce, where numbers rose dramatically in the 1770s and continued to rise inexorably after that.

Figure 1: Declarator Actions Raised 1700–1829

Is there an explanation for this pattern? In the principality of Neuchâtel (now part of Switzerland), divorce was allowed from the mid-sixteenth century onwards, and the same courts ruled in all questions regarding marriage in Neuchâtel. Jeffrey Watt, looking at the court records, found a dramatic rise in marital litigation during the eighteenth century, but whereas between 1550 and 1700 disputed promises of marriage were the commonest cases, during the eighteenth century they were far outstripped by divorce suits (426 to 218).[26] Divorce spelled freedom, and an increasing desire for personal freedom is one explanation for the rise in divorce actions. In many cases both parties wanted a divorce, and the action was in reality collusive and very easily accomplished. The rise in litigation over irregular marriages (in many cases constituted without any ceremony) was part of an overall rise in litigation in Scotland, but it could never parallel divorce because it could never become routine and straightforward.

Of the 506 Scottish cases, 417 were for declarator of marriage and 89 were for freedom. Thirty-eight (7.5 %) were raised as counter-processes to an action initiated by the other party. Most of those (29) were raised by a defender in a suit of freedom finding herself (or, in seven cases, himself) forced to prove a marriage. Raising a counter-suit of freedom was usually a pointless exercise seemingly motivated by bloody-mindedness, since if the marriage action failed freedom would be automatic. Twenty-one of the 506 cases were rival suits, where two women or two men fought to be recognised as the rightful spouse.[27] (The uneven number is because one woman fought in the English courts, while her rival raised her action in Scotland.)[28]

Apart from rival suits, no less than 96 other litigants married someone else before or during the legal action. In actions for freedom the connection is usually obvious: after a marriage, or the intention to marry, was made public another individual would claim to be the true spouse, and the only way to rebuff them was to raise such an action. But 65 of those – 57 of them men – married to someone else were involved in declarator of marriage cases. Several reasons could apply. One is that the marriage provoked the action by the 'wronged' party. A second is that a defender thought that by marrying someone else he or she would influence the court. Lawrence Stone provides examples of this in English marriage litigation, remarking:

> *A common way of short-circuiting litigation about a disputed marriage was for one of the parties publicly to marry another person while the trial was still in progress. The ecclesiastical courts did their best to stop such marriages by issuing injunctions against them. In practice, however, when faced with a litigant's legal marriage in church, and often with a family on the way, they were usually reluctant to break up such a union and would recognise it as valid.*[29]

However, the Scottish situation was different. The Commissary Court had no right to intercede in any way if a litigant chose to marry someone else while fighting a declarator of marriage action, and a regular marriage celebrated during the course of the process would certainly not be favoured over an earlier irregular one.

A third reason was that legal actions could go on for years, and some defenders simply wanted to get on with their lives – even if it did mean gambling that the action against them would fail. And finally, some actions raised were in hopes that a newly married man would be willing to pay off a woman from his past. Only 14 (22 %) of the 65 cases with second marriages were successful.

A spouse did not have to be alive for a declarator of marriage case to be raised against him or her. A woman finding her claim to be a widow disputed by his kin could raise such an action against them, and 25 of them did so (and another defender died during the course of the action which was then carried on against his relatives).[30]

There were cases where the pursuer had raised a divorce suit on the grounds of adultery but, finding the marriage challenged in that action, had to prove a valid marriage before proceeding to obtain a divorce.[31]

The gender stereotype was that women sought declarators of marriage, on the grounds of having been sexually prevailed upon and then betrayed, while men sought declarators of freedom, on the grounds of being pestered and battened upon by women with romantic delusions. The figures confirm this. Of declarator of marriage cases, 371 were raised by women and 46 by men. Of freedom cases, 69 were raised by men and 20 by women.

This picture is likely to have been period-specific. Watt, who looked at marriage contract litigation in Neuchâtel from 1550 to 1806, commented that 'the most striking contrast between eighteenth-century litigation and that of the previous period is the remarkable increase in the proportion of female plaintiffs.' Up till then men had 'slightly outnumbered women among plaintiffs who sought to enforce contracts [the equivalent of Scots pursuers seeking a declarator of marriage]. In the eighteenth century, however, women were an unambiguous majority.'[32]

There was also a social class stereotype – the young laird versus the servant girl – but the definition of social class is problematic in this period. For divorce cases a crude division has been made between aristocracy, gentry, and 'common'.[33] This did not prove possible for marriage cases. For one thing, in divorce cases the assumption of the time could be adopted: that a woman, whatever her own social background, was raised to a man's status by marrying him. This obviously could not be done in declarator of marriage cases when the fact of that marriage, and hence her status, was the point of the dispute. Also, in divorce and separation cases the rank or status of either of the parties was not at issue, whereas in marriage litigation it was relevant for a woman to argue that she was of equal rank to the man she claimed as her husband, while the man argued that she was below his rank and therefore could not have believed that he meant to marry her. The disputed facts and interpretations over this issue, which feature in a number of cases in this book, make it difficult to categorise litigants.

Even distinguishing between, say, tradesmen and professionals or the propertied and unpropertied was not viable. Men who began as carpenters could end up as lawyers, and when it came to assessing financial circumstances for aliment or damages a humble weaver could turn out to be receiving rents from houses or hold bonds and securities. The distinction between gentry and non-gentry was also a non-starter because of the way litigants dragged in relationships, however distant, with members of the gentry class. The only category that proved quantifiable was that where both parties were designated servants or labourers: 80 were counted. But the extent to which this is a meaningful category is questionable.

The other way in which social class is important is in access to justice. A legal action before the Commissary Court, in theory, was meant to be available to all, but in practice the costs varied enormously, deterring some and causing others to drop their cases. In a two-and-a-half-year case, commencing in 1790, where the man raised a declarator of freedom and the woman a declarator of marriage, after the woman proved her marriage the man was found liable for expenses of about £15, and in 1796 a man who lost a case of declarator of marriage was found liable for expenses of £21. But in 1825 a man who had successfully refuted a declarator of marriage, but had been found liable for damages for seduction, had to pay £77 expenses, and in a similar case of 1828 the man was found liable for £145. Naturally the more complex the case, the more paperwork, witnesses etc were required, the more it would end up costing.[34]

Table 1: Success Rates

Marriage

	Total	Female	Male
Successful	174	156	18
Unsuccessful	168	148	20
Abandoned	75	67	8
TOTAL	417	371	46

Freedom

	Total	Female	Male
Successful	76	19	57
Unsuccessful	9	0	9
Abandoned	4	0	4
TOTAL	89	19	70

Table 2: Contested Marriage Cases that Reached a Conclusion

	Total	Female	Male
Successful	81	73	8
Unsuccessful	168	148	20
TOTAL	249	221	28

Table 3: Effects of Pregnancy on Success Rates

	Women pregnant or bore children		Women not pregnant or bearing children	
Successful	47	(26%)	26	(30%)
Unsuccessful	103	(58%)	45	(52%)
Abandoned	28	(16%)	15	(17%)
TOTAL	178		86	

There were, in fact, still some small amounts in the early nineteenth century: two men who lost cases in 1805 had to pay £8 and £12 (equivalent to about £230 and £350 at today's prices).[35] Also, under Scottish law, litigants who could prove poverty (normally by a certificate from the parish minister) could fight a case under 'benefit of the poor's roll', and have all costs met.[36] In marriage and freedom cases 9 % of litigants did so.[37] Twelve of those were lower-class couples, meaning that both partners of 68 lower-class couples had sufficient means to pay for the legal action themselves. Not surprisingly, 41 of the 43 who received the benefit were women.

One might expect that men and women would go to the trouble and expense of a legal action only if they had a good chance of success, and that was certainly true in divorce cases, where 84 % were successful.[38] But, as revealed in Table 1, while this was also true for cases of freedom, where 85 % were successful, it was not so for marriage cases, where only 42 % succeeded.

Another contrast with divorce suits is the proportion contested. Less than a third of divorce suits were contested.[39] In marriage cases, leaving aside 27 cases abandoned too soon after commencement to be contested, the 297 contested cases are 76 % of the total. (The percentage of contested freedom cases is much lower, at 53 %.)

Unlike divorce actions, which by the beginning of the nineteenth century were often routine and dispatched within three months, most declarator of marriage suits involved a genuine legal battle. In a few of the cases where the husband was dead and his relatives refused to recognise the woman as his widow, the mere raising of a legal action was enough to persuade relatives to concede her rights, and those cases were uncontested. Most uncontested cases, however, were in reality simple adherence cases in which a lawyer mistakenly believed it necessary to include a conclusion for declarator of marriage as well. If we look only at contested cases which reached a conclusion – in Table 2 – the picture for pursuers is much starker. Only one-third of the women who raised marriage suits that were contested won; and the success rate was similarly low among the small number of men in the parallel situation.

Studying marriage litigation in eighteenth-century Neuchâtel, Watt found that a pregnant woman was far more likely to win.[40] The Commissary Court was always mindful that a declarator of marriage suit could concern the children as much as their parents, and in at least one case when a woman settled her case out of court, the commissaries insisted that her lawyer continue the action on behalf of the child, who was not a party to the woman's decision.[41] Nevertheless, as can be seen in Table 3, in contested cases pregnancy or bearing a child did not aid women pursuers.

As noted earlier, however, women did have a fallback: if they could not prove marriage they might still win damages for seduction. Of the 371 female-initiated marriage cases, 126 contained the alternative clause. Nineteen of them were successful in proving a marriage; 25 out of the 107 unsuccessful were granted damages for seduction.

Motives for raising a declarator of freedom action were usually obvious: apart from the embarrassment and annoyance of having someone going around claiming to be your spouse, he or she might incur debts or sign documents in this guise. The motives for declarator of marriage suits could be more complex. As noted earlier, some women raised a declarator of marriage suit only as a prelude to one for divorce. It seems unlikely that many women would have believed, or even desired, that the men who had deserted them would again cohabit with them, particularly after a long and bitter court battle. Nevertheless, they would possess the status of a 'wife'. So, that was one motive. Another was financial. If a husband refused to cohabit with his wife then the court would order him to pay her aliment (alimony) for the rest of his life. Under Scottish law a man had to maintain his illegitimate children, and in nearly all cases where children were involved the man was already paying maintenance, but a woman would be awarded much more if she was his wife and the mother of his legitimate children. And the claim of many male defenders that the woman knew perfectly well that she was not married to him but hoped only to extort money was in at least a few cases well grounded.

The question of how many pursuers genuinely believed they were married is not straightforward. Very few set out with deliberately false claims, though the belief might arise only after the end of the relationship, when a deserted woman learned of her rights under the law. Given legal advice that, unless she had good written or verbal evidence, the case might turn on the man's admission or denial under oath, most female pursuers presumably not only believed in the marriage, but that their man in his heart of hearts also believed in it. Such women would learn the hard way about pillow talk, words spoken in drink, and selective memory.

The following chapters present the material thematically rather than chrono-logically which, inevitably, obscures changes over time (though cases are presented chronologically within each relevant section). This was, of course, a period of massive change, of proto-industrialisation, enclosure and agricultural revolution, the breakdown of a monolithic church structure, and rapid urbanisation. It was also the period of the Enlightenment, of new ideas and of new ideals of behaviour. The latter, more than any other aspect of change, is manifest in marriage litigation. During the first half of the eighteenth century both sexes were outspoken about sexual matters, and women could be as rowdy and as bawdy as men. The rise in the cult of 'sensibility' (a cultivated state of emotional engagement with the pleasures and woes of others) and an Enlightenment belief in progress from the vulgar 'animal' passions toward greater refinement and delicacy redefined the feminine as embodying the desirable qualities.[42] Thus frank or bawdy language had to be confined to masculine company and was certainly not to be used in court.[43]

In the court records there are types of language and behaviour acceptable during the first half of the century but shunned by the end of it. Two words which crop up only occasionally in the eighteenth century but which constantly recur in the nineteenth are 'respectable' and 'respectability'. With the rise in literacy and the sentimental novel, love letters were likelier to contain poetry and, indeed, toward the end of our period a Valentine card formed part of the evidence in one case.[44] Nevertheless, as indicated in the Introduction, readers looking for evidence of a seismic shift in the marital relationship will be hard put to find it in this source.

Two particular questions arise. In the nineteenth century it was generally believed that marriage was so easily constituted in Scotland that a word spoken in jest could tie a man for life.[45] The figures above, showing the high proportion of failures, suggest that it could not really have been that easy after all. But the belief was so very strong that a more in-depth look at a variety of cases is needed before determining whether it had any validity at all.

Second is the question of whether irregular marriage was, overall, a 'good thing' or a 'bad thing' — and whether this was equally so for both sexes. Some English historians view irregular marriage as a 'problem' that was solved by Hardwicke's Marriage Act.[46] But this view has been questioned, one writer claiming that it greatly disadvantaged women, and another arguing that the pre-1753 system 'was better attuned to reality, more sensitive to the needs of women and men of all statuses'.[47] Again, this is a question better left until the evidence is assimilated. Meanwhile, in the intervening chapters and case studies we will enter into the minutiae of relationships, both licit and illicit.

Notes

1   R B Outhwaite, *Clandestine Marriage in England 1500–1850* (London and Rio Grande, 1995), 54; Jeremy Boulton, 'Clandestine marriages in London: an examination of a neglected urban variable', *Urban History*, Vol 20, No 2 (Oct 1993), 209; Rosalind Mitchison and Leah Leneman, *Girls in Trouble – Sexuality and Social Control in Rural Scotland 1660–1780* (Edinburgh, 1998), 70.

2   Lawrence Stone, *Uncertain Unions – Marriage in England 1660–1753* (Oxford, 1992), 24–5.

3   Martin Ingram, 'Spousals Litigation in the English Ecclesiastical Courts c.1350–1640', in R B Outhwaite ed, *Marriage and Society – Studies in the Social History of Marriage* (London, 1981), 50; John R Gillis, *For Better, For Worse – British Marriages 1600 to the Present* (Oxford, 1985), 96, 101.

4   John R Gillis, 'Conjugal Settlements: Resort to Clandestine and Common Law Marriage in England and Wales, 1650–1850', in John Bossy ed, *Disputes and Settlements – Law and Human Relations in the West* (Cambridge, 1983), 268; Stone, *Uncertain Unions*, 24.

5   CC8/5/9.

6   CC8/5/6. Although Margaret managed to prove her marriage, Dr Young found evidence of her adultery and procured a divorce. The story is told in Rab Houston and Manon van der Heijden, 'Hands Across the Water: The Making and Breaking of Marriage Between Dutch and Scots in the Mid Eighteenth Century', *Law and History Review* 15 (1997), 215–42.

7   Mitchison and Leneman, *Girls in Trouble*, c.4; Leah Leneman and Rosalind Mitchison, *Sin in the City – Sexuality and Social Control in Urban Scotland 1660–1780* (Edinburgh, 1998), c.8.

8   Ibid.

9   Boulton, 'Clandestine marriages in London', 203; Leneman and Mitchison, *Sin in the City*, 132; T C Smout, 'Scottish Marriage, Regular and Irregular 1500–1940' in Outhwaite ed, *Marriage and Society*, 218.

10 Outhwaite, *Clandestine Marriage in England*, 131–5; Gillis, *For Better, For Worse*, 195; 'Claverhouse' (Meliora C Smith), *Irregular Border Marriages* (Edinburgh, 1934).

11 Gillis, *For Better, For Worse*, 196–228. Gillis is convinced that a substantial proportion of couples in early nineteenth-century England and Wales were not legally married but were considered to be common-law spouses by their communities; Outhwaite, *Clandestine Marriage in England*, 139, disagrees.

12 The phrase appears in the Commissary Court records in – among others – the case of Trotter v. Muirhead in 1783, CC8/5/17. It is mentioned in William Chambers, *The Book of Scotland* (Edinburgh, 1830), 215. I am grateful to Tristram Clarke for this reference.

13 Fowlis v. Kinloch, CC8/5/4; Nairn v. Richardson, CC8/6/14; Miller v. Bogle, CC8/5/14; Mackalpin v. Thomson, CC8/6/34.

14 Steedman v. Miller, CC8/6/37; Watson v. Ferguson, CC8/6/45; Gray v. Anderson, CC8/6/62; William v. Lindsay, CC8/5/36; Thomson v. Rankin, CC8/5/41; MacGregor v. MacNeill, CC8/6/159 and 160.

15 High Court of Justiciary records, Scottish Record Office, JC4/9 and AD14/17/139. The encyclopedia of ministers, the *Fasti*, states that Robertson died in 1801, but the author also thought that he did not adopt the name Joseph Robertson Macgregor until 1784, whereas in fact he was using it in 1777 (though he later dropped it), and it seems safe to assume that this was the same man. (Hew Scott, *Fasti Ecclesiae Scoticanae*, Vol 1, (Edinburgh, 1915), 30.) According to James Fergusson other celebrators of irregular marriages were treated similarly by the High Court in 1812 and 1818, but the names he mentioned do not appear in Commissary Court records. (James Fergusson, *Treatise on the Present State of Consistorial Law in Scotland* (Edinburgh, 1829), 115.) In the 1930s one author wrote: 'There is record of one Joseph Robertson, who, finding it no longer possible to make a living by marrying in Edinburgh, migrated to London, and died miserably there of hunger, 1830–1840.' ('Claverhouse', *Irregular Border Marriages*, 18.)

16 Leah Leneman and Rosalind Mitchison, 'Clandestine Marriage in the Scottish Cities 1660–1780', *Journal of Social History* Vol. 26, No 4, 859.

17 Baleangall v. Monach, CC8/5/39.

18 Creech v. Yuille, CC8/6/166.

19 Wylie v. Hamilton, CC8/6/155.

20 Patrick Fraser, *Treatise on the Law of Scotland as applicable to The Personal and Domestic Relations* (Edinburgh, 1846), Vol I, 148.

21 Lawrence Stone, *Road to Divorce – England 1530–1987* (Oxford, 1992), 79–81.

22 Ingram, 'Spousals Litigation', 41; Stone, *Road to Divorce*, 192. According to the latter, jacitation was quite widely used in the seventeenth century.

23 Obviously the word came to have a very different meaning in English legal terminology, though both have their roots in canon law and the Latin *libellum*, or little book (ie written rather than oral evidence). I owe this point to W D H Sellar.

24 Volumes of extracted decreets in the Scottish Record Office have the prefix CC8/5; boxes of process papers have the prefix CC8/6.

25 Leah Leneman, *Alienated Affections – The Scottish Experience of Divorce and Separation 1684–1830* (Edinburgh, 1998), 14.

26 Jeffrey R Watt, *The Making of Modern Marriage – Matrimonial Control and the Rise of Sentiment in Neuchâtel, 1550–1800* (Ithaca and London, 1992), 174–5, 199.

27 Such cases were also found by Ingram in his study of England 1350–1640. Ingram, 'Spousals Litigation', 41.

28 Laura Manners v. John William Henry Dalrymple and Johanna Gordon, CC8/6/96 and CC8/6/100. This exceptionally complex case, in which the future Earl of Stair was found by English courts to have been legally married under Scottish law to Johanna in 1804, although he subsequently married Laura in England, is summarised in John W Cairns, 'A Note on The Bride of Lammermoor: Why Scott Did Not Mention the Dalrymple Legend until 1830', *Scottish Literary Journal*, Vol 20, No 1 (May 1993), 19–36.

29 Stone, *Uncertain Unions*, 198.

30 If both parents were dead, and their kin disputed the children's legitimacy, it was possible to raise a declarator of legitimacy to prove the parents' marriage (or, alternatively, the relatives could raise a declarator of bastardy to disprove it). Such cases have been collected, and transcribed onto disk, by me, but do not form part of this book, as they go off on different tangents.

31 Examples are Young v. MacLauchlane, 1777, CC8/6/35; McCulloch v. Stevenson, 1798, CC8/6/64; Baleangall v. Monach, 1820, CC8/5/39.

32 Watt, *The Making of Modern Marriage*, 200.

33 Leneman, *Alienated Affections*, 15.

34 Thomson v. Tweedie *et contra*, CC8/6/55; Callander v. Fraser, CC8/6/62; Turphy v. McCandie, CC8/6/146; Buchanan v. Lindsay, CC8/6/156.

35 Ferguson v. Peacock, CC8/6/81; Henderson v. Pitbladdo, CC8/6/79. The comparison with today's prices comes from a table of equivalent contemporary values of the pound, a copy of which was kindly supplied to me by Ann McCrum.

36 Such a provision, *la loi des pauvres*, was introduced into the courts of Neuchâtel in the eighteenth century. Watt, *The Making of Modern Marriage*, 175.

37 In the early period a few of those applied for, and were granted, a 'gratis warrand', ie not to have to pay to have witnesses summoned, and I have counted them as equivalent to receiving the benefit of the poor's roll. Not all litigants applied when they raised their actions; some did so only after it became clear that the case would not be over quickly and would therefore cost more than a minimal amount. The equivalent percentages for divorce and separation actions were 7 and 8. Leneman, *Alienated Affections*, 15.

38 Ibid, 13.

39 Ibid.

40 Watt, *The Making of Modern Marriage*, 202–3.

41 Aiken v. Bartholomew, 1792, CC8/5/20.

42 Stana Nenadic, 'The Enlightenment and the Passion for Portraits', *University of Edinburgh Journal*, Vol 37, No 3 (June 1996), 172–3.

43 Cf. 'Consider every species of indelicacy in conversation as shameful in itself, and as highly disgusting to us. All double entendre is of this sort. The dissoluteness of men's education allows them to be diverted with a kind of wit, which yet they have delicacy enough to be shocked at when it comes from your mouths, or even when you hear it without pain and contempt. Virgin purity is of that delicate nature, that it cannot hear certain things without contamination.' Dr Gregory, *A Father's Legacy to His Daughters* (London, 1826 edn), 28–9. This treatise first appeared in 1770 and went through numerous editions after that.

44 Miller v. Martin, 1825–8, CC8/6/156.

45 *Report of the Select Committee on Marriage (Scotland)*, PP 1849, XII, 7; Chambers, *The Book of Scotland*, 213; 'An Advocate' (F P Walton), *Marriage Regular and Irregular* (Glasgow, 1893), 19.

46 Outhwaite, *Clandestine Marriage in England*, 17; Boulton, 'Clandestine marriages in London', 192.

47 Eve Tavor Bannet, 'The Marriage Act of 1753: "A Most Cruel Law for the Fair Sex"', *Eighteenth-Century Studies*, Vol 30, No 3 (1997), 233–54 (I am grateful to Mary Prior for bringing this to my attention); John R Gillis's review of Outhwaite, *Clandestine Marriage*, in *Women's History Review*, Vol 6 (1997), 294.

CASE STUDY 1

STEWART V. BARBOUR: A MARRIAGE AT MIDNIGHT

THIS early case is typical of its time (1731) in the language used and in the hurly burly behaviour, almost impossible to imagine amongst members of the gentry class later in the century. But it is also archetypal in concerning a young man knowing that his family would disapprove of his choice of spouse and marrying clandestinely to achieve his end.

John Stewart was the Earl of Moray's nephew and heir. In 1730 he fell in love with Sibilla Barbour, whose deceased father had been a baillie of Inverness. Obviously she was not of his rank, and he knew that his family would have a more exalted marriage in mind for him. Indeed, when he first told her brother, Daniel, of his intention of marrying her, asking 'his Consent and Concurrance', Daniel 'thanked him for the honour he did his family, and at the same time desired him to give over thoughts of it, Because of the Consequences which would ruine both the defender and pursuer To which the defender made answer he very well knew the Consequences if such a thing should come to his friends their knowledge, but that he would keep the affair secret.' Daniel continued reluctant the second time John asked him, but the third time, seeing the young man's determination, he agreed, provided a minister could be found to marry them. At John's request he wrote a letter to be delivered 'to any man who would undertake to marry the pursuer and defender, and the Letter bore that the Gentleman to be married was a Gentleman of the Army not Nameing him'.

On the night in question, in November 1730, the couple crossed the Moray Firth and shortly after midnight awakened the minister of Logie, Angus Morison. There is no indication why this minister was chosen, and he greatly regretted his involvement subsequently. He later told those who questioned him that a young gentleman 'whom he did not know but Called himself an English officer with whose Countenance Morison was frighted came to his Bed side at Logie desiring the Minister to marry him with a Young Lady who was at the door … which Mr Morison refused at first but that the Gentleman pressed him so hard being flushed with some passion … at last he agreed.' But it was not all stick and no carrot, for he was also heard later to complain that he had been cheated by them, 'as he got only Three Guineas and Seventeen Shillings in Silver, but Expecting he would have got Twenty Guineas'.

In any case, he was hustled out of bed, and on a spot of ground near the house the couple 'joined hands and mutual vowes past betwixt them'. They were in such haste, he said, 'they would neither take the Doctrinal part nor benedictory part That he only said God bless them'. Later Morison wrote to the Commissary

Court: 'I told them Expressly That they might Marry if they pleased but that they needed not Expect the Ceremony of me ... they may be married or not married but I refused my part viz The Ceremony, Now that which I call the Ceremony viz first a proper prayer concluding with the Lords prayer Secondly a sermon on the reall notion and Incumbent dutys of marriage and to end with the proper Benediction viz The Grace of our Lord &c which I absolutely refused .... It is true I saw them join hands and Interchanging the Matrimoniall vow If that be a reall Marriage before God, in case they come togither, I Leave that decision to divines, I fancie Isaak had no more, but how can I be Called in Question when I denyed my part.' When a neighbouring minister of the gospel 'said to him That if he had Celebrat such a Clandestine Marriage it would be a Grievance to him and a reproch upon the Clergie To which Mr Morison Answered That it would be a marriage in Moses time, or in time of the Councill of Neice [sic] whatever might be made of it by the Laws of Scotland.'

Within a few days of the marriage rumours were circulating. Shaw Mcintosh of Borlum, John's 'Intimate Commerade', eventually got the truth out of him, when John told him that he was indeed married to Sibilla 'and would own her as his wife in spyt of all the world, and Expressed himselfe on that Occasion in strong and affectionate Terms Towards the pursuer, But that in the mean time it was proper for him to conceall it'. Shaw told him that since the report of the marriage was spreading, 'it was Idle for him' to go on trying to keep it secret. John said that 'he Expected by the Duke of Argyle, the Earle of Islay and the Lord Advocate their Influence to have a Commission in the Army, and how soon he obtained it, and was settled he would be in a Condition to Live without the assistance of his parents if they Continued to be disobliged, and untill then he thought it proper to Conceall his marriage but then he would own it and Live with the pursuer all his Life.'

There had been no chance to consummate the marriage until then, but John now enlisted the help of Shaw. He asked his friend 'to press him in publick Company to sleep with him that Night Telling him at the same time he designed to bed with the pursuer ... owning that tho he had been married to her for Two or three Days, he had not yet got an opportunity of bedding with her.' Shaw's only problem was that another man, a Mr Draper, had arranged to call round that night. He came very late, along with the quartermaster, after Shaw and John had already gone to bed. The two of them 'had concerted that should feigne themselves asleep that they might go away But Master Draper sat down on the bedside and waked the defender ... they Drunk a Bottle of Wine Togither, and then Mr Draper and the Quartermaster went off.' It is easy to imagine John's impatience through all this, and as soon as the others had gone he leapt out of bed and dressed; Shaw accompanied him to Daniel's Barbour's house and left him there, keeping his door unlocked so that John could return at any hour of the morning. He got back at about five and told Shaw that he had been to bed with Sibilla 'and had been the happiest man alive ever since he left him and that he had consummatt the marriage … and particularly said he had Fuck't her Five severall times'.

A day or two after this pressure was being put on John. Baillie John Stewart of Inverness asked him to disclaim the marriage, 'To which he answered that he had rather be torn to peices betwixt horses before he would do the Young Lady such an act of Injustice.' The baillie and another John Stewart, quartermaster, then went to Sibilla asking her to deny the marriage 'to save her husband', but neither she nor John would agree. They then 'Concerted he the husband should go south and Endeavour to Conceall his marriage for some time from his friends and if he prevailed she was also to conceal it But if that could not be done they were both to own their marriage and she to stay at home with her friends and he to go abroad to push for himself.'

But John did not have the courage to confess to John Forbes of Culloden, who, aged 60, seems to have been the figure of authority in Inverness most feared by him. Culloden (as he was known) testified that John had denied the marriage 'in the most solemn manner, and with the most horrid Oaths and Imprecations with his hands Lifted up to Heaven'. On the following day Culloden 'Examined him more Closely because he suspected Notwithstanding of what he had Swore That he had not told him the Truth And thereupon he … renewed the same Oaths Denying the Marriage and asserting his Innocency Upon which the deponent said to him, John, goe in to town this night to this assembly take your Leave of the Ladies in publick, and as you wish me or your self well, or Ever Expect to Find Favour with My Lord Morray and his Family Return to me this Night and I shall have horses and Servants ready for you that you may goe off tomorrow morning and if possible be with your Father before this Villainous Idle story come to his Ears.'

John did just that and played no part in the court proceedings, being far, far away. His relatives then got to work. First they tried to bribe Daniel Barbour with 'a Large Sume of money' to be given to his sister if she would not contest a declarator of freedom action. One of them, 'Commissary Stewart', got together a lawyer and several other gentlemen to question Angus Morison, the minister. John's relatives also threatened and tried to bribe Morison. Indeed, Morison himself never appeared in court, being too fearful of his safety. His servant, Donald Chisholm, who had been present when the couple were married, did appear and testified 'that Mr Angus Morison his old master told him That if he came up to Edinburgh to be a witness in this Case he would be taken and hanged'. Donald spoke no English and his testimony was translated by an interpreter. When one of John's relatives asked Morison if his servant had not witnessed the marriage he 'answered Yes, but he understood English as well as Greek or Hebrew'. However, Donald 'had seen severall marriages celebrated' and had no doubt 'that this was a marriage'.

The quartermaster John Stewart, aged 29, was another to whom John eventually confessed his marriage, and he was present just before John left Inverness when the witness heard John say to his wife, 'Dear Sibby, Conceall it from all the world till you hear from me from the South,' and when they parted the quartermaster saw them 'Embrace one another affectionatly and shade [sic] Tears each of them, at the seeing of which the deponent owned he was affected'. The Earl of Seaforth testified that 'it was commonly reported and believed in that Country That the pursuer and defender were married togither and the deponent himself believed it from the common report.' He added that Sibilla 'had the Character in the Country and amongst all his acquaintances of a virtuous Young Lady without any blemish'.

John's relatives initially raised an action of declarator of freedom, hoping, perhaps, that Sibilla's relatives would not contest it, but she raised a counter-process of declarator of marriage. The weight of evidence was so great that attempts to deny it were futile. The commissaries found 'The saids John Stewart ... and Sibilla Barbour husband and Wife' and ordained him to adhere to her. As with virtually all of our cases, we do not know what happened after that, but given the apparent strength of feeling displayed by both parties, it is to be hoped that his relations eventually accepted this *fait accompli*, and that the couple lived happily ever after.

CC8/5/2

CASE STUDY 2

LOWE V. ALLARDYCE: FUTURE PROMISE = PRESENT MARRIAGE

THIS case must have fuelled the myth that it was easy to 'trap' a man into marriage in Scotland, for an Englishwoman in a similar situation would not have been considered married. The action ran from March 1791 until November 1797, being appealed to the Court of Session and up to the House of Lords, but all the courts concurred in declaring a marriage.

Katharine Lowe was the daughter of a physician in Brechin. William Allardyce, aged 23, who also lived in Brechin, was in the service of the East India Company. After a brief but passionate courtship, in March 1791 William, according to Katharine, 'read over the marriage service from the Book of common prayer, and made the pursuer do the same thus mutually pledging and vowing themselves to be married persons ... and by actually declaring himself her husband he prevailed upon her to submit to his embraces,' and they slept together for several nights at her father's house. William was seen leaving the house at 'untimeous' hours and was caught in bed with Katharine by a servant, so word got out and Katharine said that they were married. A family meeting was called when William insisted he still intended to marry her in the future but was in no position to do so now and was about to embark for the East Indies. He wrote to her father: 'I take the first opportunity of avowing My regard for Miss Lowe to you, but to enter into matrimony in my present situation would be absolute ruin to both her and me, and if we should have any progeny entailing misery on them for ever.' And after the family meeting he reiterated this. It was something of a shock to him when she raised an action of declarator of marriage – and got a warrant stopping him from leaving the country.

'It is with extreme sorrow that I see you have been induced to adopt such a measure', he wrote to her, 'from which in honor to you I should imagine had you followed your own inclination common delicacy would have restrained you. I shall only observe that instead of gaining the end proposed it will irritate me beyond any possibility of a reconciliation, at the same time if you consider a law suit in this case must prove extremely detrimental to your character, as in vindication of myself I must mention some circumstances that I should otherwise be shocked to utter of any young lady.' He also rehearsed his own version of events, 'reminding' her that in December her father 'repeatedly urged me to go to you which I at last did, and being inflamed with liquor and your appearance in a loose dress I ventured to take some innocent freedoms, but without saying any thing that could induce you to think I had any affection for you.' There were many things 'falsely stated' in the summons he had received: 'It is said that you consented to submit to my embraces in consequence of my promising to marry you and of vowing perpetual fidelity to you both by words and in writing. This I positively deny as I never wrote to you till after the circumstance took place and in no one of my letters did I promise to marry you, on the contrary I declared that at present I would not, but hoped that in a few years by improving my fortune I might be enabled to do so. With regard to my verbal promises, they were extremely vague as I never specified any time, and you continually declared you did not believe them.' He now believed that 'this plan has been concerted long ago', and concluded, 'I am sorry to think that you could with so little delicacy proclaim to the world that we had slept together for two nights especially as you know that it was at your instigation that I did so the first night.'

Fortunately for Katharine he had also preserved her letters to him. On 12 March she wrote to him: 'Sir You must be confident to yourself how much you have injured me, and taken every opportunity to betray my honour which to me is preferable to life, and must appear in the same light to every virtuous woman. [I] therefore think it incumbent on you to make your words good, and perform what you so often promised.' On 31 March she wrote of her 'great surprise and astonishment' at reading his letter: 'In trying to vindicate yourself you would insinuate that … your visits were in consequence of my invitations when my father was from home. You surely cannot forget how you prevailed on me the Sunday evening before I sent you the Card to promise to inform you when my father went away or was engaged. From my earliest infancy I was taught to regard a promise in the most sacred light, and accordingly I kept mine to you. I wish to God I could rely with as much ease on the performance of your promises to me. As to any concerted plan I solemnly declare, it never once entered into my head. So far from it, I did as you desired me and kept every thing secret. Your being seen go out of my fathers house at untimeous hours soon spread and my sister Mrs Sievewright soon hearing of it, enquired the particulars and finding it no longer possible to conceal our correspondence, I was obliged to inform her that your professions were honourable. She having told her husband he informed my father that there had been proposals of marriage between us, and not till after you wrote him, denying what you well know to be truth did any one hear from me of our having slept together and I never would have spoke of it but trusted altogether to your honor …. Consider my Dear Sir what could I do. It was public in the world that you had been seen leave my fathers house at improper hours, the maid had seen us in bed, you had refused the connection – I was obliged to speak out the truth or be turned out of doors. My situation was and is truly deplorable.'

Her appeal fell on deaf ears, and when William appeared in court for his examination he depicted his view of the sexual double standard with breathtaking candour. 'Being interrogated when he expressed his attachment to Miss Lowe, was it in such a manner that she might understand it to be that of an honorable lover, or such as one that wished only for her favors without marriage might employ?

Declares That in the beginning of their acquaintance .... Miss Lowe must have understood the attachment which the Declarant expressed for her to be that of an honorable lover but after the liberties which she allowed him to take without his having given her any promise of marriage or having given her any reason to understand that he was to marry her she from the tenor of his behaviour must have altered her opinion and must have seen that the Declarant had other views than those of marriage.' He insisted that he had not promised her marriage before their first intercourse, 'but afterwards he might have asked her to marry him, and this he might have done to avoid a lawsuit which was threatened when he was under orders to join his Regiment in India'. He admitted that 'the answer that the Pursuer gave to this proposition of marriage was that she was willing to marry him.'

With regard to her allegation about his reading to her the marriage service, he said that 'sometime after the declarant had enjoyed the pursuer they being together in the house of her father and rumaging over some books that were lying on a table they lighted on a Prayer book which they looked into and read part of the marriage ceremony, but in reading altered some of the words in a jocular manner, as for example when they came to the passage "I plight to thee my troth" they together exclaimed "I plight to thee my kiss" and upon this they kissed each other.'

The first time he asked her to have sex with him she declined, and when she finally agreed he admitted that 'they had been a considerable time in the room together and had been professing mutual regard. That the Declarant had said to the Pursuer at this time that he liked her better than any other woman and being interrogated on the part of the Court whether from what passed on this occasion the pursuer must not have conceived that his intentions were honorable Declared that any other lady must have conceived that opinion but he does not think that the pursuer ought to have done so, as she had before allowed him to take liberties which appeared to him inconsistent with decency but the Declarant at this time did not mention marriage.' At the meeting with her relatives he 'acknowledged in presence of this company that he had paid honorable addresses to Miss Lowe, but that his purpose for doing so was to get liberty to go and join his Regiment in India but this purpose he did not mention'.

It is rare to find a man prepared to damn himself so unwittingly but compre-hensively as this. Nevertheless, Katharine decided not to rely just on the written evidence and his oath but to call witnesses as well. The first four whom she proposed were his counsel and agents; the fifth was her own agent. She realised that this was unusual but argued that after the action had been raised those witnesses alone had heard him not only declare his honourable intentions but also admit that he had promised to marry her. Naturally his side strongly protested, on the grounds that anything that occurred after the 'libel' was inadmissible evidence. The commissaries concurred, but after an appeal to the Court of Session – on the

23

grounds that 'events may occur subsequent to the period comprehended in a lybel which may tend most materially to support … allegations made in the lybel with regard to the grounds of Action set forth in it' – she was allowed to cite those witnesses. In the meantime she had produced a number of witnesses from Brechin who all testified to her virtuous character since childhood.

The first of his 'agents', an Edinburgh lawyer named Black, described receiving a letter from a Brechin lawyer about William who, when he left Brechin, had been seized under warrant in Perth and taken to Edinburgh. Black and the Brechin lawyer went to Charles Hay, advocate, for advice, who suggested they also took the advice of the Dean of the Faculty of Advocates, Henry Erskine. It was suggested that William be allowed to go north again to discuss the situation with his mother, brother and relations, and, according to Black, the Dean (Erskine) said 'that if there was a chance of a marriage being declared betwixt the pursuer and defender it was surely best to avoid as far as possible the Defenders criminating the woman who was to be his companion for life and that the Defender ought to advise coolly with his friends before proceeding at all in any kind of litigation on the business.' William himself seemed to Black at this time 'willing to do whatever his counsel and the deponent should advise him, though he did not appear to the deponent at that time to have any fixed resolution on the subject nor indeed as far as the deponent could recollect seemed very well to understand his then situation nor said much on the subject except that he never would marry Miss Lowe in answer to which the Dean informed him that that was by no means the question, for that the question to be determined by the Commissaries was not whether he should marry her but find that [sic] whether he was already married.'

The Honourable Henry Erskine, Dean of the Faculty of Advocates, told the court that 'from the multiplicity of business in which he is engaged, and the period that has elapsed' he could remember very little of the meeting, though he recollected that he had advised William 'to return to Brechin with Mr Sievewright and to act towards the lady as a gentleman and a man of honour in his circumstances ought to do.' He did not explain at the time 'what he meant by that advice … but when advising a Gentleman to conduct himself towards a woman as a man of honour ought to do, he the deponent certainly meant, and is incapable of meaning any thing else than that he should fulfill any promise or promises under which he was conscious of having come to her.'

Katharine's family members also appeared as witnesses. They all said that he had promised to marry her. Her sister remembered that 'during the course of that evening Mr Allardice said very often that he would marry the pursuer at some future time, but would not marry her immediately on account of his circumstances, Dr Lowe said that need be no stop because the pursuer should live in family with him as she had done formerly till his situation enabled him to take her home to a house of his own to which Mr Allardice answered that he did not wish to marry till he could afford to take his wife with him.'

It is clear from the above interchange that at this time Katharine and her family did not believe that William was married to her any more than he did and it was only the advice of lawyers that made her realise how strong a claim she had. (Her libel included the alternative conclusion of damages for seduction if she was unable to prove a marriage.) In April 1793 the commissaries found it 'clearly proven that a *copula* took place betwixt the parties in the course of an honourable courtship and in consequence of a solemn promise of marriage' and that those facts were 'relevant to infer marriage between the parties', therefore finding them married persons. William could not accept this and appealed to higher courts but simply ran up higher expenses doing so.

We have here been presented with two very different views of sexual standards. One held that a woman who slept with a man, no matter what the circumstances, could not expect the same regard from him, and the other that a man, if need be, must protect the woman's virtue by marrying her. Scottish marriage law went even further along the lines of the second view, by making sexual intercourse after a promise actually constitute the marriage.

CC8/5/22

CHAPTER 2

MODES OF PROOF

Looking at the types of proof used in declarator of marriage cases opens a window into perceptions of what went into making a particular relationship a marriage. Lawyers may have seized on the more legally satisfying modes, but witnesses talked about the things that spelled marriage to them.

If some kind of 'ceremony' had taken place, then witnesses to that ceremony were important (though, as we will see in the course of the book, a 'ceremony' of itself was not enough to constitute a marriage). The idea that a marriage was not complete until the couple were publicly 'bedded', although it had no basis in law, continued in popular culture during the eighteenth century, and witnesses to a 'bedding' were as important as those to a 'ceremony'.

Couples irregularly married were normally given some kind of certificate or 'marriage lines'. So-called 'marriage lines' were important modes of proof in many cases, but of course they could be forged – and they could also be stolen or burnt. Another form of written evidence (sometimes also referred to as 'marriage lines') would be an acknowledgement by the man that he promised to marry, or considered himself already married to, the woman. Then there were the contents of letters. If a man addressed a woman in his correspondence with her as his wife, or signed himself her loving husband, this was very strong evidence that he considered himself to be married to her, though, inevitably, words in letters could be ambiguous, with each side interpreting them differently. The next best thing to having had a ceremony witnessed, or possessing something in writing, was for witnesses to have heard the man acknowledging himself married.

If a couple had been cohabiting for some time before the man left her and claimed that he had never been married to her, then another important strand of evidence concerned his behaviour toward her. In all classes, people had ideas about the conduct of a husband and wife toward each other, and if a man and a woman conformed to their ideas then witnesses would consider them to have been a married couple. The point was not that a certain type of behaviour constituted a marriage, but that this behaviour revealed that the man was lying when he stated that he had never considered himself married to the woman.

From a legal viewpoint the usefulness of such evidence would vary, but it is always revealing of perceptions of marriage.

All those modes of proof are discussed in this chapter.

Ceremony and Bedding

In the 1771 case of Janet Miller (daughter of a wright in Glasgow) against James Bogle (a farmer's servant), James Ballantyne, weaver, was asked, one evening in December 1766, to accompany the couple as a witness to their marriage.[1] He 'at first declined this as he never had been witness to any such private marriages but … he at last agreed.' Not only that, but he fetched 'one Robert Liddell a Soldier whom this deponent knew was in use to marry people together'. When Liddell arrived

he was desired by the pursuer and defender to marry them together which Accordingly he Liddell did after the form and practice of the Church of England by reading the Office in the Prayer Book – That the pursuer and defender declared themselves single persons and agreed to accept of one another as husband and wife and he the said Liddell declared them married persons and the deponent also saw the said Liddell write marriage lines which he thinks he subscribed not with his own Name but by the name of William Clark and saw him deliver the said Lines to this pursuer.

Ballantyne subsequently heard James Bogle 'say that he would go next day to a Justice of Peace and get himself fined for his irregular marriage'. Afterwards it was agreed that they should be bedded in the house of William Ranken, baker in the Gorbals, so Ballantyne and the other witnesses to the marriage accompanied them there, 'where this deponent saw the pursuer and defender in naked Bed together and that William Ranken and his wife were then also present'.

We have here a marriage 'ceremony' carried out by a soldier, who gave them a marriage certificate (signed in a false name), followed by a 'bedding', and with the intention of registering this irregular marriage by going to a JP to be fined. Yet James Bogle raised an action of freedom against Janet Miller, forcing her to raise a counter-process to prove her marriage – in this she was successful.

In a 1775 case where both parties were servants – Margaret Mackalpin against Walter Thomson – Margaret stated that a few months earlier they went to Edinburgh and in a house in the Pleasance which she understood to be possessed by Charles Johnston they were privately married 'by the person whom she then took to be the said Charles Johnston, but whom she now understands to be one Thomas Herd'. Charles Stewart, 'journeyman gingerbread maker in Portsburgh [Edinburgh]' met the couple, whom he knew by sight, at Dalkeith fair, when William talked of marriage and asked Stewart if he 'would direct him to a proper person to celebrate their marriage'. According to Stewart, William 'was so impatient to have the ceremony performed that he would not stop when the deponents Master proposed to take a little refreshment on the road'. Stewart took them 'to the house of one Herd who lives at the head of the plaisance with whom he was a little acquainted and who as the deponent had heard was one of the people who made half mark marriages'. Stewart saw that Herd 'joined their hands together and declared them married persons'. Thomson denied all this, and the case was abandoned.[2]

A 'bedding' was not necessarily preceded by any kind of ceremony. A couple who had privately acknowledged themselves married to one another could use the 'bedding' ritual to make this public. In the 1760 case of Charlotte Armstrong (daughter of John Armstrong younger of Sorbie) against John Elliot younger of Halgreen, she stated that they 'did constitute marriage between them by mutual consent and declaring their acceptance of each other for husband and wife'. John had been advised by John Scott, a friend, to acknowledge Charlotte as his wife, so, taking Scott with him, he roused her father from his bed and 'said to the Company "this is my wife" and in a Little time thereafter proposed going to bed with her, to which the pursuers Father said he had no Objection since they Acknowledged themselves to be man and wife.' Once they were in bed together Charlotte's father

> took a bottle of Brandy in his hand and invited the Company to go along with him and drink to the young folks good Luck, which being done the said John Scott sate down upon the side of the bed wherein the defender and pursuer were lying and spoke first to the defender thus 'John do you acknowledge Charlotte Armstrong for your lawfull wife' to which he the defender answered yes and then put the same question to the Complainer 'do you Acknowledge John Elliot to be your lawfull husband' to which she also answered Yes and thereupon the said John Scott declared them married persons, and the next morning being friday the said John Scott went into the room wherein he and the other company left them the night before in bed and found them still in bed, and having asked the pursuer how she liked to lye with a man, the defender made answer this is not the first time we have slept together, we have slept together often before now.[3]

This was one of two rival suits (the successful one) and is discussed further in Chapter 7.

Alan Macfarlane argues (for England) that consummation was essential to marriage, and the bedding ritual was meant to demonstrate this.[4] Under Scottish law consummation was not necessary unless the marriage had been constituted by a promise only, but the idea of viewing a newly married couple in bed goes back centuries in both countries, though by the eighteenth century the bawdy element had been removed, and it had been turned into a polite ritual.

In the 1795 case of Janet McCulloch (daughter of a 'cow keeper', ie dairy farmer, in Glasgow) against Robert Stevenson, brush maker, Alexander Paterson, who kept a shop opposite Janet's father's house, testified that in February 1794 he *was Invited by Joseph McCulloch to be present at the bedding of the pursuer and defender And to Supper on that Occasion, That accordingly he went to McCullochs house in the Evening and Saw the parties bedded as husband and Wife That he heard the defender when in bed after taking a Glass from the hand of the witness drink to Janet McCulloch as his Wife and then to the pursuers Father and Mother as his Father and Mother in law.*[5]

During the supper (which clearly took place *after* the bedding) Paterson 'drank to the health of the parties as New Married persons and the Entertainment was considered as a Marriage Supper'. Robert married another woman – regularly – after this, but the commissaries found his irregular marriage to Janet valid.

Something in Writing

Before the end of the eighteenth century the commonest form of written evidence was a marriage certificate. Because of its importance in helping to prove a marriage, a man attempting to disprove a marriage might steal or destroy it. In the above case of Janet Miller who was married to James Bogle by a soldier called Liddell, she appeared in court and declared that the man who married them gave them marriage lines which she put 'in her Bible but in a Fortnight thereafter she missed them out of her Bible and believed they were stolen'. She was a servant at the time to a cousin of James Bogle and thought that his relatives took it. Fortunately, there was so much other evidence that the certificate was unnecessary.[6]

The 1762 case of Helen Adam against William Lauder, eldest son of Sir Andrew Lauder of Fountainhall, baronet, was a classic one of a wealthy heir falling in love with a servant, marrying her clandestinely, falling foul of his relatives, and regretting the deed.[7] William was sent abroad and his family fought the case on his behalf. According to Helen, before going he had broken open her 'Chest or Trunk at Fountainhall and taken away or abstracted the forsaid Certification or Declaration of their marriage thereby vainly thinking to have Deprived the pursuer of that evidence of their marriage'.

William's brother, Andrew, testified that William had admitted the marriage and then subsequently denied it.[8] Andrew was in the dining room at Fountainhall when Helen 'came in and made a Great noise', crying out that William 'had taken away a paper out of her Chest, upon which her happiness in a great measure depended'. William, according to Andrew, 'said nothing, but as she made a hideous noise she was turned out of the room' (and, next day, out of the house). But Andrew testified that William 'did acknowledge to the deponent that there had been marriage lines between him and the pursuer And that she once had them in her possession.' And William's sister, Anne, testified that Mr Hall, the children's tutor at Fountainhall, told her that he had taken the lines out of Helen's chest at William's request, and that 'the said marriage lines were destroyed'. Helen's lawyer pointed out that 'the Examination of Miss Lauder furnished proof of fresh ground of complaint, of the unjustifiable measures, taken by the defender and his freinds by employing Mr Hall the young divine in a Service so unsuitable to his character.' (Hall himself 'had after he was personally Cited as a witness, either been put out of the way or absconded and fled to England, in order that the pursuer might be deprived of the benefit of his evidence'.) Helen won her case, and the theft of the certificate proved evidence as powerful as the certificate itself would have been.

The above were examples of a marriage certificate being destroyed, but not all marriage claims were genuine, and women sometimes produced forged certificates. In response to the action of freedom raised by George Lobban in Aberdeen, Isabell Wilson produced a marriage certificate allegedly signed by the couple and by David Strang and witnesses. George declared that the signature was not his and that he had never been married by Strang or anyone else. Strang himself appeared in court and declared that he had not signed the certificate or married the couple. So where did this certificate come from? Elizabeth Murraylees, who did not like George and did not think that Isabell should marry him, testified that David Strang had at one time lodged with her. Subsequently George came to her enquiring after Strang, saying that 'Strang was a damned Villain for he had heard that he had given lines that he was married to the defender which was not true.' (Elizabeth's response to this was 'are you going to deny your marriage with Bell Wilson I am sorry she had Ever any thing to do with you you have ruined many young women are you going to ruin her too.') Subsequently George told Elizabeth that 'he had been with Strang and drunk a Bowll of punch with him and his wife and Strang said That he should meet with no trouble for he would do the pursuer any service that was in his power.' So it seems that Isabell paid Strang to produce a false certificate but George paid him more to repudiate the certificate in court. Perhaps Isabell should have raised her offer, for George's action for freedom was successful.[9]

In 1782 Elizabeth Smith produced a certificate of marriage to William Cockburn, tenant in Monktonhall. He claimed that the marriage lines were 'a gross forgery and fabrication being all of one person's write and not signed by different parties and witnesses as therein pretended'. The commissaries found that 'the Certificate of Marriage now produced Appears to Ocular Inspection a Manifest forgery' and assoilzied the defender.[10]

By the end of the century the term 'marriage lines' came to mean a written acknowledgement of the marriage rather than a certificate. A sensible woman, however passionately in love, would obtain such a document before she went to bed with her beloved.

In the 1790 case of Elizabeth Ritchie against James Wallace in Ayrshire, Elizabeth produced the following, dated 7 January 1785: 'I James Wallace son to John Wallace of Wallace Grove do hereby acknowledge that you Elizabeth Ritchie daughter to Alexr Ritchie in Drumley is my lawful wife and will Solemnize the

Marriage regularly between us in the terms of the rules of the Church as soon as convenient for us and I am your Loving Husband.'[11] He claimed that this was a forgery and did all he could to stop the crucial witness, Janet Telfer, from testifying. Janet Telfer declared that in midsummer 1785 the couple asked for her help. Elizabeth was pregnant and James wanted her to go to Edinburgh to bear the child; he asked Janet to accompany her and offered her money for the expenses. Janet 'told him she had a greater regard for her Character than to employ her time or attention upon his or any other mans Miss, but that if he intended to make her his wife and would do so She would do every thing in her power to serve him'. At James's suggestion, Janet then went into Ayr and got a copy of 'marriage lines', which James then copied out, inserting their names, which he signed, as did Janet as a witness. When Elizabeth said 'she was affraid the lines were not sufficiently binding' James 'lifted up his hand and said "He wished he might never see Gods face in Mercy if he would not fulfill every article of the Marriage lines",' and gave the document to Janet to keep.

But a few days later James had second thoughts and asked Janet to return the lines to him, 'for that if she did not he would either drown himself or leave the Country as his friends were enraged at the Marriage'. Janet refused. James then tried to get Elizabeth to put pressure on Janet, and once again demanded the lines from Janet: 'he appeared then to be in a passion and stamped with his foot saying what right had she to keep possession of them.' Janet gave the document to the parish minister. James left the country for some years, but on his return Elizabeth raised her declarator of marriage action and was successful.[12]

In the 1790 case of William Thom(p)son, clock and watchmaker in Biggar, against Jean Tweedie, William had regularly married another woman and raised a declarator of freedom against Jean for saying that he was already to married to her, whereupon she raised a counter-action of declarator of marriage against him.[13] Jean, who had been his uncle's servant, possessed no less than three written declarations from him. The first read: 'Biggar 25 – 1787. I give you these few lines to prove that I intend to marry you when time and (here is a blot) is most convenient to this I certify you to be my lawfull wife (signed) William Thompson clockmaker.' She was not satisfied with this, so he granted her another written declaration on 27 January 1788: 'That you are to be my lawfull wife and I your lawfull husband till death'. Jean showed those declarations to her brother who doubted if they were 'strong enough expressed', so she asked for yet another, which he granted on 24 February 1788: 'That you are my lawfull wife and I your lawfull husband from this date till death.' After that she felt secure enough to go to bed with him, 'and he often Slept with her'. He told her that his reason for concealing the marriage 'was the dependance he had on his friends from whom he expected money'.

But some time later William asked for the declarations back, when Jean 'expressed her surprise and said, "Will are you changed now." He 'answered no "If there be a God in heaven I will never change till death.'" However, after that he 'behaved in a Cold and indifferent manner and drew up with another young woman in the Country with whom he even went the length to be proclaimed'. In his defences William insisted that he did

> not remember of being concerned with any of the lines produced, or of giving them to this pursuer altho he may have scribbled some such writings upon loose Bits of paper, which she might perhaps have picked up or taken out of his pocket, when he chanced to change his cloaths at his uncles house.

He also claimed that he had never had intercourse with her; she responded that she could even prove that he had 'told this Circumstance to different persons of his Acquaintance, adding at the same time what was very base that the lines (as he termed them) had been given for this purpose to have his will of the pursuer which he had obtained'.

When William appeared in court he could not sustain his lawyer's nonsense of remembering nothing about the declarations. He stated that 'when he granted the two first lines he Understood them to imply no More than a promise of Marriage to take place when convenient for himself or after the lapse of some years And being Interrogated by the Court what he Understood by the words contained in the third writing … Declares that as the pursuer had threatned to drown herself, he Wrote the line to pacify her And that he was in Such confusion of Mind that he did not know the Meaning of what he had written.' The marriage was declared to be valid.

In the 1814 case of a lower-class couple in the Bo'ness area, Margaret Kindred against David Grant, labourer, the following 'lines' were not written by the man but still proved the marriage: 'This lines do testify that I David Grant do take this woman Margaret Kindred to wife to this I do solemnly promise before God (signed) David Grant May 18th 1812.'[14] In his defences David stated that he could 'neither write, nor read write' (this phrase, which occurs quite often, meant he could read print but not handwriting). She responded that after she agreed to marry him he

> went to a most intimate acquaintance of his own, and solicited him to write and subscribe for him, a copy of the lines which he had received when he was married, as he said he was intending to marry the Pursuer, but that as they had not yet been able to procure the necessary articles for a house, they meant to keep the marriage secret for half a year thereafter.

David got the lines from his friend, Robert Cuthbertson, and gave them to Margaret, 'assuring her at the same time, that these lines established a marriage to all intents and purposes as valid and effectual as if the ceremony had been performed in the regular way'. She 'believed this assurance, and not only admitted the Defender to all the privileges of a husband but actually left her service and went to her Mother's house to provide the necessary articles for her own house, which was intended by the parties to be taken up at the term of Martinmas 1812'.

As the document was admitted not to be in his hand, the proof had to depend on his testimony in court. He declared that 'Robert Cuthbertson labourer one time when he was in company with him advised him to make out marriage lines and to get himself married by them as he had done himself.' David had said that 'he did not think persons could marry themselves in that way' – but Cuthbertson told him he had done so himself, and gave David a copy of his own marriage lines. David 'was unwilling to take them, but at last was prevailed upon to do it and that "through bare silliness and ignorance of the world" he gave the lines he received from Cuthbertson to the Pursuer'. David was then asked by the court what his intention had been and replied that 'in giving the Lines "he meant marriage at the time", being incited to it by the persuasion of Cuthbertson.'

> Interrogated whether after delivering the Lines to the Pursuer he considered himself married to her, Depones and answers, 'Yes at that time' – Interrogated at what time he began to think he was not married to her, Depones that it was about a twelvemonth after when he saw that he could not live happy with her and 'that therefore it was better to leave her then, than at an after period' – Interrogated how he came to discover that he could not live happy with her, and whether he had lived with her during the twelvemonth after giving her the lines. Depones that he did not live with her, but that he went to see her occasionally in order to pay his best respects to her and in that way discovered that he could not live with her, as his wife.

This was found to be a valid marriage, and David had to pay her an annual aliment of £6 (and expenses of £17).

The case of Jean Laing against George Reid Esquire of Ratho Bank was classic insofar as she was his servant at the time of the secret marriage in 1808, but unusual insofar as she continued to be employed as a servant in various other households in the years that followed, with only occasional meetings between them, until she raised her action of declarator of marriage in 1817.[15] The 'lines' which he gave her in October 1808 stated: 'I hereby engage to be a true a faithful a kind and an affectionate Husband to you on conditions you are the same to me and I further engage to shew this to no person, and to make it known to nobody whatever without your consent.' She entered his service in 1803, and said that he started talking of marriage as early as 1804.

> Mr Reid was much under the influence of his mother and sisters and perhaps also of 'The world's dread laugh / Which scarce the firm Philosopher can scorn'. He was therefore extremely anxious to keep secret his attachment to the Pursuer but flattered himself, and

her with the expectation that he would one day have the fortitude boldly to come forward and avow it in the face of the world.

George could not deny that he had written the declaration, but 'It certainly was not meant to constitute a marriage at that time, and the parties never considered themselves as married …. A marriage did not consist in writing foolish pieces of paper without any date …. It was altogether incredible that if the defender had married her and acknowledged her as his wife … he would have allowed her to go into service and wished her to remain there.' Furthermore, the declaration 'did nothing more than describe the conduct that he would oblige himself to observe if he should become a married man. It said that he engaged to be a true a faithful a kind and an affectionate husband ….That was no act of marriage *de presenti*. It was a declaration that might be made fifty times to any person without any marriage taking place or any intention of a marriage.' But the commissaries, taking into account other evidence, such as letters (discussed below), declared them to be man and wife.

John Martin gave Jean Miller the following in January 1825: 'I hereby sware and aledge that Jane Miller is my Lawful Wife from this date hereafter, and that no female has or will have any clame to me after this said date but her, and I say before as many wittnesses as the frinds of Jane Miller wishes to bring forward, to clame her as my wife,' after which they were publicly bedded.[16] His defence was that on the day in question

> *when he was about to Sail from Greenock as Mate of a vessel proceeding on a foreign voyage, the Pursuer came from her place of residence at Port Glasgow down to the Quay at Greenock, a distance of three Miles, and threw herself into the Water near the place where the Vessel was lying, and in the view of the Defender and the rest of the Crew, who with great difficulty succeeded in getting the Pursuer out of the Sea.*

She was taken to the house of a relative nearby. John (he claimed) was forced to go there and threatened with imprisonment 'unless he instantly signed a paper acknowledging her to be his wife'. He had 'no recollection whatever of writing or subscribing any paper … and if he either wrote or signed it, he was unconscious of what he was doing at the time, thro' the fear of being sent to Jail and of loosing [sic] his situation in the Vessel, which was then on the eve of her departure.' He also denied any public bedding.

It was admitted that David's threats 'to go to sea without acknowledging his marriage so distressed and distracted the Pursuer [who was pregnant] that she was indifferent as to what should befall her and she did throw herself into the Sea.' But David came to her relative's house 'of his own accord and there expressed his regret and his readiness to acknowledge his marriage with the Pursuer', and he freely and willingly wrote out the declaration at that time. Apart from Jean's father and sister, the witnesses 'were all neutral and disinterested persons, and in presence of the same witnesses the parties were bedded as husband and wife'. The testimony of those witnesses bore this out, and in 1827 the commissaries found them to be married persons and the child she had borne a lawful child.[17]

The written acknowledgement was a comparatively late development, but letters were a consistent feature of evidence throughout. Such letters did not have to be between the parties themselves but could be to a third party. For example, the crucial evidence in the 1757 case of Jean Macdonald against Angus Macalister of Loup Esquire was the following letter he wrote to his friend, Dr Alexander Douglas, when Jean became very ill with a venereal disease:

> *Dear Sandie, The bearer of this and I being married but wants to conceall it for some time, so therefore beggs you will not speak of it to any person whatsomever, You know Sandy I had the Cpt [sic] and most unluckily gave it to her, I beg for Gods sake you'll get her Instantly Cured and you shall be handsomly rewarded.*

After the news broke out he wrote again:

> *Dear Sandy, You may Remember sometime ago I wrote you That I was married to a Certain person and desired you not to speak of it. The story is broke out, and makes a Damn'd noise in this Countrey Although by God I am as much married to her as you are, but you know Sandy a body will say a great many things to save a poor Girl And if I had the least thoughts that ever you would have mentioned it I never would have wrote you any such things But I beg if ever you spoke of it to any body that you'll Endeavour to suppress such a Report as it does me a damned deal of harm. I beg if ever you see her to let nothing on for Gods sake nor ever that I wrote you this Letter.*

The case was bitterly contested, and initially the commissaries did not find a marriage proven, but after an appeal to the Court of Session the decision was reversed and a marriage was declared.[18]

Of course, most letters adduced as evidence were between the couple. In a 1734 case Mr James Kinloch (eldest lawful son to Sir Francis Kinloch of Gilmerton Baronet) fled to the Continent after secretly marrying Margaret Fowlis (daughter of Mr William Fowlis of Woodhall, advocate). He wrote to her from a series of places, hoping that, although his sister and other members of the family knew of the marriage it could still be kept from his father, 'for they are all of oppinion that the moment my father hears of it my bills will be stoped and what will become of me in a forreign country without money you must deny it to the last …. If it is known at this time I am sure to be disinherite and all the misery that possibly can fall upon a poor Creature will happen [to] me. All that wee have for it is to keep it secret a litle longer.' Later he wrote from Strasbourg that he had not received a letter from her for three months: 'for Gods Sake write to me for I cannot live if

I hear not from you I have left Swis [sic] some time ago and I am at present in my way to the South of France and I hope before I am much older to have the pleasure of seeing you.' A month later he wrote: 'there is not a day that passes that you are not a hundred times in my thoughts and I hope to be home sooner than you think but to sett a day is what I cannot do My dear life your afflicted husband for ever and ever.' There could be no doubt that they were a married couple.[19]

In 1779 and 1780 Elizabeth Richardson, from Cumberland, was a chamber-maid in the King's Arms Tavern in Annan, where she met John Irving, an Edinburgh lawyer.[20] He fell in love with her and asked her to marry him, but because of the difference in their ranks in society he persuaded her to keep their marriage a secret, 'perhaps till his father's death, which, by the course of nature, could be at no great distance'. After she became pregnant her relatives came to Annan, when John assured them that the marriage 'was as valid, by the law of Scotland, as if the most public celebration had taken place'. And to prove his sincerity, he wrote the following letter, dated at Annan 13 November 1780:

> *My dear Betty, As I was married to you in the month of May last, at which time was agreed betwixt us to conceal the marriage for three or four years, from motives of prudence, I think it necessary, however, for your security, to give you this acknowledgement, that you and your children, in case of my dying before it is made public, may succeed to my estate, as I hereby declare you to be my lawful wife. If you friends have any doubts about the matter, I hereby engage to come to the country from Edinburgh against Christmas, and marry you in consequence of a licence to be obtained in England: But I consider myself as much your husband at present as I can be thereafter. I am, my dearest Betty, your most affectionate husband.*

Yet John contested the case. After various delaying tactics his main argument was that the letter was granted 'at the earnest desire of her mother, and to protect her from the parish officers, who would have sent her under the charge of a constable, from parish to parish, till she was brought back to Annan', and was not meant to constitute a marriage. But the letter was unambiguous and he could not wriggle out of the marriage.

The unusual aspect of the case of Helen McLauchlan (daughter of Dugald McLauchlan Esquire of Ballwill) against Thomas Dobson, an Irishman sent by his father to be educated as a merchant in Greenock in 1787, was the extent to which he swithered.[21] After initially denying the marriage, in July 1791 he acknowl-edged it before witnesses, so that Helen withdrew the action, but then he changed his mind and again denied it. In January 1792 Helen wrote to her agent:

> *You no doubt was astonished, in so short a time, and thinking every thing settled between Mr Dobson and I, that matters have taken so extraordinary a change. However, Mr Dobson, by the unfriendly advice of one Campbell, writer in Greenock, has got it*

quite into his head that our marriage is not good; a circumstance which to me, and every other person, appears impossible.

The couple, who had carried on a lengthy correspondence after they had 'mutually and solemnly engaged to hold each other as married persons', never found an opportunity of consummating the marriage, and Thomas thought this meant he could not be declared married to her. As mentioned earlier, that was not the position under Scottish law.

The families on both sides disapproved of the match (though hers, it seems, did so only because they were offended at his treatment of her). In August 1790 Helen, 'overcome for a time by the influence of her friends' agreed to a meeting between the families on the Isle of Bute, 'in order that they might mutually deliver up to each other the written correspondence which had passed between them, as if by such a measure their connection of marriage, already established, could have been dissolved.' But after both sides handed over their letters, she repented and took hers back; as he did not want his she took them too, and indeed they formed the ground for her action.

His first letter to her, on 3 November 1787, began: 'My Love, Yours of yesterday came to hand, I found sacred happiness in looking at your super-scription. My dear wife, you may expect to see me to-morrow, with God's assistance, at 11 o'clock …. I had letters from my father the day you left. He has made me very good promises. I hope that our happiness will commence sooner than we expect. I am, my dearest wife, your faithful husband, Thomas Dobson.' In January 1788 he wrote: 'My dearest Love, The day I parted with you and your two sisters, was a scene I would never wish to see again, as my love for you is so great, that parting for such a long period distresses me to the greatest extreme …. I am, my dearest Helena, your faithful husband, Thomas Dobson.' And so on. His only defence was that 'the letters were not intended to establish a marriage; and that they were written merely at the desire of the pursuer, without any other meaning than to gratify her humour.' Her lawyer argued that this was 'too ridiculous an account of the matter, to require any answer from the pursuer'. The courts agreed.

Lord Neave's nineteenth-century poem, 'The Tourist's Matrimonial Guide Through Scotland', advised:

You'd better keep clear of love-letters,
  Or write them with caution and care;
For, faith, they may fasten your fetters,
  If wearing a conjugal air.[22]

In the unusual case of Jean Laing, discussed above, who spent years working as a servant in various households after marrying George Reid Esquire of Ratho

Bank, Jean was able to produce a great quantity of letters inspired by romantic prose of the time, as in the following (30 November 1808):

As the Heart panteth after water brooks in a desert Land so panteth my heart after thee my beloved. I sit down with mingled emotions of delight and sorrow to unbosom myself to my love, and to pour forth the anguish of my soul torn with the most violent sensations of love heightened by the thoughts of the darling object of all my wishes torn from my embraces, and placed at a cruel distance from my view. Sometimes perplexed with the idea, that removed from my protection she may be exposed to the rude attacks and insults of other men, and separated from all the endearments which would result from the exercise of mutual affection between two congenial souls framed and moulded by nature to make each other happy. Two such souls united and living together with the more perfect unanimity of heart and sentiments would enjoy happiness flowing from the reciprocal exchange of kind offices, and the constant exercise of sympathy esteem and love which no human language can describe nor the boldest imagination conceive.

Later in the same letter he asked a favour of her, 'that you will write me weekly a journal of the way in which you have spent the preceding week you need not care one farthing about how you write it if it is only from you it is enough to me. Bye the bye I observe you are very much improved in your way of both writing and spelling of late.'

George argued that there were letters from him 'in which marriage was in his contemplation, but there was no celebration of marriage in any way'. He did admit that she gave him an acknowledgement of marriage as well but said he had destroyed it. He declared that he had also destroyed most of her letters to him, but he did produce a few which bore out her assertion that his influence over her was so great that 'she submitted for years to the situation in which he requested her to remain. In the meantime she consoled herself with the conviction that she was beloved and by the sentiment that her apparent station was a disguise which was one day to be laid aside when her true rank was to appear and be avowed.' In her final letters she revealed that her patience with his endless delaying tactics was at an end. In July 1816 she wrote that she would wait until Martinmas

providing you give me your hand of write as security of your promes to me dating the month year and your own name in full, and if you dont agree to this I will have no more to say to the question but procid on my plan .... If you cannot agree to my request I will put off no longer I am agravated to the utmost when I think on the way you have used me .... George I must say it is very mean in you keeping me in such a way working for myself if you could allow yourself to think for one moment you could not bear the idea of it the thoughts of another winter living in misery is what I never could bear.

As noted above, she won her case.

Verbal Acknowledgments

In the very first case in the volume of decreets, that of Jean Cook (daughter of a deceased minister at Prestonpans) against William Johnstoun of Corehead, in 1698, the man destroyed the written acknowledgement he had given her, but she was able to prove verbal acknowledgements.[23] After she had promised to marry him, she said, her relations enquired into 'the Circumstances of his fortune, and finding the same to be bad' they tried to dissuade her from marrying him, but because of her promise she would not heed them. He, coming to Edinburgh and 'getting notice how her freinds were searching after his condition and were beginning to slight him and Call him a broken Laird' got very angry and 'went out of the Town in a pett', but afterwards he wrote to her apologising. They met in town to be married, but he refused to have any kind of ceremony, telling her that 'his mother was ane old dieing woman and could wrong him exceedingly, and that his Creditors would be upon him for marrying without money, so that there was a necessity for marrying without any person knowing of it.' His 'gravity and behaving allwayes with so much respect and kindnes to her, made her at length to condescend to marry privatly'. They 'were married als solemnly as ever any marriage was done on earth, by joyning of hands with all the words and Ceremonies of marriage'. But afterwards William insisted that she had only been his mistress.

Fortunately Jean had witnesses to the contrary. David Spence, minister of the gospel, baptised the child and testified that Jean's health was drunk as William's 'Lady' and that William 'Pledged the said health and acquiesced therein'. Prior to that when the minister happened to meet William he 'did ask the pursuers health as his Lady and that the defender did never quarrell the same, bot gave the deponent a bow and Return of thanks'. And various other witnesses heard him 'own the pursuer to be his wife and treat entertain and cherish her as such', so that the witnesses 'never doubted bot that they wer man and wife' and 'always called them Laird and Lady'. The commissaries found them to be married persons.

Seventy years later George Scott went to London and left his relations to fight the action brought by Margaret Scott (daughter of James Scott of Howden) in 1768. They alleged that during their whole association the couple had never cohabited as husband and wife and he had never introduced her to anyone in that light.[24] But Patrick Hutchison, an Edinburgh lawyer, testified that George had taken a great deal of interest in a legal case concerning Margaret's father and over a drink he acknowledged his marriage to her, 'And furder added that tho he was married to the pursuer, he did not choose to give any of her friends the satisfaction of knowing that it was so.' Marion Dallas, in whose house they lodged, testified that when Margaret became pregnant Marion told George that he should acknowledge his marriage to her 'and received for answer from the defender that he could not acknowledge it publickly at that time because his Mother and Mr Bruce his stepfather were against the marriage'. She asked him when he would acknowledge it and he 'answered that he would do it in the space of a twelve months'. But he did not, and finally Marion asked him

> whether the pursuer was the defenders Mistress or his wife, adding at the same time that if she was the former, he the defender was possessed of a deal of assurance to introduce her to the deponent, and the best Company that frequented her house as such That the defender Answered No, by God she is not a whore, but a virtuous woman. That thereupon Mr Cuming the deponents husband observed that the defender then was a Scoundrel for not publishing his Marriage.

The commissaries found them to be married, and he had to pay her an annual aliment of £40.

Janet Colquhoun alleged that Alexander Walker, journeyman engraver in Edinburgh, had, on at least one occasion, introduced her to an acquaintance as his wife. In response Alexander insisted that this 'was merely an introduction in jest, when the defender was tipsy'. However, in court, when he was asked under oath if Janet had heard him tell his friend that he was only joking he admitted that she probably had not, whereas he knew that she *had* heard him say to his friend that she was his wife. In this case the acknowledgement was not sufficient to prove a marriage, but in 1829 she was awarded damages for seduction of £50.[25]

Of course, the commissaries were well aware that a man might very well call a woman his wife simply to obtain lodgings, and, as will be seen in subsequent chapters, landladies were often called as witnesses and swore that they believed the couple to be married or they would not have given them a room. Such an assertion was never taken seriously, and at the end of the nineteenth century a Scottish advocate wrote:

> If two people agree to pretend to be husband and wife for some ulterior purpose, the fact that a waiter and a landlady took them to be such will have no more effect in marrying them than the belief in witchcraft will enable an old woman to ride through the air on a broomstick ... many people stay together at hotels and lodging houses who are neither married nor have the least intention of marrying. To avoid scandal and to obtain quarters they call each other husband and wife, and there the matter ends ... the view is fundamentally erroneous that in such a case the law of Scotland will hold them married.[26]

A very different situation was one in which a long-term relationship had existed, and witnesses testified to behaviour patterns that convinced them that the couple in question were married.

What the Neighbours Thought

Most women pursuers cited witnesses who testified that they considered the couple in question to be married. From the beginning of the period until the end of it certain types of behaviour implied marriage to those who witnessed it. They were all illustrated in the 1735 case of Susana Gordon against the children of George Kinnaird by his first marriage, who disputed her claim to be his widow.[27] Alexander Colvill, late collector of the customs at Dundee, often dined and supped with them, and he always heard and saw them

> behave each of them to the other as is usuall betwixt husband and wife That his usuall Compelation to her was my dear That she allways did sitt at the head of his Table and Carved and distributed the Dishes That the Servants behaved Towards her as their mistress that she gave them their orders in presence of Mr Kinnaird anent the affairs of his family and other business that frequently there were other Strangers at Table that upon these occasions the deponent had drunken the pursuers health under the denomination of Mr Kinnairds Lady and the health went about so.

Furthermore, when the witness

> had occasion to see the said Mr Kinnaird in other places than his own house the deponent was in use to ask him how Mrs Kinnaird was he returned the deponent thanks deponed that frequently when the deponent had occasion to Converse with people in Dundee he had heard them when speaking of the pursuer Call her Mrs Kinnaird.

A husband and wife dined and supped together publicly; a wife ran the household; visitors would drink their health as Mr and Mrs, and everyone who knew them would refer to them in those terms. Those were the ritualistic aspects of the relationship; naturally there was also the personal side. George Colvil, a doctor, testified that Susana's

> behaviour to Mr Kinnaird in his last sickness was in the most affectionate and tender manner as any wife could have to a husband by frequently asking my life shall I get this or the other Cordiall or Victualls for you That he Mr Kinnaird showed a Tenderness and regaird for her by useing such kindly epithets as dear or poor Susie and desireing the deponent and others about him that they would take care of her for that he was affraid she would distroy herself by the great fatigue and Trouble she took about him.

It was a powerful example of conjugal love. Though affection in itself was never sufficient to prove a marriage, it was often adduced as evidence.

In 1799 Mary Macfarlane alleged that Angus McDonald, cook in Edinburgh, had married her twelve years earlier; she had borne him four children, of whom two were still alive, but in 1798 he left her and regularly married another woman.[28] Angus appeared in court and denied under oath any courtship or marriage, swearing that she had been his 'Kept Mistress' and that 'every body in the Neighbourhood knew that she was not his wife That she was never called Mrs McDonald in presence of the Declarant nor was she considered as such by his Brother the Bookseller nor by his Customers all of whom were in the perfect knowledge That she was not his wife.'

The neighbours told a different tale. Margaret Galbraith testified that the couple 'sold drink and spirits and made ready dinners to people who came to eat in the house', and Mary was always known as Mrs McDonald and referred to by everyone as his wife. The witness never considered them 'to be other than husband and wife and was surprised at finding any doubt entertained about it'. Charles McIntosh, writer to the signet, testified that the couple lived in a house of his, and that he 'understood them to be married persons' otherwise he 'would not have let the house to them.' When Mary came to the house McIntosh's servants 'would have said "Mrs MacDonald wants to speak to you" and that the deponent himself used to call the pursuer "Mrs MacDonald"'. Jean Laidlaw testified that 'the Neighbours in Canal Street used to call the Pursuer Mrs McDonald And people who would have knocked at the door would have asked if Mrs McDonald was in, and the neighbours on meeting the deponent would have said to her "I hear you have been at Mrs McDonalds"'. Lewis Murray, porter dealer, 'frequently heard the Defender giving orders that said Porter should be carried home to his wife'. Many more witnesses deponed along the same lines.

Yet two witnesses testified that Mary had confided to them that she had never been married to Angus. When the relationship deteriorated Angus employed a lawyer, William Waugh, to draw up a summons which

> set forth That altho' the ceremony of marriage had never passed between the parties ... yet they had lived together for about seven or eight years as husband and wife, and had during that period been acknowledged as such by their friends and acquaintances That he the raiser of that Summons, and Defender in this cause, would have been willing to continue to live with her on the footing of husband and wife, but that he found it impossible to do so on account of her unhappy temper.

Angus had hoped to obtain a judicial separation, but presumably he discovered that this was only granted when one party was in danger of their life.[29] At a meeting between them, Waugh said, 'a good deal of disagreeable altercation took place ... in the course of which the present pursuer frequently said that tho' she was not actually married to the Defender, yet they had lived together and acknowledged each other as husband and wife, and you Angus (addressing the Defender) know that it was all the same.' Waugh 'was a good deal surprised when he heard that the present defender was married to another woman'.

This was a classic case of marriage having been established by habit and repute.

Angus continued to live with his second 'wife', but he was forced to pay Mary an annual aliment for the rest of his life.

The main modes of proof having been discussed, the next question is how a man could defend himself against a claim of being married.

Notes

1   CC8/5/14.
2   CC/8/6/34.
3   CC8/5/11.
4   Alan Macfarlane, *Marriage and Love in England – Modes of Reproduction 1300-1840* (Oxford, 1986), 315.
5   CC8/6/64.
6   CC8/5/14.
7   CC8/5/9.
8   The witness was designated Andrew Dick alias Lauder, feuar of Grange, but Anne Lauder, the defender's sister, referred to him as 'her brother Mr Dick'. According to the Complete Baronetage, Sir Andrew Lauder, the fifth baronet, married his cousin, Isobel, only child and heiress of William Dick Esquire, and their son Andrew was the first Dick of Grange. Andrew was apparently the only one of his three sons to survive Sir Andrew so he, not William, became the sixth baronet.
9   CC8/5/6.
10 CC8/6/62.
11 CC8/5/20.
12 When James first returned to the country Elizabeth's father raised an action on her behalf against him in the Sheriff Court which was dismissed, as that court was not competent to decide the matter. CC8/6/51. A witness, Daniel Dick, declared that after James returned Daniel asked him 'why he had left the Country on account of his begetting a bastard Child, That the defender answered that the Bastard Child was neither here nor there but that he had signed a Line which vexed him more than a bastard Child.' James appealed to the Court of Session against the commissaries' decision but was unsuccessful.
13 CC8/6/55.
14 CC8/6/100.
15 CC8/5/37.
16 CC8/6/156.
17 The defender appealed to the Court of Session but his appeal was unsuccessful. While he did not adhere to her he had to pay her £100 a year plus an additional £20 for the child, and she could claim for more if his circumstances improved. And he had to pay expenses of £115.
18 CC8/6/22.
19 CC8/5/4. There were also witnesses to a 'ceremony', including the celebrator. Mr Alexander Hamilton of Pencaitland testified that after his wife told Sir Francis of the marriage the witness 'did say to Sir Francis what he judged proper to reconcile him to his son telling him that he had married a good Gentlewoman and that he ought then to make the best of it', and sometime later he found Sir Francis 'better disposed to be reconciled to his son than when first spoke to'.
20 Papers for this case, which was appealed to the Court of Session, have not survived amongst the Commissary Court records. (It is mentioned in Patrick Fraser, *Treatise on the Law of Scotland as applicable to The Personal and Domestic Relations* (Edinburgh, 1846), Vol I, 147.) But it is in the Session Papers, Signet Library, 182; 36 (1785).

21 CC8/5/37.
22 'Claverhouse' (Meliora C Smith), *Irregular Border Marriages* (Edinburgh, 1934), 154.
23 CC8/5/1 and CC8/6/3. The claim was one for adherence, but the gist was proving marriage.
24 CC8/5/12.
25 CC8/6/162.
26 'An Advocate' (F P Walton), *Marriage Regular and Irregular* (Glasgow, 1893), 43.
27 CC8/5/4.
28 CC8/5/25.
29 See Leah Leneman, *Alienated Affections – The Scottish Experience of Divorce and Separation 1684–1830* (Edinburgh, 1998).

CASE STUDY 3

MURRAY V. CRANSTON: THE DISOWNED WIFE

A MARRIAGE ceremony took place, and there was voluminous written evidence in this case, which ran from 1746 to 1748, but the woman's uncertainty about her own status encouraged the man to fight it. Both parties were of relatively high rank, and the reason for keeping the marriage secret – the man's fear that it might 'prevent or Retard the promotion he was then in quest and hopes of in the army' – was not unusual. But in fact it is a unique case as it was the woman's adherence to her religion that was the real bone of contention.

Lieutenant William Henry Cranston courted Ann Murray, granddaughter of Sir David Murray of Stenhope, but procrastinated 'by reason of the lowness of their fortunes untill he should attain to a post and Commission in the army whereby to be enabled to make them live in a way more suitable to their birth'. However, in 1744 he learned that 'a Gentleman of considerable fortune' was in suit of her and would obtain her mother's consent to a marriage, and therefore he renewed his courtship and persuaded her to enter into a secret marriage. He brought someone 'of the appearance of a Clergyman', whom he 'called a Chaplain to a Regiment', and a ceremony was conducted. She bore a daughter to him in February 1745, but from August 1746 he refused to have anything to do with her, insisting that he was not married to her, thereby forcing her to raise a declarator of marriage action.

The first letter produced was the one written after he learned of the other gentleman's suit of her. 'Dearest Miss Murray,' he wrote to her, 'Don't imagine that love can follow upon your giving yourself away when your affections is otherways fixed, that never can happen in my opinion. All the love you can possibly give to a husband is in itself little enough, but in what a situation must you be in, when a second has your affections, and tied during life to the man you cannot equally esteem, this would be a state that I earnestly pray you may be saved from venturing on.' She was also able to produce a letter he wrote to her uncle, John Murray of Broughton, in October 1744, after she became pregnant, assuring him that his niece 'is Mistres Cranstoun'. He still hoped that this would not be known 'before I had gott a Company, And if it can by any means be kept from the Ears of the rest of the world untill that happen, It would be the greatest happiness to us both, for did my friends know of it my promotion in the army would quite stop upon the Account of her way of thinking, and what I have besides is only Eleven hundred pounds being obliged to give Three hundred for the Captain Lieutenancy.'

Ann also produced many letters addressed to her as Mrs Cranston, and the following from William's brother to William: 'Dr Brother, I would not delay the first opportunity to assure you that I wish you with the utmost sincerity all happiness and shall forever endeavour so far as is in my power to contribute to it so soon as you think proper to make publick your marriage, my Sister in Law shall be as acceptable to live in my family as any of my Sisters.'

With so much written evidence, how could William deny a marriage?

Ann's 'way of thinking' that he feared would stop his promotion was Roman Catholicism. Anti-Catholic prejudice was deeply embedded in all classes of society in eighteenth-century Scotland, and in the 1740s laws were still in force denying Catholics the right to inherit property. The Stuart allegiance to that religion had been the cause of King James VII's overthrow, and while the couple were courting, a rising headed by the son of the Catholic pretender to the throne was being defeated. At the time she married him Ann was so much in love she believed that she might convert to Protestantism. 'As to the Story of Religion, I shall leave it entirely to yourself,' she wrote, 'for I can't bring myself to go and break my brain with Controversy, So what I doe in that is Just to please you, but at the same time if you can think we can be happy another way I hope you'll not insist on it, but if not, I shall go to either kirk or meeting house, As I think all Religions are much alike, if I quit my own, altho the Episcopils has a greater look of serving God than the other.' Shortly thereafter she wrote to his mother, assuring her Ladyship that 'I shall endeavour to behave so as neither your Ladyship or Mr C shall ever have reason to repent his chuse. To be sure I come in to your family, with a great many disadvantages, having neither Religion friends or money, which I'm sensible is very necessary to his preferment. Two of these things is not in my power to Correct, but as to the part of Religion, I shall lay by the prejudice of Education, And see my Errors as soon as I can.'

As far as William was concerned, Ann had promised him that when their child was born she would renounce her religion, but when that time came she found herself unable to do so. Nor did she believe that she had come under such an obligation, though she had agreed that the children would be brought up as Protestants. 'Now my Dearest life I need not put you in mind of the frequent Conversations we have had on that Subject,' she wrote, 'And the many promises we made never to disturb one another with our private sentiments on that head, for what does it signifie to your Friends what I am since I give you my word I shall never disturb your quiet nor your Childrens, with any such thing, and whatever I wrote on the Subject, and you know the reasons. You was to go for the Indies, you laid it all on that footing, that nobody would make any Interest for you in case they knew what you had done … the dreadfull prospect of losing the man in whom my heart was bound up, And he laying all on that footing might have forced me to give up my own ease, God only knows, for to be sure, I nere should have been easy after the Renounceing my Religion for it's by that only I can expect to be happy hereafter, and instead of being able to convince myself to the Contrary, I have grounded myself more firmly than ever by pretending to read myself out of it.' Three months later she wrote: 'My Dearest had you but desired me to undergone any other hardships, how happy should I have been to share, my Dear Willie how strong my love is, but that only thing in which you seem to build your happiness on to have it out of my power, makes me double miserable but shall torment you no more with my misery, Since you say you suffer yourself, but prays that God may either take me to himself or soften your heart.'

William convinced himself that the marriage was conditional on her becoming a Protestant, and when she engaged a lawyer to raise an action of declarator William wrote to him, 'It's true I had the misfortune of being deluded so far as to have Carnall dealings with her a misfortune I often regrated, And as an evidence of my sorrow, I went great lengths to make all the atonment in my power, but she obstinatly refused to disavow the Roman Catholick Religion, for this I gave her six weeks and upwards to think of it, and upon receiving a letter to this purpose from her, I then declared of and determined with myself to have nothing further to do with her .... She knew she never was Mrs Cranstoun nor never should be, except she obeyed me in this, I have it under her hand in answer to this, that She had committed sin enough, but She was determined never to add to her Sins by turning Protestant, not even if She were to suffer death upon that Accompt, Sir from the time I received this sentiment of hers, it entirely freed me from all I was determined to doe for her both in the Sight of God and Man.'

William relied on Ann's own confused belief that she was not actually married to him, for in July 1745 she wrote to him: 'no further petitions after this, but for this once, I must needs beg of you to grant, which is that before you declare me infamous to the world which I suppose won't be long that you may show me so much mercy as to let me know, so as I may get out of the way, and not see the shame and concern I put me friends to, At the same time allow me to take my infant alongst with me, this I'm sure you can't deny me ... she will be my greatest comfort, I may say all I shall have in this world ....When you marry may you gett a wife every way to your mind, but may she not love you so well as I have done for fear of being as miserable.' She continued: 'when I gett your Commands to gett out of the way, I intend to go for a Convent ....There's no doubt but from that moment I gett your orders, I shall endeavour to forgett you, And even to hate you if possible for my own ease. I have taken care of that all this time, not to let myself have the least Reflection on you, for fear of what it might have done, but I repent of this As I find my Affections As Strong As ever for you when you are away from me, but needs own myself a grater fool than ever I thought And has showen myself ane Idiot in your behalf all along, but I find there's nothing but experience that will make young Girls believe all men changeable alike.'

Perhaps Ann's relations raised the action on her behalf, or perhaps someone pointed out to her the legal implications of William's Protestantism. When the case came to court Margaret Park (daughter of John Park of Forfithis) testified that on 22 May 1744 William brought someone whom he called a minister, and

Margaret was present when the parties were married. She 'saw them join hands together and heard them distinctly take the marriage vows and thereupon the Minister pronounced them married persons'. Margaret also testified that the couple slept together that night and she breakfasted with them in the morning. William had asked her 'to keep his marriage secrete assigning this reason for it, that the pursuer being of different principles of Religion from him, if his marriage with her was soon published it might marr his promotion in the army, which he had then in view, by the Interests of his friends'. But soon after that she learned that Lord Cranston had been present at an 'entertainment' on account of the marriage and then felt herself at liberty to tell others of it.

Margaret also testified that 'the Child was held up in baptism by Mr Charles Cranston brother to the Defender that she was named Jean, after Lady Cranston, That Mr Murray of Broughton Sir David Murray, Miss Jeanie Cranston the Defenders Sister and Mrs Dunbar were all present at the Baptism,' and that 'during her Inlying and while she was in Mrs Dunbars she was visited by Lady Charles Ker and her Daughters, Lady Jean Home sister to the Earl of Home, Lady Dalswinton and her Daughters, Two of the Earl of Traquairs Sisters, Mrs Campbell an Aunt or Great Aunt of the Defenders and by severall other persons of respect.'

Even William's sister, Jeanie, testified that she had heard of the marriage about a month before Ann's child was born and 'wrote a congratulatory letter to the pursuer, Wishing her much joy as her Sister in Law'. She treated her as such until March 1746 when her brother first denied the marriage. At that time William told his brother George that he had agreed to declare that they were married before the birth of the child but only if she changed her religion, which she at last refused to do, and William 'said he thought himself at liberty upon that account to disown her as his wife, and that he had done all that a Man of honour was bound to do in such a case'.

Ann's lawyer argued: 'Mr Cranston not having prevailled with his wife to be converted so soon as he proposed, he bethought himself of ane ungenerous and base expedient of denying his marriage.' Ann, 'not knowing what would amount to the proof of a marriage or what would be held to be a legal marriage, She believed what Mr Cranston had averred that she could not prove her marriage and therefore looked upon herself as in the most dismal situation if he persisted in his Intention of denying it.'

Scottish law would recognise a conditional promise of marriage but not a conditional marriage, and the commissaries found them to be married persons.

CC8/5/6

CASE STUDY 4

CURRIE V. TURNBULL: THE MEANINGFUL SCRAP

THE main evidence in this case, which ran from December 1803 until December 1807, was a written acknowledgement combined with the verbal evidence of what occurred on the night it was granted. And though the action was not raised until some two years later, a year after the man had regularly married another woman, the marriage was declared valid. Thus summarised, the story seems straightforward. It was not.

David Turnbull was a drover or cattle dealer living at Carfrae Mill, Berwickshire. According to Elspeth Currie, David's relations were against his marrying her, so their marriage was kept a secret. There was no ceremony, but on 1 October 1801 he delivered the following to her: 'I hereby acknowledge that I am married to Elspeth Currie as soon as I get all things put to rights or my affairs are that I am not to see you in noways distress until that I provide for you which I hope will not be long – that is all from yours (signed) David Turnbull.' They went to bed that same night, and he introduced her to the people in the house they were in as his wife.

David's lawyer claimed that when Elspeth became pregnant she took him to a public house and got him drunk, and that the document bore 'tolerable evidence' of that – 'indeed he was so very much overtaken with liquor that he does not recollect a single circumstance about the Letter but he is informed by the person who wrote it that he did write it, and the Pursuer prevailed on the Defender to copy it with the intention as the Pursuer then said to deceive her friends but which is now attempted to be used to a very different purpose.' The writing, he argued, 'neither expresses that the Defender is husband to the Pursuer nor does it contain any obligation to marry her. It speaks of something to be done when all "things are put to rights or his affairs are" – are what?… But without descanting more on this unmeaning scrap it seems sufficient to say that it is downright nonsense.' Everyone knew that they were not married; he was publicly rebuked for fornication without her objecting, and a year earlier he had been regularly married to another woman without any challenge from her.

Her response was that in October 1801 they went to an inn in Edinburgh, and though Mr Nicol, the innkeeper, could not accommodate them, he took them 'across the Street to a Mrs Bells a person of respectable character where they were drunk to as married persons and where they went to bed and staid several days during which they were held and reputed and did own and acknowledge each other as man and wife'. Before that bedding 'the Defender wrote with his own hand and delivered to the Pursuer the letter quoted in the libel which if not satisfactory itself at least will amount to a promise, and should the Pursuer prove a Copula thereafter, she will be entitled to have a marriage declared.' His marrying another woman after that was irrelevant.

When David appeared in court he swore under oath that he 'got intoxicated the night he was in Nicols house with the Pursuer and next morning found himself in the house of one Mrs Bell in the Lawnmarket in bed with the Pursuer without being sensible of the way in which he came there'. Though when shown the acknowledgement he had to admit that it looked like his handwriting, he had 'no recollection of giving the Pursuer a Letter on that occasion'. His lawyer then alleged that after he had given in his defences, 'so sensible was the Pursuer of her action being totally groundless that she then relinquished it altogether avowing to every body whom she knew that she had only raised the action from bad advice and that she would never proceed farther with it.' Five months passed, after which it 'no doubt would have been dismissed but from the circumstance of there being a child in the field in whose name the process was also raised'.

Nevertheless, the commissaries allowed Elspeth to adduce proof. David asked that she be examined in court, but he gained nothing by this, for she declared under oath that David wrote the acknowledgement in Nicol's inn, 'and that on this occasion the Defender wrote said line twice over in her presence, as the first he wrote did not please him. Declares that at the time he wrote these lines the Defender was perfectly sober.' She also declared that 'he Called her by his name, and addressed her as his wife in presence both of Mr and Mrs Nicol.' She said that 'her reason for not sooner bringing the present action against the Defender was the Confusion in his affairs and that she wished him to have them settled before she claimed him as her husband.' She had heard of his relationship with another woman, but he had denied it. If she had known of his 'intention of marrying said woman or of acknowledging her as his wife she would have endeavoured to have prevented it, but she did not know it till afterwards having been residing with a Sister at Carlisle when said marriage or acknowledgement took place'.

She had neither received nor applied for further money from him since her child was born, as they had quarrelled at the time. Clearly David really did not regard what had occurred on the night in question as constituting a marriage, and it may be that Elspeth had doubts herself until someone informed her of her rights in law.

Her witnesses added to the confusion. John Nicol, the innkeeper, had known David for several years and remembered him asking for supper for himself and his wife, 'and while they were at supper his wife as well as himself called the Pursuer Mrs. Turnbull and his wife said to the Defender that she would get Gloves and Ribbons now.' (Gloves and ribbons were traditional wedding gifts.) After supper, 'having taken a chearful glass, David 'was hearty but could not be called drunk, and the witness never at any time saw him so drunk but that he could manage business.' Two days later (during which time they had been sleeping together as husband and wife at Mrs Bell's) David asked him 'for paper pen and ink, as he said he was not then married to the Pursuer and wished to give her a letter. That the paper pen and ink was brought him accordingly and he wrote different letters which did not seem to please him as he tore them upon the witness gave him some sort of scrol which he said would satisfy the Pursuer and her friends.' He 'was perfectly sober at this time'. Nicol did not give his wife this information, 'as he was apprehensive had she received it she would not have allowed them to remain in the house'.

Ann Wilson, Mrs Nicol, was adamant that David had told her that Elspeth was 'Mrs Turnbull', and she introduced her as such to Mrs Bell. But about a week later David came with his brother and 'told the witness that he was not married to the Pursuer upon which the witness called him several bad names'. Mrs Bell, of course, 'would not have allowed them to have lodged in her house unless she had believed they were man and wife'.

In spite of all the ambiguities surrounding this case (including the child being baptised as illegitimate), in August 1805 the commissaries found the marriage sufficiently proven and the child legitimate. The law, after all, was clear: a written promise of marriage followed by intercourse constituted a marriage. David appealed against the decision to the Court of Session, but his appeal was unsuccessful. In the meantime, Elspeth (in September 1805) had borne David a second child.

After the Court of Session's decision a two-year argument started over the amount of aliment he should have to pay her. He argued that he should not have to pay anything at all for the children as he had offered to take custody of them. Her response to this was that David was living and running a tavern with his second 'wife', Miss Cowan, and that if the child were put under her care Miss Cowan 'would extend to it some of those regards which she had shewn to their mother who she assaulted more than once and particularly when the Respondent was near her inlying of that very Child'. The amount of £35 a year awarded was 'well founded Considering the whole conduct of the petitioner from first to last and the indecent resolution which he speaks out without reserve and even attempts to justify vizt that he will Continue to abandon his wife and children and live in an adulterous intercourse with "the lady whom he married" after being more than a year married to the Respondent.'

Her own habits, Elspeth argued, 'have been always those of virtue and industry – had she not exerted her utmost industry she and her children might have starved. At Whitsunday she took a Beef Stake [sic] Shop in the Flesh market Close of Edinburgh and has not yet had time to know how she will Succeed Whatever attention and industry can accomplish will be hers to rear and educate her Children and she knows that a happiness will flow therefrom which cannot be found in the revels of a Bagnio or the riot of a Tavern.'

The law may have been clear that David's written 'scrap' followed by inter-course constituted marriage, but the morals of the parties are anything but clear.

Did Elspeth really consider herself married to David in the year before she raised her action? And despite her lawyer's strictures on David's continued adultery with Miss Cowan, the fact remains that Elspeth had intercourse with him while he was cohabiting with this second 'wife', whose jealousy led to a physical attack on her. Elspeth would receive lifelong support from David and their daughter would be considered legitimate, but a conventional marriage this was not.

CC8/5/29/2

CHAPTER 3

CONTESTING A CASE

WHAT means could be used to contest a declarator of marriage action? First and foremost the man had to deny any intention of marriage, initially in his written defences and then, if necessary, under oath in court. Case Study 2 was one example of a man's denial under oath, and more occur in this chapter. He might attempt to blacken the woman's character. The legal relevance was that he could not be presumed to have ever intended marriage with her, but often it was an expression of resentment. He could claim to have been so drunk at the time of the celebration that free consent to marriage had not been given, or that the celebration had been nothing more than a jest or joke. A technical defence was lack of jurisdiction by the court. And there was the usual spectrum of legal delaying tactics, trying to get inconvenient testimony rejected, and bribery and threats against witnesses.

The Oath

One verse of Lord Neave's nineteenth-century poem, 'The Tourist's Matrimonial Guide Through Scotland', warned that a promise to marry followed by certain behaviour would make a marriage:

> But if when the promise you're plighting,
> To keep it you think you'd be loath,
> Just see that it isn't in writing,
> And then it must come to your oath.[1]

The implication is that if it comes to the oath, the man can cheerfully lie through his teeth – as many did. But the judicial oath or declaration is worth a careful look, as it is here that the voices of the parties are heard most directly.

In an early case (1731), that of Katharine Harvie against John Crawfurd alias Stewart of Milntoun, the commissaries refused to allow Katharine to bring proof of her allegations that John had

again and again acknowledged to his mother and other friends he had made her promise of marriage and that he was bound to perform it, and that they did meet with Mr James Boswal of Affleck her Lawier and made offer of a peice of money to her If she the Supplicant would pass from her pretensions as they were Called and desired and Intreated Mr Boswall to use his Endeavours to prevail with her to accept of it.

The commissaries demanded either a written document or verbal declaration from him, and when he appeared in court and denied ever promising her marriage, they assoilzied him.[2]

The commissaries were summarily ruling out a large category of evidence, and had the court continued to take this line few women would have won a declarator of marriage. But in later cases the court was not so quick to take the man's word for it, especially after the alternative conclusion of damages for seduction became established, when the woman's belief in a marriage became more relevant.

In 1740 Barbara Nairn (daughter of a glover in Banff) became a servant to William Richardson, 'the King's Smith in the Mint' at Edinburgh, and within a short time William Richardson Junior fell in love with her. Well aware that his father would not approve of the match, William Junior was married to Barbara clandestinely by David Strang (under the alias 'William Milne'). Word of it got out, and 'att length coming to the Ears of his father, he it seems was highly displeased att it, and the young man stood so much in awe and terror of his displeasure, that he was brought to take the Resolution of disowning his marriage for fear of the consequences.' Barbara therefore raised a declarator of marriage action. As will be seen much later in the chapter, William Senior used unsavoury methods to try and circumvent the course of justice, and William Junior in court 'denied every thing, even the particular facts that are proved against him by Concurring Witnesses, such as his ever being in the house of James Neil att the Netherbow along with the pursuer or his ever having acknowledged to Thomas Gifford his Unkle and to Mrs Gifford that he was married to the pursuer.' But in this case witnesses' testimony proved the actual marriage, so in spite of his denial under oath the commissaries declared them to be married.[3]

In 1757 Jean Low abandoned her action against Francis McFarlane (both were servants) after Francis declared under oath that after she bore his child, Jean, he declared,

pressed him very much to allow her to say to such Folks as came about her, that she was married to the defender, and did likeways as he understands sollicite other people to endeavour to prevaill on him to allow her the pursuer for to say she was married to the defender, but that he the defender always refused to allow her to take his name or to give it out to any body that she was married to him.[4]

By the early nineteenth century the examination in court tended to be much lengthier and more detailed, and both the questions and answers were recorded, as well as impressions of the man's behaviour.

In 1818 James Cheape Gray was a servant to John Thomson's father in Glasgow (Jacobite sympathisers often named their daughters Jacobina, but this is not the only instance of a woman called James). She alleged that he courted her and promised to 'have the marriage ceremony performed when his father died, and who was then on his deathbed'. She bore his child, but he refused to acknowledge her as his wife. In court he denied every asking her to marry him.[5] The examination proceeded thus:

> *Interrogated whether he was ever in Bed with the Pursuer in his own room Depones and Answers I have been on the top of the Bed with her but not in Bed under the Bed Cloaths Interrogated If he is certain he never was in Bed with her under the Bed Cloaths Depones and Answers I think not – I do not recollect that I was Interrogated Whether he remembers going to the Kitchen one night after the Pursuer had gone to Bed and of going to her Bedside Depones and Answers yes I did.*

At that point the judge examinator thought it 'necessary to enter upon the record that the Deponent made the answer after Considerable hesitation and repeated evasions of the question'. When asked if he had 'carnal connection' with her at that time he replied, 'No I do not think I had – I do not recollect if I did.' The judge examinator again admonished him

> *to tell the whole truth upon the great Oath he had taken and the question being again put to him Depones and Answers yes I had Connection with her upon that Occasion Interrogated Whether he was under the Bed Clothes with the Pursuer [or] on the top of the Bed Clothes Depones and Answers upon the top of the Bed Clothes Interrogated Whether the Pursuer was under the Bed Clothes and with her Clothes off Depones and Answers She might have had her clothes off – The question being put a second time to the Deponent and he being desired to say explicitly in answer to the question after Considerable hesitation Depones and Answers Well she was under the bed Clothes and her Clothes off Interrogated again Whether he went under the Bed Clothes when he went into Bed with the Pursuer Depones and Answers yes I did and the question formerly put being again put to the deponent Whether he went Completely into Bed to the Pursuer or whether he was only partly into Bed Depones and Answers I was completely into Bed.*

But when it came to the crucial question – 'Whether upon this Occasion he said to the Pursuer that he would marry her' – he continued to assert, 'No I never said any such thing,' and she lost her case.

In another 1818 case Robert Gentle, cattle dealer and butcher in Dunfermline, was, by contrast, eager to assert that Catherine Glen had yielded to him at an early stage in their relationship. However, when he was examined under oath he admitted that the first time he had claimed 'connection' with her, this amounted only to 'a great deal of touzling' and 'freedoms'. On the next occasion of 'carnal connection' he 'did nothing by which a Child could be got'. He did 'not mean to say that I then entered the Pursuers body carnally but I was as much gratified as if I had ....Through excitement from her, secretion took place from me.' The couple certainly proceeded to full intercourse, for she was pregnant when the action was raised but, once again, the man denied any promise of marriage, and the woman lost her case.[6]

In 1825 Elizabeth Addison also lost her case against Daniel Robertson, baker in Edinburgh.[7] She was his servant and bore his child. In court he was asked when he first had sex with her:

About two months as I think after she had come to my service I happened to be engaged out at a wedding and came home in the morning between four and five as I think – she opened the door to me and shewed me to my room – I took some freedoms with her which were not much resisted and then had connexion with her the first time Interrogated What did you say to her and she to you upon that occasion Depones and Answers I remember nothing in particular except our speaking about the wedding – Interrogated What did you say about the wedding? Depones and Answers our conversation was about who was there whether it was agreeable and the like .... Interrogated Did you make no profession to herself of love or the like then? Depones and Answers Never at any time Interrogated Did you say any thing of marrying her Depones and Answers Never.

After she became pregnant he took a room for her and gave her money to live on. On one occasion when he went to see her, he declared, she 'said to me "Now that my parents have found out that I am with Child the only thing you have to do was to marry me" I answered "I will not marry you – I have nothing farther to do but to take the Child" She Replied "Remember my word will be taken before yours".' She was wrong.

Joseph Couper, commissary clerk depute in Glasgow, was minutely examined in the case brought against him by Margaret Smith in 1824.[8] When asked if he had ever stated to Margaret that 'it was his intention to marry her', he replied, 'No I never did, nor did I ever speak of marriage to her'. He tried to blacken Margaret's character, alleging that 'she was in the habit of lending herself to acts of prostitution.' When it came to his judicial examination, however, this allegation apparently concerned only one other man:

Interrogated If he heard who the young man was Declares 'No I never did' Interrogated Where the criminal intercourse was stated to him to be carrying on Declares one of the persons told me that it was carrying on in Glasgow Interrogated Where the others told you it was carrying on Declares with considerable hesitation 'O the others told me it was in Glasgow too.'

At this point the judge examinator warned Joseph 'to be careful to answer the Interrogatories put to him in a very different manner from what he had hitherto done as his manner of answering the questions appeared to mark a very decided wish to keep back the truth and not to make a fair and explicit statement.' The questioning continued, and he declared that 'he never stated either verbally or in writing to the Pursuer before she made any surrender of her person that she was to consider herself as his wife or that he held that they were married persons in reality or that the marriage would be regularly solemnized when circumstances permitted.'

The questions then turned to the letters he had written to her. For example, in one he had referred to her as 'my Margaret', which he said was simply 'a term of endearment'. In another one he had written that he would 'always wish and endeavour to make you happy in mind and protect you against the impertinence of slander or the insolence of either friends or foes', and in court he was 'desired to say whether he did not mean to convey by these expressions that he was to make the Pursuer happy in the character of a husband and Defend her from slander by making her his wife or declaring his marriage with her'. He denied any such meaning and when asked 'How he could protect her from slander if he did not make her his wife,' he replied, 'I would defend her if I heard her defamed by stating that many young women had committed the same error.' Margaret was unable to bring any other proof, and Joseph was assoilzied.

A simple denial of marriage was a universal defence, but in some cases other defences – legitimate if true – were put forward.

She Got Me Drunk

Lord Neave wrote:

If people are drunk or delirious
The marriage of course would be bad;
Or if they're not sober and serious,
But acting a play or charade.

In cases that came before kirk sessions in the eighteenth century, men often claimed they did not remember committing fornication because they were too drunk at the time.[10] It also occurred in declarator of marriage cases. (However, claims that the man was 'delirious', ie insane, at the time of the marriage occur only in cases where he was dead, and these are discussed in Chapter 8.)

In 1769, in response to Mary Galloway's charge that she and David Laidlaw, flesher (butcher) in Dalkeith, had been married by a minister in Edinburgh and bedded in the presence of witnesses, David claimed he had been drunk that night, and at her father's house the next day he 'again gott himself drunk ... declares that he staid there all night and next morning found himself in bed with the Pursuer'.

When shown the marriage certificate and asked if the signature was in his handwriting he declared that 'it is his Name but that he does not remember his having adhibited the same Declares he never did acknowledge to any person his being married to the Pursuer because he never was sensible of his being married to her.' Witnesses to the ceremony and bedding testified that he appeared sober on both occasions, and David was declared to be Mary's husband.[11]

In 1776 Janet Law, living in Edinburgh, raised a counter-action against David Hill, clock and watch maker in Thurso.[12] He had married another woman there and raised a declarator of freedom action against Janet when she wrote to the parish minister after learning of his second marriage. After bearing him a child some years earlier Janet alleged that she had been regularly married to him in Dysart, Fife, in 1773. David claimed that after being absent from his native country for some years he revisited Dysart on 'a jaunt, where unluckily for him he was again introduced to this pursuer who kept him in a state of intoxication during his whole stay in that place being only four days ....What past during this period of intoxication the defender cannot say only he is certain that during that time he was incapable to give a consent that would have been binding in the smallest mercantile affair.' As to the marriage certificate she produced,

> *If this Minister did marry the Defender as He alledges, it is certainly one of the most extraordinary marriages ever celebrated by a Clergyman of the established Church of Scotland. To marry a Stranger at first sight without a Certificate or recommendation from any Person, and for ought he the Clergyman could know, might have had a wife in every one of the three Kingdoms throu' which he had passed, and that stranger too in a visible state of intoxication without proclamation of banns and absent from any one friend, was a step that cannot be paralleled in the Annals of the Church of Scotland.*

Once again, witnesses testified to seeing the marriage ceremony and no drunkenness in the man, and the marriage was declared valid.

In a case of rival claims, discussed also in Chapter 7, Isobel Robertson produced a certificate of having been fined by Lanarkshire JPs for irregular marriage in 1802 to Andrew Hamilton, carter in Airdrie.[13] Andrew claimed that he was drunk at the time. Isobel's lawyer called his story 'utterly incredible.'

> *Was the defender drunk and insensible of what he was doing for four days and four nights together. Was he intoxicated when he appeared before the Justices of Peace, and will it be believed that these Justices declared a marriage when they found the man in a state of total insensibility from drunkenness. Was he drunk when he carried the Respondent to Airdrie, and introduced her as his wife to his friends?*

Of course he was not, and this marriage too was declared valid.

In 1816 Marion Williams and George Lindsay, baker or victual dealer in Edinburgh, were married by Joseph Robertson after 'marriage lines' (ie of banns having been proclaimed) were procured from the session clerk.[14] George's story was that he had seen her only once before, 'in the Tavern in which she served', when, on 19 August, 'on his return from Portobello Races', he met her in the High Street and she asked him to go with her to her master's tavern for a drink. He then accompanied her to her master's house, 'where he consumed not less than four gills of ardent spirits'. In the course of a jocular conversation with others Marion said that she would be married that night and asked George, by then very drunk, to accompany her to a friend's house. She then took him to Joseph Robertson's house. 'Marriage lines were most improperly issued by the Session Clerk .... The marriage it would seem then proceeded notwithstanding the inebriated State of the Defender.' They then went on to a bawdy house where there was a bed in every room but stayed only ten minutes: 'when he had recovered his senses on the morning after this alleged marriage or rather Conspiracy he thought no more about it, never viewing it in any other light than as a jest or at least as an Artful trick on the Part of the Pursuer.' Marion's lawyer said of George's defences:

> though he pretends to be in such a state from drink as to be incapable of giving Consent yet he gave a very Particular Statement of what he alledged to have happened – the jocular conversation in her master's house – the Parties going to Mr Robertsons – what passed there – the sending for the lines, the parties going to Mrs Stewarts and what passed there – but says they did not remain longer there 'than ten minutes' and that the allegations of the bedding 'is completely false' – Can it be for a moment supposed that a man so completely intoxicated as to be incapable of giving consent as was here alleged could recollect all the Circumstances stated by him so distinctly nay so very minutely told as to ascertain to a minute the time he staid in Mrs Stewarts house?

Joseph Robertson himself was one of the witnesses and testified that George did not appear to be drunk, and Mrs Stewart testified about the bedding and that 'she did not see any appearance of his being in liquor.' That marriage also was declared valid.

However, some men genuinely were too drunk to know what was happening. Irregular marriages in London got a bad reputation because of incidents like the one 'when a youth named Hill was persuaded to drink himself into a state of intoxication at an alehouse near the Fleet Prison, and was then drawn into a marriage with a woman "in mean circumstances and of a bad character".'[15] Such things also happened in Scotland.

At first sight Catherine Leitch's story (in 1792) is more plausible than that of Alexander Torrance (formerly of Greenock, by then merchant in Limerick, Ireland).[16] She alleged that he had given her a written acknowledgement of marriage, that they had been bedded in the presence of witnesses, that the next morning he acknowledged her as his wife in the presence of those witnesses, and he then visited her as a husband as often as he could while keeping the marriage secret until he was no longer financially dependent on his uncle; and she bore his child.

In his defence Alexander said that when he was 19 and Catherine was a menial servant in his uncle's house and much older than him, she enlisted the help of a fellow servant and another man to get him drunk. She came to his bed that night 'when inebriety had deprived him of all judgement and steadiness while at the same time it had excited his passions' and he then had sex with her for the first time. Soon after that, when he was again drunk, she asked him to write out some lines in case she became pregnant, admitting paternity. He had no intention of denying such a thing if she did bear a child, so he 'wrote a paper at a time when his senses were not in a situation to admit of his chusing proper expressions to convey his ideas'. He added: 'Very luckily however the paper he wrote conveyed no ideas at all and bears internal evidence of the inebriation of the writer.' Catherine had not made the document part of her evidence, but Alexander now supplied it:

> Greenock 22d Jan[y] 1785 These is to certifying and declaring that the bearers hereof Alexr Torrance and Katrine Leitch came before me craving them to be married and gave solemn oaths and whom God put together let mine not asunder This I do before these witnesses.

Two fictitious names had been inserted as witnesses, and though she came to his bed on the two following nights he never acknowledged her as his wife. Catherine was unable to prove a valid marriage.

Although in a case mentioned above, a marriage ceremony conducted by Joseph Robertson was considered to be valid, that of Sarah Dow and William Eadie, in 1802, was not. The couple had come to Edinburgh from Kinross, along with her brother and brother-in-law, and Eadie claimed that the latter had kept him continually drunk. One of several witnesses, John Burgess, described meeting Eadie in Edinburgh and declared that 'he was what is vulgarly called fou'. William had taken Burgess into a public house 'and told him a story about an attempt that had been made to seduce him into what he called a damned marriage'. The witness did not remember the exact particulars, 'but it was something about a servant girl that had run away from him; and her friends, he said, had insisted upon his seeking her; and he said the friends had kept him fou ever since he had left Dunning, and he was fou yet'. When they brought marriage lines and wanted to go to a minister, he said, 'he made an excuse that he wished to make water, and having got out of the house, left them.' The commissaries found that Sarah had not proved a marriage.[17]

Heavy drinking was common in eighteenth-century Scotland, but those cases hinged on lack of consent because of drunkenness. (There were two cases in which a woman successfully contested a declarator of marriage action raised by a man on the grounds that she had been made drunk, but discussion of these is reserved for Chapter 9.)

Only Joking

Free consent was also not present if the so-called marriage ceremony was nothing but a lark. 'It is commonly believed in England that there is a considerable risk in Scotland of being married without knowing it', wrote a Scottish advocate:

> *Perhaps in a charade a mock ceremony is gone through, and afterwards the parties to it are horrified to find that what they meant in jest has turned into earnest, and that they are validly married to each other. Or it may be that a man, by way of a foolish jest, or for some other reason, speaks of a lady of the company as 'my wife,' or as 'Mrs A.,' and though neither the one nor the other of them has any intention to marry, they find themselves married by force of law.[18]*

The author took pains to point out that there was no real danger of this occurring.

In January 1745 Elizabeth McNaughton, a widow, raised an action against Mr William Clugston, surgeon apothecary in Stranraer, alleging that the previous May he had brought William Maxwell of Ardwell, a Justice of the Peace, to her, and they joined hands and were married by him.[19] William replied that all that had happened on that day was that Maxwell and others took him to Elizabeth's tavern

> *and having drunk pretty liberally a frolick came in their heads to have the pursuer the Landlady and the Defender married together who were altogether strangers to one another And some Discourse past on that head in Jest.*

That was all the 'courtship' amounted to.

> *And the next Day the same Jest was renewed and push'd so far that Ardual as a Justice of the peace pretended to officat as the Celebrator of a marriage betwixt them which was looked upon by the parties and all present as no other than a Jest nor did the parties give any mutual Consent to accept one another as married Spouses before him whatever words he might have pronounced And if there was any congratulations on the occasion it was no more than carrying on the jest But which never turned into Earnest by the parties bedding together on the Contrary the Defender went off with the rest of the Company having been only at Portpatrick on his return from Ireland And soon thereafter made his Addresses of Courtship to a Young Lady in the Neighbourhood –*

and was married in October. Elizabeth abandoned her case.

In 1804 Ann Archer, daughter of a weaver in Ferryparton Craigs, raised an action against Andrew Berrie, corn dealer there, alleging a marriage ceremony in the presence of witnesses.[20] Andrew explained that in October he was among a number of farmers who 'were superintending the Shipping at Ferryparton Craigs of some grain which they had sold'. Shipping grain, 'by bringing a number of people together with servants and horses and detaining them a long time, is generally attended with a treat of meat and drink', and on this occasion 'the farmers and merchants met in the morning and frequently adjourned to the house of Thomas Gorrie Innkeeper in Ferryparton craigs, whose servant the pursuer then was.' In the afternoon, once all the grain was on board ship, 'those concerned in the Cargo retired to Gorrie's house to settle the money part of the transaction,' and Ann, as the only servant there, was occasionally in the room.

> Towards evening the Company became merry, and some of them endeavoured to force a kiss from the pursuer, which produced much noise and laughing, the pursuer in the meantime being sometimes in the hands of one, and sometimes of another of the Company. The defender upon one occasion having got hold of the pursuer, one of the farmers who was disappointed, cried he would marry them, and without farther ceremony declared them man and wife as well as he could articulate, being much overcome with drink The Company next tumbled the pursuer and defender with their Cloaths upon them just as they sat into the bed which was in the room At this time the pursuer had as little idea of a marriage as the defender, and was not consulted being in some respects passive to the frolick and seemingly pleased with the contention of the Company about her.

However, Gorrie and his wife were Ann's uncle and aunt, and when this 'bedding' occurred, they apparently

> conceived the plan which is now operating upon. They came into the room and witnesses at their backs crying out 'see there they lye married man and wife, and we take you to be witnesses,' after which the pursuer left the event and went about her household employment. Next day the company that had been in Gorrie's had much laughter about the frolick but it appears that Gorrie was resolved to make as much of it as possible, for on the thirtieth of October he caused take out the present Summons.

Ann was unable to prove a valid marriage.

No Jurisdiction

The court's jurisdiction covered Scotland, but what if one party had left the country? After 1753 England accepted only 'regular' marriages as valid (and even before then English courts were not accepting 'contract' marriages), so a man wishing to repudiate a marriage might move south of the border and then argue that he could not be subject to a Scottish court. In divorce cases, when English couples came before the commissaries they had to prove a Scottish domicile.[21] Contradictory judgments were made in declarator of marriage cases.

In one that ran from 1742 until 1746 Rebecca Dodds claimed William Wescomb as her husband on the grounds of a marriage ceremony conducted by David Paterson, followed by cohabitation, plus a child always known as their lawful child, and a letter signed as her 'most loveing Husband'. William had been a registrar in the Court of Exchequer for some years before returning to London, and his lawyer asked 'how far by the Rules of Law it is competent to proceed in this Action of Declarator and Adherence against the Petitioner in his present situation, where he has no longer either Residence, office, or Estate within Scotland.' But her lawyer replied that as the marriage was celebrated in Scotland, 'The same and whole Consequences thereof must be regulate according to the Laws where the Contract had its use and foundation just in the same manner as any Civil Contract wou'd be.' The commissaries agreed and repelled his defence. Rebecca had witnesses to the marriage, and William had to pay her an annual aliment, dated back to the time of the marriage.[22] This case was always cited subsequently where lack of jurisdiction was argued, but of course defenders always insisted on the difference between that situation and their own.

John Gray Esquire was a student at the University of Glasgow when he was alleged to have married Margaret Scruton but was at home in Ireland when she raised her action against him in 1772.[23] The commissaries repelled his defence of lack of jurisdiction, but he appealed against this to the Court of Session:

I only came to the country with the intention of attending the college, and returning to Ireland from whence I came: I was under age when the folly stated in the libel is said to have been committed; I never had any office, or lived in the country in any other character than as a boarder at the college; it is not said that I ever cohabited with the pursuer as my wife; and it is not pretended that she is with child.

Her lawyer argued eloquently: 'The marriage was perfected in this country, and the defender by entering, in Scotland, into that most solemn contract of divine institution, did thereby subject himself to the jurisdiction of your Lordships.' John had resided in Scotland

eighteen months and more before his marriage, and this action was raised; he had no intention to remove out of it for a long time, and yielded only to a scheme devised by others for escaping your Lordships jurisdiction, by flying Scotland, which, on common principles, cannot be allowed to benefit him ... were the doctrine contended for in the bill to be established as the law of this country, the consequences would be dreadful. It would at one blow deprive our women of that defence which our law has with so much propriety given them, by opening our ports to an inundation of foreigners ... not over scrupulous in their dealings with the fair sex, and who, under the appearance of husbands, might seduce and debauch our women at pleasure, and afterwards walk off exulting at the havoc they had made, and laughing at the laws of our country.

However, in this case the Court of Session reversed the commissaries' decision, and John was assoilzied.[24]

How complex the question could be is shown in the 1779 case of Mary Key, daughter of a weaver in Paisley, against Peter-James Bennet junior, son of a silk weaver in London. Initially, as he was not a native of Scotland, the commissaries sustained his defence of lack of jurisdiction. Mary appealed against this decision, and the commissaries asked Peter-James to state how long he had resided in Scotland before receiving the citation and what his employment had been at that time. He stated that when he was 15 he became an apprentice to silk manufacturers in London and soon after that was sent by his employers to Paisley, 'to get some insight in the business of silk-weaving', where he remained for two years. The commissaries reversed their original decision and sustained the jurisdiction of the court. Peter-James appealed to the Court of Session and that court instructed the commissaries to revert to their original decision. Mary appealed to the Court of Session, pointing out particularly that Peter-James had been residing in Scotland at the time she raised her action when he had been personally cited to appear as a defender in the cause. The Court of Session once again sustained the jurisdiction of the court.[25]

In declarator of marriage actions the court does not appear to have had a clear-cut rule about jurisdiction, and therefore it was worth trying that as a defence. However, most of the men contesting such actions were living in Scotland, and some of them were not too scrupulous about the means they used.

Unsavoury Tactics

One unpleasant aspect of many declarator of marriage cases is the man's attempt to depict the woman as a whore. This was a key tactic if the woman was claiming damages for seduction, because it was held that a woman could not be damaged by 'seduction' if she was not virtuous to begin with; therefore this aspect will surface again in Chapter 6. But it was also used in a number of straightforward marriage cases, to persuade the court that the woman could not have anticipated marriage.

The extent to which the allegations came from the man and the extent to which they were dreamed up by his lawyer cannot always be untangled. But it is clear enough in a case like that of Katharine Malcolm against John Lessells, weaver in Pathhead, in 1781, because his judicial declaration did not support the picture painted in his defences. In the latter it was stated that Katharine's 'behaviour was very light', and her 'virtue was but slender, having it's believed in the Course of her Galantrey bestowed favours upon other young men'. When personally examined in court he still insisted that he had never intended marriage, and therefore Katharine, who had no proof, lost her case. But when asked about her character he no longer defamed it: he 'had no bad opinion of her' and 'looked upon her as a Neighbour as good as himself but had no thoughts of Marriage'.[26]

By contrast, in the 1804 case of Frances Henderson against John Pitbladdo, shipmaster in Charleston, Fife, the man had already physically abused her and broken her thumb, 'whereby she was prevented from doing any needlework, at which she was in use formerly to gain her livelihood', and the abuse continued in court.[27] She was an Englishwoman, and they met in Egypt when he was in the navy and she was housekeeper to a carpenter, James Braye. They cohabited and he eventually brought her to Scotland where he introduced her to his parents and others as his wife. After he maltreated her she left him and went to London. He begged her to return, promising to treat her 'more kindly', and she did so, but a few months later he deserted her and refused to acknowledge her as his wife.

According to John, Frances had been married twelve years earlier to James Baxter, a joiner, with whom she sailed, and

> it was only when she was discharged from that ship [the Diadem], on account of Drunkenness and firing a Pistol at the Master of Arms that she lived on Shore in Egypt, first with a Mr Baillie and afterwards with this Mr Braye, in the capacity of Mistress to each in their turn.

Furthermore, it was well known that

> whenever a Sailor picks up a Girl to his Mind, he uniformly calls her his Wife, and holds himself out as her husband, although their connection may last not for twenty four hours; this Fact is peculiarly remarkable on occasion of a Ships coming to an Anchor in the Roads after a Cruize, where it never fails to happen that a number of Prostitutes contrive to get on board, and it is most certainly true that every Man immediately singles out his Girl whom he denominates his Wife, and so they continue in their own phrase Husband and Wife as long as the Ship remains at her Station; but it is believed, a Seaman would rather be astonished from this circumstance, to find himself sued as the lawfull husband of a Prostitute whom he only retained for the gratification of his Passions, and considered himself to be no longer tied to her than the Ship was to her Moorings.

Frances's lawyer commented that John had failed to answer 'the particular facts libelled, but given Your Lordships a very rude account of the treatment of Seamen in general to Women, which he has introduced in a very indelicate manner, rather unbecoming the Dignity of this Court'. She had never heard of James Baxter and had never been married to anyone before John. She

> was never on board of the Diadem, so could not possibly be dismissed from that Ship on

any account whatever, and She never in her lifetime fired a pistol, indeed she is of too timid and gentle a nature to do any such thing. And being of a weakly constitution She could never take any Drink, even if she had been inclined to do so, which she never was.

She never knew Mr Baillie and was Mr Braye's servant, not his mistress. And, finally,

It is only necessary to inform Your Lordship further that the Pursuer is at present in the house of the Defenders Aunt, to whom the Defender introduced the Pursuer as his wife, and owned and acknowledged her as Such, a fact which almost every person in Charleston and Limekilns can prove was it necessary … and what will appear Still Stranger to Your Lordships, he even introduced the Pursuer as his Wife, to the woman he is Since married to, and to her family.

Frances was unquestionably John's lawful wife (making him a bigamist), and he was ordered to pay her an annual aliment.

In the action raised in 1814 by Elizabeth Dunn against David Ewart Junior (former collector of the customs at Arbroath, then residing in Edinburgh), David claimed that he had had an 'illicit connection with her in the fields and places about her fathers house, and she had also upon sundry occasions clandestinely admitted him into the place where she slept in her fathers house where he had had illicit connection with her and likewise clandestinely in the Town of Arbroath and Dundee'. Her lawyer responded that his defences were 'calculated to add insult to keep lasting and unmerited injury'. She 'never had any connection with him in the fields' and 'never secretly or clandestinely admitted him to her Fathers house – there was no necessity for doing so as he was openly acknowledged as her husband in the family and in general the Pursuer could safely lay her hand to her heart and with a pure and unsullied conscience say she never slept a night with the Defender in a stolen or hidden manner but openly as her husband.' Elizabeth's marriage was declared valid.[28]

Another unsavoury tactic was to threaten key witnesses. In the 1741 case of Barbara Nairn against William Richardson Younger, featured earlier in this chapter, William Senior tried to bully Barbara into signing a document claiming she had never been married to his son. When she refused he threatened David Strang, the celebrator of the marriage, with prison if he did not sign a document stating that he had not married them to each other. But Strang did not succumb to this pressure and testified in court that he had celebrated the marriage.[29]

In a male declarator case, that of David McKie, a teacher in Maybole, Ayrshire, against Margaret Ferguson in 1778, a witness testified that 'it was the report of Maybole And the Country around that the deponent was to be hanged in the Grass Market of Edinburgh if the deponent came into Edinburgh to be a witness in this Cause for the pursuer.' The defender's family were furious with him, and the parish minister 'seemed to be Apprehensive for the deponents safety when he went to Edinburgh'.[30]

Apart from threats, bribery was also attempted. In a 1784 case Alexander Goodwin said that Catharine Goodwin had been married some eight or nine years earlier to a man named Barker or Parker. She denied this, but the entire case hinged on whether Catharine was already married, and Alexander or his agents persuaded a man called Tap and his wife to find witnesses to testify that she was. Catharine on her part found a witness who established that 'a Mrs Fraser was brought into Tap's house several times and offered Money and the witness heard Tap say That if he could get Mrs Fraser in Liquor he would make her swear any thing ....The Witness also heard Tap say to Mrs Fraser that if she would swear to the pursuer's being married to another Man than the defender she would be well rewarded.' And when Tap 'observed the witnesses reluctant to accept of a Bribe, "He said damn him, he knew nothing about the pursuer's being married to another man than the defender but if he wanted to get rid of his wife, meaning the pursuer, he would find abundance of people who would swear for Money".'The commissaries therefore refused to allow Tap to appear as a witness, but they did allow his wife to do so. She 'was accordingly brought forward and the Oath begun to be administered to her when she was discovered to be so very drunk as to be incapable of giving a distinct Answer to any question'.[31] Such skulduggery was far less frequent in marriage cases than in divorce cases, but it certainly existed.

The previous chapter, on modes of proof, and this one, on ways of contesting a case, plus their attendant case studies, have revealed how far from straightforward it could be to prove a valid marriage. The strongest evidence was something in writing, but even that depended on what the 'something' actually was. No woman could depend on what a man would declare under oath in court. And because it was possible to get a young man drunk and inveigled into marriage, men could claim this story in defence. The lengths that some individuals would go in threatening or bribing witnesses shows how hard they resisted being pronounced legally married.

For the most part, however, the modern reader will have agreed with the commissaries' decisions about which relationships should, under Scottish law, be judged valid marriages, and this will continue throughout the book.

Notes

1   'Claverhouse' (Meliora C Smith), *Irregular Border Marriages* (Edinburgh, 1934), 154-5.
2   CC8/5/3.
3   CC8/6/14. He had to pay her £20 for bygone aliment since their marriage, but no subsequent aliment was set, so clearly it was assumed that he would live with her as her husband.
4   CC8/6/21. Jean alleged that at the time of the Leith races Francis 'Solemnly swore he was then to make amends for all he had done and would furthwith Marry her promise-

ing and Engageing to Compleat and Solemnize the Bond of Matrimonie ... upon which the Complainer told him that none but God was witnes to their Agreement and accordingly Accepted of the said promise and again gave the use of her body in Carnal Copulation.' But in court Francis declared that at that time he 'coming to understand that the pursuer gave herself out to be his wife, went to the place where she was lodged And finding her was very angry with her and complained much of her spreading abroad such a story as that of the Deponents being married to her, and discharged her to do so any more, upon which she averr'd that she had never spread any such story nor called herself the Deponents wife'.

5   CC8/6/123.
6   CC8/6/119.
7   CC8/6/147.
8   CC8/6/144.
9   'Claverhouse', *Irregular Border Marriages*, 154.
10 Leah Leneman and Rosalind Mitchison, *Sin in the City – Sexuality and Social Control in Urban Scotland 1660–1780* (Edinburgh, 1998), 102.
11 CC8/5/12.
12 CC8/6/36.
13 CC8/6/83.
14 CC8/5/36.
15 Roger Lee Brown, 'The Rise and Fall of the Fleet Marriages', in R B Outhwaite ed, *Marriage and Society – Studies in the Social History of Marriage* (London, 1981), 132.
16 CC8/5/22.
17 No papers appear to have survived for this case, details of which come from James Fergusson, *Treatise on the Present State of Consistorial Law in Scotland* (Edinburgh, 1829), Reports, 43–50. The decreet was not issued until December 1814.
18 'An Advocate' (F P Walton), *Marriage Regular and Irregular* (Glasgow, 1893), 19.
19 CC8/6/15. Elizabeth embellished the bare bones of this story. She had said to him that 'she had a family of Children, he answered that he would do the best he could for them, and she further telling him that she had taken care of her family these severall years and was in debt, he answered that he would pay it all, and further said It is hard I must force you to your own good, for I will take you from a publick house which I think a Hellish life to One in your Station and the said Mr William Maxwell interposeing and saying that he was surprised that she the Complainer should sitt so fare [sic] in her own light that few in Galloway would refuse Mr Clugstoune and that tho he Mr Maxwell had never done the lyke before he as a Justice of the peace would marry them'.
20 CC8/5/28.
21 Leah Leneman, 'English Marriages and Scottish Divorces in the Early Nineteenth Century', *Journal of Legal History* Vol 17, No 3, and *Alienated Affections – The Scottish Experience of Divorce and Separation 1684–1830* (Edinburgh, 1998), c.11.
22 C8/5/6. One witness testified that she thought William was joking when he said that Rebecca was his wife, but he swore that she 'was truely his wife, and he wondered the deponent had not heard of his marriage before that time That the deponent said Mr Wescomb I thought you would have married one of your own Country women but he said that he Loved the pursuer better than any of his Country Women.'
23 Papers for this case do not appear to have survived in the Commissary Court records, but it is summarised in Session Papers, Signet Library, 159; 23 (1772).
24 There is no note attached to explain how the judges came to this decision, and I have not found the case discussed by legal commentators.
25 It is perhaps not surprising that lawyers should have borrowed cases concerning jurisdiction and failed to return them; the process papers for this case too appear to be missing. It is summarised in Session Papers, Signet Library 349; 6 (1780). From handwritten notes it is clear that one of the judges disagreed with the majority decision, but though none of them thought Mary had any hope of establishing the marriage, 'on the

Jurisdiction they were clear and entirely upon his having been personally cited.' It appears that Mary then abandoned the case.

26 CC8/6/39.

27 CC8/6/79.

28 CC8/5/36. During the course of the process David persuaded Elizabeth to sign a paper voluntarily withdrawing from the action, but as her infant son was also a pursuer the court insisted on the case continuing on his behalf. Subsequently she insisted that she had signed the paper only because David told her that it was his relations who were fighting the case, not him, and that she never had any 'idea of withdrawing the claims which she and her Child held against him as a lawful husband and parent. These claims she never departed from, nor did the Defender require she should do so; on the contrary at the very time he obtained from her the disclamation, he acknowledged her to be his lawful wife, and declared his readiness to live and cohabit with her as such.' But after bearing him another child she was again deserted and therefore fought the case anew, and won.

29 CC8/6/14.

30 CC8/6/38.

31 CC8/6/44. But Catharine's action was eventually abandoned.

CASE STUDY 5

STEWART V. LINDSAY: THE EQUIVOCATOR

SOME men lied outright under oath, denying well attested facts, while others shrank from the outright lie, and equivocated instead. Robert Lindsay of the Excise was in the latter category.

At the time Elizabeth Stewart raised her action in 1814 her father and brother had for some years been prisoners of the French, so that Elizabeth and her mother had to support themselves and the younger children. Elizabeth worked as a milliner and dressmaker, and her mother rented out one of the rooms in their house in Kirkcaldy. Robert Lindsay became their lodger in 1811. He was aged about thirty and 'a man of a good appearance'. He persuaded her, she said, that it was not a sin to yield to him, even quoting the Bible (1 Corinthians 7.36 – 'let him do what he will, he sinneth not; let them marry') and promising that he would marry her if she became pregnant. She had thought he would only marry someone 'of the same age with himself from the nature of the widows' fund to which he belonged', but he assured her that 'he only had to pay a pound to the Society for each year of the difference of ages and that he would pay it all up at once, so that they would not after-wards be troubled with it.' And he gave her a copy of the book detailing what an exciseman's widow would receive. But in December 1813 he was posted to Bannockburn and, though she was pregnant by then, refused to 'fulfil his repeated promises of marriage'. And thus, 'When her Father and her Brother sharing the common deliverance of Europe returned to this Country, they had the mortification to find their Daughter and Sister scarsely entering her 20th year in a state of pregnancy, dishonoured by a denial of marriage by a man who at the best could only found his denial on a very gross self accusation.'

Robert underwent a lengthy interrogation in court, part of which went as follows: 'Interrogated when he began to pay particular attention to the Pursuer? Depones and answers "I do not recollect paying particular attention to her at any time" Interrogated if about March [1813] he asked the Pursuer if she would take him for a husband? Depones and answers "No, I do not recollect of having done it." Being specially interrogated and desired to give a positive answer whether he ever put such a question to the Pursuer? Depones and answers "Not at that time that I recollect of." Interrogated at what time he put such a question? Depones and answers "at no time".... Interrogated what expressions about marriage he ever made to her? Depones and answers "I do not recollect I ever made any expressions of marriage to her." ... Interrogated if in particular he did not say on a Sunday evening that as he and the Pursuer were to be married there could be no sin in a connection between them and that he could prove this from the Scriptures? Depones and answers "I did not say that at that time." Interrogated If he said so at any time to her? Depones and answers "Not in that case." Interrogated in what case he said so? Depones and answers "I recollect once but I cannot specify the time that I said to her I thought it was not much sin." Interrogated If he did not point out a certain passage in the Bible in support of his argument? Depones and answers "No I did not, I recollect I mentioned a chapter and bid her look at it but I do not remember the time or any thing further than doing that.'"

Eventually he admitted that the passage was in Corinthians but denied that he asked her to submit to his embraces after showing her the verse and when asked 'If he did not say that the Bible itself showed that as he and the Pursuer were to be married a connection between them would not be sinful?' he replied, 'I never said that we were to be married.' The examination continued: 'Interrogated if at any time when he was endeavouring to persuade her to yield to his embraces she answered him in words to the following purpose "Mr Lindsay you have no regard for me or you would never ask any thing of the kind"? Depones and answers "Yes, I recollect her saying so" Interrogated if upon that occasion he professed strong attachment to the Pursuer? Depones and answers "I don't think that I did." Interrogated if after she had said so to the Deponent he did not say to her when parties considered themselves as married the ceremony signified nothing? Depones and answers "I do not recollect positively the expressions that might have passed at the time." Specially interrogated whether he used such expressions at that time? Depones and answers "I really could not say positively whether I used such expressions or not at the time, I never considered myself as married.'"

Later he was questioned about the widows' fund, and whether he had had any conversations about it with her and her mother, and he claimed that he had been talking generally, not specifically. 'Being shown a Book entitled "List of Acceders to the Incorporation of the Officers of Excise in Scotland at fifth of July Eighteen hundred and nine" and Interrogated If he gave that to the Pursuer or her Mother? Depones and answers "I do not recollect of whether I gave it her or left it in the room." Specially Interrogated upon the solemn oath he had taken, and desired to give a positive answer, Depones and answers "I cannot say whether I gave it into her hand or not." ... Interrogated if when he gave her the book he said to her that she would see from it what she would have from the fund if she were his widow? Depones and answers "I said to her she would see what she would have if she was a younger widow.'"

After all this the commissaries found that 'altho' the Defender denies that he ever made any explicit promise of marriage to the pursuer, Yet the Admissions made by him in other parts of his Deposition with evident reluctance and equivocation as to what passed in conversations with the pursuer go far to establish a virtual promise, or offer of marriage to her on his part: Find it explicitly admitted by him that on one occasion previous to the copula he pointed out to the pursuer and desired her to peruse a chapter of the New Testament which expressly treats of Marriage and that he afterwards conversed with her on the subject of it. Find that on another occasion he gave to, or left with her a copy (in process) of a printed List of the Acceders to the Incorporation of the Officers of Excise in which his own name is inserted and which relates to the provisions for Excisemen's Widows and that he had different conversations with the pursuer and her Mother on the subject. Find that these facts when viewed in connection with the Defender's other Admissions can be regarded in no other light than as fully equivalent to an explicit promise or offer of Marriage, and as thus sufficient along with the subsequent copula likewise admitted by him to constitute a valid marriage betwixt the parties by the Law of Scotland'.

Robert appealed against the decision to the Court of Session and the higher court instructed the commissaries to examine him further. Part of that examination went as follows: 'The Deponent being admonished that in his former Deposition he said he had mentioned to the Pursuer the seventh chapter of First Corinthians and bid her look at it and being Interrogated for what purpose he did this Depones and answers "It was one Sabbath I had been looking over it and I just desired her to look at it." The Court having observed that this was no answer to the question and he being desired to give a direct answer for what purpose he did so Depones and answers "Just to hear her opinion." ... Interrogated if he was aware that it contained descriptions relative to marriage when he gave it to her Depones and answers "Yes I was aware that it treated on that." ... Interrogated if when he conversed with her afterwards about the chapter he understood that she had perused those parts of the chapter which relate to marriage Depones and answers "Yes." Interrogated if when he desired the Pursuer to read the chapter above mentioned he thereby meant that she should reflect on the subject of marriage Depones and answers "I meant that she might consider it." ... Interrogated if he thinks that a person can peruse the chapter in question without reflecting on the subject of marriage Depones and answers "I should rather think not." Interrogated if it did not occur to him that the Pursuer when she read that chapter must have been led to consider the subject of marriage Depones and answers "I should suppose she would." Interrogated what was his intention in desiring the Pursuer to peruse that chapter Depones and answers "It was necessary for me to mention it to hear her opinion upon it – I mentioned it for the purpose to hear her opinion upon it."' And so on.

Another question produced a surprising answer: 'Interrogated how long before he had connection with her he had any conversation with her about marriage Depones and answers "I had been speaking to her about marriage both before and after I had connection with her." Interrogated if he is certain of this Depones and answers "Yes" – And the Answer to the Interrogatory being read over to him and he being asked if that was his answer Depones and answers "Respecting marriage in general I have, both before and after I had connection with her." And being desired to explain these last answers with the Answer ... in which he says "I do not recollect I ever made any expressions about marriage to her" Depones and answers "that was not meant by me – it was expressions of marriage between her and me.'" So, according to his declaration, he had had various conversations with her about marriage but never meant to imply that he intended to marry her.

He was also asked more about the widows' fund. 'Interrogated for what purpose he left the book with her Depones and answers "for no particular purpose." Being desired to explain for what purpose Depones and answers "Just if she thought proper to look at it she would see what a Gauger's widow would have as I was a Gauger myself." ... Interrogated if a woman can derive any benefit from the widows' fund without having first been married to an officer of Excise Depones and answers "No, she cannot.'" At this point the commissaries thought it 'proper to certify, that the deposition which has been just now given by the defender, has been emitted with a very great degree of hesitation, and with an evident desire to conceal, in so far as the deponent could, every thing which, as he conceived, might have a tendency to injure him in the present cause.'

Not surprisingly, the commissaries stuck by their original decision, and a further appeal to the Court of Session was refused. However, the final decree was not issued until 1826 when she awakened the case and successfully sued for her annual aliment, dating back to 1814, as he had never adhered to her.

CC8/6/152

CASE STUDY 6

YOUNG V. ARROT: THE GREATEST VILLAIN THAT EVER WAS

IN this case the man told several people that he was married, while at the same time doing his best to keep his options for deception wide open. He tried to blacken the woman's character, but his viciousness did his cause no good.

In the early 1730s Elizabeth (Betty) Young and her older sister, Katharine, the daughters of a deceased writer (lawyer) in Edinburgh, were, with their mother, on the fringes of gentry society. They were made acquainted with John Arrot of Fofarty by Lady Home of Renton, and 'by doing them severall good offices' they became friendly, so that the Young daughters and mothers were invited to the house of Fofarty to stay, and John Arrot of Fofarty and his lady stayed with the Youngs when they came to Edinburgh. Thomas Arrot was John's younger brother who returned from a long stay abroad in spring 1736. Having met them at Fofarty he too was invited to stay with the Youngs in Edinburgh, and by this time he had already told Betty that 'there was no woman in the world he would so much wish to be under the care of as she, nor any he had such a value for.'

While staying with them, one evening in February 1737, while Katharine was out of town, Thomas brought to the house 'a Gentleman in Dark blew Cloaths mounted with black', and said that to Betty that 'he could no longer Deferr marrying her And that he brought there with him for that end a friend of his own one Mr Gordon a Churchman who was in the next room.' Betty naturally objected to all this, not knowing the minister and wishing for witnesses, but Thomas 'in the most serious manner Called Heaven to Witness, and used the most solemn oaths and imprecations that his intentions were no other than Honourable and that he would never Deceive her And that it was only for Certain Causes with respect to his private affairs that he wanted his marriage not to be published for some time.' The minister joined in the pleas and assurances, and in the presence of her mother they were married by him and went to bed together.

When Betty's sister, Katharine, returned, Thomas told her of the marriage but begged her to keep it a secret. He had to go north to Fofarty then but said he would arrange matters so that Betty was invited to stay there, which she was, and together with Thomas and his lady, and Lady Renton, she went 'to the Goat Milk'. (Taking goats' milk or whey was meant to be health-giving, the equivalent of taking the waters at Bath or Harrogate.) Back in Edinburgh Thomas told Betty's aunt about the marriage and thereafter visited her as a relation. By February 1738 Betty was heavily pregnant and getting worried, but in response to Katharine's pleas Thomas replied that though Betty was her sister 'Yet she was his wife and that the Child was his Child.' Before leaving her to go north again in March he acknowledged the marriage to a minister of the gospel (so that the child could be baptised) and to a midwife. But when the child was born he denied that she was his wife.

Thomas's version of the story was scurrilous. When he first met her at his brother's house, he said, he soon discovered that she 'was not of difficult access She informed him that her Sister and She were Mantuamakers together to Trade that they stayed in family with their Mother ane old aged widow woman, and had a spare Room in their house which they lett to lodgers for rent and invited the defender when he had occasion to come to Edinburgh to be their Lodger and gave so many broad hints that the defender was led to make advances towards the obtaining of certain favours which were but faintly refused under pretext that her honour and reputation would suffer but gave no positive denyall on the contrary pressed the defender to come to Edinburgh to lodge in her Mothers house which was a reasonable encouragement upon so short ane acquaintance for the defender to go on in pursuite of this Game.'

When he stayed there (as a paying lodger rather than as a guest by his account) Betty at first gave herself 'airs of great virtue and reputation and under that pretext would gladely have buckled the Defender under a promise of Marriage before she should consent', but when he refused to consider marriage, he said, she at last went to bed with him and he 'was soon made Sensible from undoubted prooffs that the pursuers former pretensions to great virtue and reputation were all Grimace'. In his version the fact that Katharine (who normally shared a bed with her sister) was out of town at this time was part of the Youngs' plot to trap him, for Katharine finding him in bed with Betty said that 'her sister was ruined unless he would Marry her and therefore pressed a promise of Marriage which he positively refused to give.'

He did not know what means Betty and Katharine had used to persuade Mr Logan, the minister, that 'the Child was the produce of a private Marriage ....But thus far he was certain, that when they brought Mr Logan in upon him ... he carefully avoided saying the least word that might seem to import ane acknowledgement of Marriage.' As for her story about an actual ceremony, he said that she was not 'so simple as to be so easily Imposed upon to believe that no witnesses were necessary for proof of the Marriage and if she had been that simple could it be thought that her mother would have witnessed a form of Marriage liable to so plain ane Objection, She did not so much as pretend to have used that common precaution which even the most ignorant woman is carefull to do that of provideing herself with Marriage lines which is the strongest naturall evidence that it is all a fiction.'

Betty's response must have come as much from her heart as from her lawyer's pen: she 'could not but Testifie her surprise as weel as affliction at the usage she meets with from the defender. It is a deploreable misfortune for her to have fallen into the hands of a person bearing the name of a Gentleman who it seems thinks himself at liberty to make free with the rules of Honour and Truth.' If his account of her had been true it would 'cast a most unbecomeing reproach upon his own Brother and his Lady who cannot be thought without dishonour to have entertained so closs a familiarity and intimacy with any person of the Character the defender gives of the pursuer.'

In his response Thomas became even more scurrilous, now alleging that Betty had 'of a long time been in the use of disposeing her favours the very same with which she indulged him to other men', and did so particularly in June 1736 'in the litle wood called the Bush of Bunzian near to where she then resided'. Her retort was that in June 1736 she was with the party in the Highlands for the goat whey – 'there was no other man in the howse with her or in the neighbourhood but [John Arrot of] Fofarty except the wild highlanders whom she could not so much as understand or converse with She was in such state of bad health that she never went further than the outter door of the howse.' Furthermore, 'if she was become a proverb for lewdness by four days residence how does this agree with the many kind respects she afterwards met with at the howse of Fofarty from the defenders Brother and his wife and with the many kind letters she has under the Lady Fofartys hand all subsequent to these pretended acts of Lewdness.'

Eventually Betty was allowed to adduce proof. Her first witness was Mr George Logan, the minister, who was told about the secret marriage first by Betty's sister Katharine, and then by Betty. He had asked Betty for her marriage certificate, but she said that Thomas had told her 'she could not get it unless she owned herself Roman Catholick and took the Sacrament upon it for the person that married them was a popish priest.' And when the minister asked her 'why she had not more witnesses present she answered it was in complyance with Mr Arrots desire'. Mr Logan called on the couple and saluted Thomas, 'Congratulated him upon his Marriage and wished him all Manner of Prosperity and farther added that altho he was dissatisfied with the pursuer for her Marrying Irregularly Yet now when he saw the defender and observed him to be a person of good behaviour and a compleat gentleman and that she had made a good choise was the best appology she could make for her Marriage.' Thomas, he said, 'thanked the deponent for the good oppinion he had of him.' They sat down to tea and Thomas told the witness 'that he had some affairs to end or settle in the North Country which would obleige him to go there for three or four weeks and therefore he desired that her Marriage might not be divulged until his return to Edinburgh when he would make it publick.' The midwife also testified to being told by Thomas that Betty was his wife and asked to keep this a secret.

The Youngs had servants who testified to Thomas acknowledging and treating Betty as his wife. One of them said that in February 1737 Thomas 'brought to her Mistresses howse about the dusk of the evening or glooming a man wearing a suite of dark blew cloaths mounted with black'. The servant maid 'suspecting there was a marriage in hand listened at the Chamber door but could not hear so as to understand distinctly what was said in the Room only from the sough and Tone of the Voice she believed there was a person praying within the Room'. Another servant testified to a change of status; although Katharine was the older of the two, after the marriage Betty 'at table and otherways took place of her sister Mrs Katharin and as any thing was wanted she had observed Mrs Kathrine rise and bring it while the pursuer satt still'.

By May 1737 the marriage was Edinburgh gossip. Mary Fullarton, a widow, testified that in that month some ladies were drinking tea in her house 'where it was told by some of them as a piece of newes that there had been a marriage in Toun, and the deponent asking whose it was They told her that Miss Beatty Young had been married to a Gentleman, who lodged in her Mothers had been long abroad was very rich worth severall thousand pounds and that his name was Mr Arratt and that he was a doctor'.

The commissaries had refused to hear any evidence on Thomas's side concerning Betty's alleged misconduct, but at this point he tried again, specifying times and places where he claimed it had occurred. Her lawyer responded that Thomas had 'arrived to such a pitch of Malice against the pursuer as to invent and offer grounds of a process of divorce against her', but the marriage would have to be established first, so she should be allowed to bring proof of this, as much for the legitimacy of her child as for herself.

In spite of Thomas's objections, the commissaries allowed Betty's aunt and sister to appear as witnesses 'cum nota' (ie reserving judgment on the admissibility of their evidence until it was heard). The aunt testified to being told of the marriage by Betty, chiding her for keeping it a secret, and Thomas then saying to her, 'Aunt, Don't be angry for I laid strict injunctions upon my wife and Katty to keep our marriage secret until I returned to Toun.'

Katharine's testimony was particularly vivid. In June 1738 Betty and she were so worried that they went to Fofarty to see Thomas. Katharine 'asked him what was the meaning of that letter he had wrote to her and why he had not come up to Toun, as he promised and that his not doing so was a strange way of treating his wife To which he answered I do not know whither I have a wife or not whereupon the pursuer said to the defender Oh! Mr Arrat are you going to deny your Marriage upon which the defender said Beatty you know there was but one witnes your mother who is now dead and you have nothing under my hand so that I can deny it when I will.' Katharine then asked him 'where the man was that married them whom he called Mr Gordon, to which he answered by God you shall go blind that day you ever see him, That thereupon the pursuer said Since you say that my mother is dead and I cannot prove my Marriage can you deny it before God and added Mr Arrat have you no Conscience in you To which he answered if he had he would swallow it, and after many expostulations betwixt them, he said he had denyed it and would deny it If he should Damn his Soul to all eternity for he was going off the Country and could be no longer tyed to a wife.'

Betty, according to her sister's testimony, then 'fell down upon her knees and said Mr Arrat God forbid you should ruin your Soul for me And said do you not remember the protestations that you made to me upon my refuseing to sleep with you after we were married till such time as my Sister Kattie returned to Toun, That you took the great God of Heaven to Witnes that I was your wife and should be your wife till the day of your death or mine upon which he cryed out Beatty do not pleague me for my Soul is racked out of me saying I have pistles and I would be glade any body would shoot me thro the head for what I have done and if you have a mind Kattie you may take one of them and shoot me and after that take another and shoot yourself for I have done the most villainous action that ever man did and I know the world will think me the Greatest Villain that ever was but I will go abroad and not hear of it.'

At this point we are provided with an extraordinary picture of the examination of those witnesses in court, for Thomas complained of their 'deportment and behaviour'. Katharine's 'during the while course of her examination which continued for many hours was so foreward keen and anxious as in his humble oppinion ... was most unbecomeing a witnes' and 'she told many storries that were not asked her by the Lord Examinator'. Her lawyer in response said that what was 'most noticeable was their care and scrupulousness that everything they remembered was recorded correctly. The aunt's examination had taken from three in the afternoon until nine at night; Katharine's first session had been from three to about five or six, the next went on from two in the afternoon until ten at night ('without stirring from her seat', when 'she was observed to turn pale and faintish'), and the third from ten till noon. And, if all that were not enough, 'upon every Interrogator made by the Judge and answer given thereto by the witnesses', Thomas 'and one or more of those who came into the Court with him ... fell a stareing giggleing and sneering in the face of the witness.' And at the final session, when Katharine was describing what happened when she and Betty went to Fofarty in June, Thomas 'appearing highly inraged at her declareing the truth called out to the Judge in ane abrupt and boistrous manner to Question her if she the witnes herself on the said occasion at Fofarty did not say that she would go and hang herself'.

Thomas tried one more time to be allowed to prove Betty's 'libidinous behaviour', but the commissaries refused, for this 'though proven could not availl the defender in the present question'. It was up to him if he wanted afterwards to raise an action for divorce (which he did not do). The commissaries declared them to be married persons and their child a lawful child. Thomas appealed to the Court of Session which upheld the decision. But his villainy was not yet at an end, for he now petitioned that she and the child come to live with him, stating that if she did not do so he should not be liable to pay her any aliment. She answered that 'after the most injurious treatment she had met with and especially the gross attacks and Calumnies that have been advanced to the prejudice of her Character and Chastity in the course of the said process she could not think herself Obleiged either in duty or law to repair to the howse of her husband from whose past behaviour she could hitherto have no sufficient reason to expect either comfort or safety in living with him.' In spite of the general dictum that a wife's duty was to live with her husband, the commissaries refused his petition.

CC8/5/4

CASE STUDY 7

AITKEN V. TOPHAM: AN UNEXPECTED TWIST

THIS 1775 case appeared to be either a seduction or an illicit relationship. But when the girl's mother pressed legal action to protect her daughter's reputation, and the man began retaliatory muck-raking, the story spun off in a very unexpected direction.

Margaret Aitken, daughter of a deceased deacon smith burgess of Edinburgh, said that Edward Topham Esquire, an Englishman, persuaded her to go to England to marry him, and on 11 December 1774, accompanied by his friend, Paul Jodderell, they set off. They stopped at a public house twelve miles from Edinburgh where he 'prevailed upon her to yield to his Embraces and to sleep with him that night as his wife, but next morning in place of proceeding on their Journey he the Defender pretended that he had received a letter by express from Edinburgh which required his immediate return', and they all trooped back to Edinburgh. Thereafter he continued to promise marriage but failed to keep that promise.

Edward's story was that his home and estate were in Yorkshire and 'he only came to Scotland to pass a little time for his Diversion.' He met Margaret at a dance, and after initially refusing to sleep with him, she succumbed a couple of nights later. He 'then askt her to Sleep with him a whole night, which she said was impossible as her Mother would discover it, but that if he would take her to England, she would agree to go with him'. He consented, and she 'requested particularly that Mr Jodderell an intimate friend of the Defender to accompany them'. She brought some things to take along, but Edward gave the bag 'to his servant to put by in his own house, as he never entertained any serious thoughts of carrying her to England'. After the night at the inn she reluctantly returned home but continued to visit him every evening until her mother found out about the escapade. Margaret threatened to kill herself if he 'did not take her away from her Mother, with whom she repeatedly said there was no living'.

Edward, unable to persuade her to stay with her mother, 'told her that there was a woman who washed linens for Mr Jodderell who had an apartment but that it was so poor that it would be impossible for her to live in it for any length of time', but Margaret nevertheless moved herself in. She continued to threaten suicide if her mother found out, 'and had actually brought Laudanum for that purpose, so she staid in this House for about two months never once saying that the Defender was to marry her but only was to take her to England and buy her fine Cloaths.'

Margaret's mother eventually traced her and fetched her home. Mother, daughter, and a relation named Robert Cairnton went round to see Edward, and asked if he had promised to marry Margaret, 'which he said he never did, They then hoped he would make her some amends for the supposed loss of her character, and that she would be obliged to leave Edinburgh and go to Perth, and hoped the Defender would contribute something to Defray the Expence of her Journey.' Edward 'said he had no objection, if they would agree among themselves, what might be proper for that purpose, when they Departed seemingly well pleased, and would speak to their friends, and inform the Defender of their Determination, in a few days, but he heard no more of the Matter untill he was apprehended upon a warrand from the Commissary Court'.

That meeting was one of the topics of Edward's lengthy interrogation in court: 'did not the Mother blame and accuse you of having carried off and seduced the pursuer under promise of marriage .... Did not you repeatedly answer it was all very true, she said; that you was sorry for it; but could not now help it.' His reply was that 'Mrs Aitken blamed the declarant for carrying off her daughter and seducing her, To which he answered that he had not, and that according to his idea of seduction he had not seduced her .... Declared that Mrs Aitken also upon this occasion observed to the declarant that her daughter had lost her Character, To which the Declarant answered that he was sorry for it, But that he could not give it her again.'

With regard to the journey, he admitted that he 'had then no thoughts of going to England as he carried no luggage with him and no servant .... But believed the pursuer understood she was going to England.' Being asked if before he slept with her the first time 'he was satisfied that she had not known Man before Declared that he could not be certain whether she had nor not, but from the ease with which the pursuer complied he was of the Contrary opinion.' He admitted pretending to receive a letter recalling him to Edinburgh.

The testimony of the innkeeper, a widow named Elizabeth Adamson, was vivid. The party of three had been given two bedrooms, and a short time after they retired 'the deponent heard a skirle of a cry, upon which she came up to the turn of the stair, and the noise immediately ceased, when the deponent went again downstairs, and from the skirl as above mentioned the deponent had reason to believe that some of the Gentlemen were in Bed with the Lady, but whether one or both she could not say, only she apprehended the skirl came from the woman. That the skirle above mentioned did not seem to be the Cry of a person in distress nor would it have induced the deponent to have gone to her assistance .... That while the deponent was on the stair she heard a Mans voice saying "hush my dear you'll alarm the house" .... Deponed that it was her belief that the Gentleman and Lady were then in bed ... and she supposed that when she heard the skirle above mentioned they were in the act of copulation.' She believed they had been privately married, since naturally 'she would not have allowed the pursuer and defender nor any other Gentleman and Lady to have bedded in her house unless she had supposed them to be married persons.'

Robert Cairnton (who had accompanied Margaret and her mother) testified that Mrs Aitken said that 'her daughter was a sort of prisoner, That she could not now walk the streets without being pointed at, and that her Character was lost, and that her daughter was come of respectable parents as any Burgher in Town, To which Mr Topham replied "Peugh! I should not mind tho' half a dozen were calling to me on the street for such a thing" That Mrs Aitken then observed that she must mind it, and that she would endeavour to recover her daughters character as much as she could.' Cairnton himself had subsequently intervened, and when he asked Edward whether 'the pursuer had never known man before her connection with him, he put his hand upon his breast and acknowledged that she never had'. But at that time he also said he did not mean to marry her.

Paul Jodderell was on Edward's list of witnesses, but Margaret's lawyer objected to him as he had been acting for Edward. Daniel Mackenzie, a brush maker who also kept 'an oyster cellar', testified that Edward and Jodderell had come to see him and that 'Mr Jodderell talked a great deal to the deponent about the cause, enquired particularly into the pursuers character, and asked the deponent, if he knew that the pursuer was a whore, and if any other men had enjoyed her before Mr Topham and added that he Mr Jodderell was very sure that other Men had enjoyed her before Mr Topham.' The commissaries sustained the objections to Jodderell as a witness.

However, Mrs Stewart, in whose house Margaret had stayed those two months and to whom Margaret's lawyer also objected, was allowed to give evidence. She testified that she had asked Margaret 'what she expected of Mr Topham and why she had left her Mother', to which Margaret answered that she expected that he 'would give her fine Cloaths pay her board and carry her to London', and that if he 'would not take her in the way she was in, she would dress herself in men's Clothes and go with the Defender as his Livery man to London'. She 'never from first to Last insinuated to the Deponent that Mr Topham the Defender was married to her or had promised her marriage', and when Mrs Stewart asked her 'why she had left her Mother, she answered that she did not choose to live with her mother, because She was confined and had not her freedom like other Young people unless when her Mother was at Perth'. Mrs Stewart also testified that she had seen Margaret 'reading an obscene book and had heard her read aloud several passages of said book more than once'. Margaret told her that it came from Mr Topham, 'and the Book was marked with the usual impression of Mrs Yairs Circulating Library'.

At one point during her stay, Margaret told Mrs Stewart 'that Mr Topham was to have no more to do with her, and that Mr Jodderell with whom the Deponent was acquainted, was to accept of her, by which the deponent understood that Mr Jodderell was to keep her.' Mrs Stewart, having asked her 'upon what terms Mr Jodderell was to take her, she answered that Mr Jodderell had promised to do every thing for her that Mr Topham had done. But said that going to Mr Jodderell would be her last refuge.' (But 'after this Mr Jodderell acknowledged to the deponent that he only wanted to try the pursuer's fidelity to Mr Topham.') Mrs Stewart could not claim that she would not have allowed Margaret to lodge there if she had known that she was not married, but she did say that 'she was ashamed of having done so base an action as to take the Pursuer into her house, having never before or since had a person lodged in her house of a bad character or in a clandestine manner.'

The next witness proposed by Edward, a woman named Eddy Moyes, was successfully objected to because it was shown that she had been offering money for witnesses to blacken Margaret's character.

But it was a witness who was not objected to, David Wilson, gardener in Roslin, formerly an Edinburgh innkeeper, who dropped the bombshell. His public house, he said, 'used to be frequented by students at the College'. A student called Downes came there one night with a young girl called Aitken and sent for a minister. The minister 'came to the house and married this Downes to one Margaret Aitken in presence of the deponent and Daniel Sutherland the waiter.' The marriage lines were 'delivered to the deponent by Downes's order, and were to be kept by him till he should receive payment of half a guinea which had been promised to the Minister', and 'Downes drank upon this occasion a Bottle of Madeira which still remains unpaid.' David Wilson then produced the marriage lines, which he had seen the parties sign and which he himself had signed as a witness. He added that since then 'he had seen Downes frequently who desired him not to speak of what had happened in his house that night, as he Downes wanted to keep it private.' Immediately afterwards, he said, there was a quarrel between the couple, and she ran away.

Margaret's lawyer, faced with this new evidence, asked whether Wilson was sure that the man was really a minister, 'and whether he believed the parties to be serious about their marriage?' Wilson replied that 'he considered him as an half merk minister and that he believed the parties to be serious, as he used all the Ceremonies and prayed after them.' Wilson's servant also testified about the marriage. After that Thomas Murray, the celebrator, testified to celebrating the marriage and that 'some nights after the marriage he went to David Wilsons in Gray's Closs where he saw Downes who then told him that he had never seen Margaret Aitken after the Ceremony and had never been bedded with her, and that he never expected to see her again and that she would not see him.'

Margaret's lawyer tried to have Arthur Downes cited as a witness, but Edward objected because 'he had a manifest interest in the Cause seeing a Clear prooff had been brought of his marriage with this pursuer. If the pursuer prevail in the present process, he would be relieved from his marriage with her which would be an evident advantage to him as his desertion showed his desire to be free of her.' The commissaries sustained the objection. Her lawyer petitioned against this. She intended to prove by him 'that after the pretended Marriage with him it was mutually agreed to pass from the same nothing further having followed upon it, and the Petitioner was informed that he since married another woman And as there was no Copula they could of consent resile, and no third party could force a marriage upon them.'

But, of course, under Scottish law, consummation was required only if a promise was made for the future; mutual consent to a present marriage was all that was required to make it legally valid. With regard to Edward Topham the commissaries found 'no facts or circumstances proven relevant to infer marriage ... and in respect of the proof of the said pursuers previous marriage' they assoilzied him. Margaret appealed to the Court of Session, but the appeal was refused.

The ramifications of irregular marriage in Scotland were strange indeed.

CC8/5/15

CHAPTER 4

MISTRESSES

IN most contested cases (as revealed in Chapter 1) the woman failed to prove a marriage. In this chapter we look at cases in which the woman was judged to have been the man's mistress. The first section deals with officers' women. The second looks at cases where the woman was the man's servant or housekeeper, while the third is about 'kept' mistresses. While cases of army mistresses span the entire period, there is a clear time division between the second two categories, the servants being confined almost entirely to the early to mid-eighteenth century and the kept mistresses to the late eighteenth and early nineteenth. In other words, before the late eighteenth century a 'gentleman' might openly have a long-term sexual relationship with his employee, while by the early nineteenth century, even if she started out as his servant, he would subsequently set her up in other lodgings where he could visit her on the quiet.

Army Mistresses

The relationship between Captain James Dalrymple and Irishwoman Mary Gainer began in 1723 and resulted in seven children, of whom five were still alive when he married another woman in 1737. In 1739 he raised an action before the Commissary Court to stop Mary calling herself his wife; she raised a counter-process of Declarator of Marriage.[1] They had met in Dublin, and she later followed him to Gibraltar. Although this was a stable relationship, his witnesses made clear how they regarded her. Sergeant Allan Burn did not even know the surname of 'Miss Mary' who 'Lived with the defender in his house at Gibraltar in the Character of his house keeper but he never heard her repute his lawfull married Wife'. And in Ireland he had 'Looked upon Miss Mary as the defenders Miss, and not as his Wife'. Colonel James Kennedy looked on her as the Captain's

> servant or house keeper, or Mistris, which was a practise much obtained there at the time, That he never Esteemed her as his Lawfull married wife nor Shewed her that respect he would have done to the Captains Lady, For in his Common Conversation with her as he had occasion he allways called her plain Mally which he would not have done had he suspected her to be the Captains Lady.

Captain David Cunningham had 'heard other Gentlemen term her Mistress Dalrymple when Capt Dalrymple was present', but it was 'the common practice at Gibraltar for Ladies to pass by the names of the Gentlemen that keep them'. Thus, in the army at this time it was considered quite normal for a relationship that on the surface resembled a marriage (Mary not only bore James's children but looked after him as well, and would not have been sexually available to any other man) to be considered an illicit one that could be terminated at will. The woman was not 'elevated' in rank or respectability, as an officer's wife would be whatever her background.[2]

In 1798 John Smith Esquire, a major in the Norfolk fencible cavalry, stated that he was 'descended of a respectable family in the other end of the Island, and is presumptive heir to a considerable fortune, from which circumstances as well as the Rank he has already attained in his military profession, he is well entitled to form a very respectable alliance in the way of marriage'.[3] He had met Jane (or Jean) Aitken, who was claiming to be his wife, 'in a common Brothel in the Town of Dumfries'. In fact, he produced witnesses who had known her there. A cornet's servant had gone to the house 'for the purpose of being accommodated with a wench'. He 'gave her a little money after which Jean Aiken told him he might lye with her, but this offer the witness at the time declined. That the witness took every liberty with her except the last from which he was deterred by the Mistress of the house giving him to understand that Jean Aitken was extremely bad of the venereal disease.' A private did have sex with her.

Robert Alexander, cornet, testified to the outrage that ensued when the major brought Jean to the barracks. Several of the married officers took great offence, and 'a meeting of officers was held to consider what was proper to be done'. The cornet was particularly friendly with the major, so after the meeting broke up in disagreement, the colonel asked him 'endeavour to make some arrangement so as to prevent a breach between the Major and the other Officers on the subject of Jean Aikens being introduced into the Barracks'. In that conversation the major

> told him that he had previously seen some of the other Officers between whom and him warm words had passed as he had declared his resolution not to suffer Jean Aiken to be turned out of the Barracks and Major Smith added that he conceived himself to be entitled to keep a housekeeper in the Barracks … in the course of that conversation the Major suggested an inclination to declare that he considered Jean Aiken as his wife in order to put an end to all disputes upon the subject.

The cornet warned the major that 'if he had any intentions of this kind he should previously Bind the woman by as strong ties as he possibly could that she should take no advantage of any such declaration which was not meant to fix any serious connection between them, but merely to prevent Jean Aikens being turned out of the Barracks on account of her bad Character.' At the next meeting with the officers the major 'said that if nothing else would satisfy them he had no difficulty to say that he considered Jean Aiken his wife while he lived in the Barracks but that she was not to be considered on the same establishment as their wives, that he did not desire they should associate with her, or that she should associate with them'.

When the major had had enough of her he gave her a bond of annuity, and the lawyer who drew up the bond testified that when he went to the barracks 'it did not appear to the witness that the Major treated Jean Aiken as a wife, but as a kept Mistress.' After she accepted the bond the lawyer heard her 'say that both the Major and her were free from one another, and he might do as he pleased, and she would do as she pleased, and the witness understood that all connection between them was altogether at an end'.

The testimony above suggests that by the end of the eighteenth century the presence of legitimate wives in barracks was introducing an air of domestic respectability into army life. The free and easy days were over – but liaisons were still carried on.

In a case of 1809, Lieutenant Colonel John Baird of the Aberdeenshire regiment of militia also gave his mistress, Christian Mennie, a bond of annuity when he had had enough of her, on various conditions: she was not to come further south than Peterhead, was to lead a virtuous life, was not to have custody of her two children by him, and if she married then the money was not to be paid to her husband. One piece of evidence which he adduced was that

> every married officer is exempted from attending the Mess of the Regiment. This the Defender never was – he messed with the officers, and could not in the nature of things be said to live at bed and board with the Pursuer nor was the Pursuer ever introduced to any officer by the Defender nor considered by any of them in any other character than as his Mistress nor was she introduced or visited by any of the officers wives.

There was 'not an officer in the Regiment who will not swear that she was by all of them considered as his Mistress and by them treated as such'.[4]

In 1826 Euphemia Inglis raised an action against Captain Charles Barry. The captain said that at the beginning of 1822 Euphemia 'resided and co-habited with Lieutenant Elliot of the 77th Regiment then stationed in the castle of Edinburgh as his mistress'. In August 1822 the lieutenant went to England on leave of absence, and Euphemia, 'having thus been left unoccupied, the Defender took her into Keeping in the same character in which Lieutenant Elliot had entertained her vizt, that of his mistress.' She went along with him when the regiment left Scotland but was never treated by him 'in any other way than as a lady of easy virtue and as his mistress – Neither was she known, esteemed or treated as any thing else, by any other person.' Her status 'was that of a Kept mistress; and even in the conversations with her associates, who were usually the wives of the common soldiers, she represented herself as the mistress, and not the wife, of the Defender'. When he was stationed at Dumbarton Castle, Euphemia 'was excluded from the Barracks under the Governors regulation which was that no mistress should be admitted within the Precincts of the Fortress.'[5]

None of the above women were able to prove a marriage, and it was only because they were advised that a marriage in Scotland could be established on 'slender grounds' that they even thought of alleging any such thing.

Servant Mistresses

For an unmarried man (or widower) who wanted a sexual partner always at hand, what could be better than to make a domestic servant his mistress? But there were shades of grey between a housekeeper and a wife.

In a 1742 case Sir Alexander Hope of Carse, baronet, said that Margaret Drummond was hired as his housekeeper at 32 pounds Scots a year.[6] Margaret called herself a 'gentlewoman' and her lawyer stated that during the eight-and-a-half years that they cohabited:

she had the absolute direction of his family of his servants and children she had the disposal of his money went about in the Town of Edinburgh the publick place in the Kingdom dressed and attended in a chair in a way and manner well becoming the defenders wife, But by no means suitable to his harlot.

She came to The Carse as a 'comrade' to his sister, said her lawyer. She was only 15 or 16 at the time, 'and of an unspotted Character', so the idea that Sir Alexander would have paid 'such an one to be his whore at the rate of £32 scots per anno … must appear wholly incredible'. (Indeed, she stated that during their time together he 'Gifted to her several Rings one of which had a part of his hair set in it and likeways a Gold Broach with a diamond in it, a pair of Gold Earings, a Silver Snuff miln, a Sponge Box, a pair of Silver Buckles' etc.)

Margaret was able to produce a woman who had been invited by her to stay at the house and who testified that the couple behaved as husband and wife. The witness was unable to mention any 'Ladys' who visited Margaret but said that 'there were several Stranger Gentlemen Both from the Country and from Edinburgh who visited and dined there'. And though the witness never heard Sir Alexander ever say that he was married to Margaret or that she was his wife, 'she remembered particularly to have heard him Express himself once in these words That God Forsake me if Ever I forsake you.'

A servant maid of Sir Alexander's testified that at first his 'behaviour was such as a master had towards his principal servant But sometime after he turned more fond of her and used frequently to come to the nursery to her and in the deponents hearing desired her to come out and speak with him pretending to want a candle to his room or some thing else which he named'. The servant did not observe anything that made her think them married until they returned from Edinburgh after she had borne him a child, 'then she suspected from their behaviour the one towards the other that they were married for she observed the defender more fond of the pursuer than formerly and the pursuer more uppish and sawcy and take more upon her than she used to do'. After that Margaret 'sat always at table with the defender at Breakfast Dinner and Supper, Except when there were a great many strangers there'. The servant maid 'saw no Ladies visit at the Kerse save Doctor Grahame's Wife and her daughters'. And neighbouring gentry, like John McLeod, advocate, testified that he sometimes dined with Sir Alexander but never saw Margaret and that 'she was not habite and repute in the Country to be his Lady but Generally considered as his housekeeper.' The Earl of Kilmarnock said the same.

Archibald Dickens, a tenant of Sir Alexander's, testified that he paid off the kirk treasurer for Margaret's children as born in fornication. On the way to Edinburgh he asked Margaret 'if she was married or expected marriage of Sir Alexander Hope, She said she was not married at the time But Sir Alexander had promised to marry her, And she would not return to Kerse untill he did it'. But two or three months later, on the way home, she admitted that he had not married her.

Although Sir Alexander had clearly been in love with Margaret Drummond, there was ample evidence that this was an illicit relationship. And the letters she produced from him did not aid her case. In one letter he asked her to write him 'a Sweet Billet', which

> will make my Business go on with the better relish received inclosed a thousand Glowing Burning Kisses, and quench them in my Sweetest Lassies moist and Rosie Lips, I am this moment straying over all her charms in my wanton ravished fancy and wish for nothing more than to repeat those delightfull Enjoyments I have often been dissolved in reality upon her lovely Bosom which I hope shall happen soon.

Those were not words which the commissaries were likely to write to their wives.

Nevertheless, the commissaries' decreet in this case was unique. They found the evidence 'not relevant to inferr marriage' and therefore assoilzied him. But because of the the witness's deposition that he had 'Imprecated That God might forsake him if he forsook Mrs Drummond', and because in one letter he wrote that 'he hoped to be Enabled to provide for all those that he thinks himself obliged in honour and duty to take Care of and always would to the utmost of his power and desires her in the meantime to take good heart', and in another letter

> he assures her that she shall never want from him as long as he is master of a shilling and by his Letter Number twenty seventh he Bids her be persuaded that nothing should be wanting upon his side that might contribute to make her Easy and happy and that he would always Love and Esteem her and take all opportunities of Convincing her that

he had no greater pleasure than in forwarding her health and prosperity and by his letter No. 29 He assures her that she shall want for nothing that he can do for her and says that if he does not make her rich until he is so himself yet he desires her to be assured that she shall have an abundance and plenty

they found him liable to pay her a aliment for the rest of her life. It was the only time a man was legally obliged to provide for a mistress in this way.

A far from 'servile' mistress was Christian Campbell, who followed an infantry regiment down from the Highlands to Edinburgh. There she was taken up as mistress by David Martin, a successful portrait painter in his forties, who lodged at the house where she had been engaged as a servant.[7] In 1781 after she was dismissed from that service for suspected theft, and David had bought himself a house, she would 'lay in wait for him in the Streets near his house till his return when she frequently fastned herself upon him more particularly if he had been taking a cheerful Glass and on these occasions the defender must acknowledge that she prevailed upon him to give her a Share of his Bed'. He was in London from autumn 1782 till March 1783 and when he returned Christian demanded that he hire her as his servant. He refused; as he rarely ate at home, and his manservant's wife looked after the house, he had no need for a female servant. But one evening he got home to find that she had managed to get inside by one of the windows. He 'severely reproved her for what she had done whereupon she burst into tears and pulling a Bottle out of her pocket told him that it contained a Dose of Poison which she was determined instantly to drink of unless he would accept of the tender of her Services'. After this drama he agreed to give her a trial, 'at the stipulated wages of Three pound per annum'. He realised his mistake almost immediately, for Christian, he said,

conducted herself precisely in the manner which he had suspected and which people of her sex and rank uniformly do when the masters condescend to use improper familiarities with them she became idle pert and dissipated staid out often till it was late and returned home attended by ugly looking fellows whom she frequently entertained and some times concealed in the house for the whole night.

She got worse and worse, and he began to miss various articles like shirts and handkerchiefs, and finally he missed his purse which contained a five guinea piece and a valuable shirt pin. She denied the theft, but one night later it turned up when he arrived home unexpectedly; there was another man in the house with whom, it appeared, she was dividing the spoils. (Later he discovered that she had also stolen linen, blankets and shirts.) He ordered her out of the house, and she went.

After that she wrote him some letters asking for money and once she even broke into his house. The legal action was raised because she thought that for someone in the public eye 'a charge of this kind might not only be disagreeable but also very pernicious in its consequences', so that 'he would rather submitt to the payment of a considerable sum of money than allow such an Accusation to be made publick.' He called her bluff, and she was unable to bring any proof at all. This case is a useful corrective to the woman-as-victim scenarios of so many of the stories in this book.

The case of Elizabeth Hutchison, daughter of a salt officer at Bo'ness, against John Ronaldson of Blairhall, Esquire, in 1794, was more typical.[8] She alleged that they cohabited as husband and wife. He said that she was his housekeeper: in the house at Culross she 'acted as a Servant in every respect in dressing and washing linen cleaning the house etc', and his manservant always called her 'Lizzy'. He was surprised at her claim that she presided at the head of his table –

> *for ever since he had a house no person whatever has sat at the head of his Table but himself, and the only circumstance which could have put any thing about sitting at table into her head, must have been that upon some occasions when her Father or any of her friends in the Council were with the Defender if she happened to come into the room, she might be asked to sit down for a little, but immediately upon anything being wanted, she either went and brought it, or sent the other servant with it.*

She was never 'considered to live with him in any capacity but as his Housekeeper, allowing him at the same time to use freedoms with her, which deprived her of that respect which otherwise she might have had from the neighbourhood'. (Though of course he did not lose any respect in the process.)

In her libel Elizabeth asserted that John, when asked to stay out late by his companions, would always say that he had to get home to his wife. He responded:

> *The truth is that when in company with Mr Johnston of Sands and some of his other companions in the Tavern at Culross it was a kind of hackneyed expression when the question was whether they should sit longer or not, that it would be best to go home to their wives; and the person who said so was generally asked which of his wives he meant to go to, by which every body present understood some of the young women (of whom there were perhaps more than there should have been) who received their visits in a private manner – The Defender has often heard the expression, and it is very probable he may in that ironical manner have used it himself; but it is certain the Company never understood any of them were going to women they really meant to be considered as their wives, and most certainly it never was understood by any body that the Defender meant the Pursuer to be considered as his wife.*

Elizabeth fought the case. She said that he told her the marriage must be kept secret because of his 'dread of offending his Mother who liferented a great part of the Estate'. She 'was not considered as House Keeper, though she confesses that owing to his embarrassed situation she often when he was out of the way assisted in menial services, such as washing and dressing his Linens, but when he came to the knowledge of it he was very much displeased at her doing so'. (John responded that he was 'very certain he never said he was displeased with her doing so on the contrary he has often thought that she did too little'.) And she still maintained that she presided at his table whenever there was company and did not act as a servant on those occasions.

Her own witnesses, alas, contradicted this. John Drysdale, a merchant in Culross, testified that 'Lizie', as he would call her, 'always acted as a Servant by doing work in the Kitchen and laying out Cloths on a Green'. When there were no other visitors than Drysdale and his wife, she would sit at the table with them, but even then 'she put down part of the Dinner with her own Hand and often rose from Table to bring whatever was wanted in the course of the Dinner.' Robert Bald, likewise, often visited and 'at times when there was no Genteel Company Elizabeth Hutchison sat at Table. That upon these occasions the Witness addressed her as "Lizie" and never by the appellation of Mrs Ronaldson.' He always thought of her 'as Mr Ronaldsons Servant and looked upon her as Such even when she was sitting at Table with Them'. Witnesses on both sides told a similar tale, so her claim of marriage was unsustainable.

From this case we see that in the closing years of the eighteenth century in the household of a landed gentleman of modest means only servants were expected to be seen to work; the wife should not have to lift a finger.

Kept Mistresses

In the cases in this section the woman was paid for one thing only: to be available for sex whenever the man desired.

Cases of that kind are much commoner in the nineteenth century but do occur earlier, as in the 1766 example of Helen Moffatt against Hugh Dalrymple Esquire of Craig.[9] Although she alleged marriage his version of events was the accepted one. He became acquainted with her in a village in East Lothian where she 'had never been in any better station than a servant or employed in knitting stockings, or shearing in the Harvest'. She did not seem averse to his 'familiaritys' and agreed to go to Edinburgh where he placed her 'in a house where Gentlemen are in use to have kept Mistresses'. After a while she complained that it 'was too publick and that some Gentlemen had been endeavouring to be introduced to her in order to ly with her', so he took a room in a private dwelling. All he did in this house 'was to sleep with her, and perhaps breakfast with her next morning, which is commonly done by Gentlemen who sleep with their Mistresses, he never had his Cloaths there, but kept a room in another house where his Cloaths were, he dined and supped else where, and in short in no respect did ever he behave as husband to the Pursuer.'

A unique case was that of Elizabeth Drummond against Alexander Stewart of Bonskeid, physician in Perth, in 1824, because he was a married man during their liaison, though the legal action was raised after his wife's death.[10] Married men with mistresses would have been common, but for that mistress to raise a declarator of marriage action was unprecedented.

Her story was that in 1804, at the age of eighteen, she went into service in his household. Her master 'was then a Married Man, and about 60 Years of Age. Notwithstanding this, she had not been long in his Servitude, when he began to fondle and caress her, and use seductive measures to corrupt her Morals'. When all those measures failed 'he solemnly and deliberately promised to Marry her upon the event of his Wifes decease, who was then and had long been in a delicate state of health'. Accordingly she 'surrendered her person in April 1806', and became pregnant. Thereafter she left his service and he paid for her upkeep, and that of the four children she bore him, for ten years in Edinburgh, and thereafter in Perth. But when his wife died in 1819 he did not marry her. A conditional promise made at a time when he could not legally contract a marriage could not subsequently bind him, and in court she was unable to prove that a promise of marriage followed by intercourse had occurred after his wife's death.

The unusual aspect of the 1822 case of Margaret Wilson against Archibald Robertson, doctor of medicine and druggist in Edinburgh, was that she was awarded damages for seduction.[11] As will be seen in Chapter 6, such damages were normally awarded to women who could prove that the nature of the courtship had caused them to believe that a marriage was in the offing, not to women who had been 'kept' by men.

In common with the last case, Margaret had started out as Archibald's servant – he was a widower with six children – but after she became pregnant he paid for her keep, and she bore him two sons. He stated that far from having been considered his wife, 'she was frequently upbraided by her neighbours for her course of life', and when that happened she did not claim that she was married to him; 'nor did she ever to her most intimate friends alledge that she lived in any other capacity than that of a *Kept Mistress*'.

One argument in court was whether the children had been baptised as legitimate or illegitimate. Archibald insisted that when the first was being baptised the Episcopal minister said he presumed they were married persons and Archibald firmly replied 'no', but that the child was crying at the time so he could not be sure that his answer was heard. James Walker, the minister in question, testified that he had no memory of the child crying and that his 'clear impression and belief' at the time was that 'Doctor Robertson made answer that they were married.' When the second child was brought to him he obviously had no reason to repeat the enquiry, and both children were entered in his register as legitimate.

When her witnesses appeared they said that Margaret told them she was married to Archibald by Dr Brown and that the marriage had to be kept secret 'because the sister of his first wife was mistress of his house and he had benefited in particular by her educating his children'. Mrs Elizabeth Imrie, a neighbour, remembered 'asking her how a good looking young woman like her came to marry so old a man who had six Children – she said he was a clear fresh man'. Mrs Imrie always considered Margaret to be married – 'I would not otherwise have kept her company' – but admitted to the court that Margaret 'had so many various ways of stating matters that I came to have my doubts.' Another neighbour testified that while she lived at Fountainbridge 'it became a common report that she was kept by Doctor Robertson … and the accounts which the Pursuer gave of herself did not hang well together and led the Deponent to think that these reports were true.'

Yet another neighbour testified to what happened on the two occasions when her uncle called. The first time

> he upbraided her for bringing shame to his face by a connexion with Doctor Robertson as he said her mother had done before her – The second time he again reproached her on the same account – very high words passed betwixt them – Both times she threatened to cleave him with the tongs before he went away – Interrogated Do you remember any phrase of reproach used to her Depones and Answers On the first of these occasions I remember he called her a damned whore.

Unexpectedly, while the case was still being heard (it dragged on for over three years), Margaret married – regularly – an Edinburgh tailor, and bore him a son. However, the legitimacy of her sons by Archibald Robertson still being at issue the legal processes continued until the commissaries declared he had not been married to her but was liable to her for £100 damages, representing the wages she had lost during the years they were together.

In an 1825 case, Alexander Haig, distiller in Edinburgh, became acquainted with Margaret Dickson in about 1816 when she was 16 or 17 and the servant of someone with whom he dined from time to time. They had sex at various time and places and then, when she was dismissed from that service, and became pregnant, he 'employed a person of the name of Francis Beattie then a Porter in the Infirmary to take a room for the Pursuer as a girl of easy virtue who was to live under the Defenders protection'. Subsequently he bought a flat for her, and when they parted he granted her 'an absolute disposition of the flatt' and some money; on 26 March 1824 she signed a formal discharge of all claims she had against him. But in March 1825 she 'heard that he was about to marry a young lady in Glasgow', followed him there and demanded a thousand pounds from him. The kirk session, when they heard what she had to say, allowed the banns to be called, and in the Commissary Court he swore under oath that he had never promised Margaret Dickson marriage.[12]

In a case that was decided in July 1829, the liaison between John Cunningham Esquire of Duchrae and Augusta Brownlow (who bore him four children), was mainly London-based and would never have been heard before the Commissary Court if he had not brought her to Scotland in the summer of 1822. The next time she came to Scotland was in spring 1825, when she told some of his relations that she was his wife. He had her summoned for declarator of freedom; she raised her declarator of marriage action in response.[13] John denied that he ever 'treated her in any other character than as his Kept Mistress'. When he allowed her to accompany him to Scotland they stayed in furnished lodgings and he did not introduce her to anyone as his wife.

Augusta's witnesses were folk connected with their lodgings in Edinburgh and Moffat. One of the landladies, Mrs Ross, testified that

> the Lady was always called Mrs Cunninghame by the Deponent, the servant and the Nurse, but the Defender used always to call her the Lady – Interrogated Whether she considered them man and wife – Depones that she always did, but upon being pressed, she said she had her suspicions .... Interrogated upon what her suspicions were formed Depones that it was from there no company or Ladies coming about the house.

The testimony from Moffat was about how everyone at first believed they were married but later had doubts.

In contrast to the chaotic relationships featured in the next chapter, the distinguishing feature of the cases featured in this one (and the two case studies that follow) is the formality of the arrangements. Being a mistress was a clearly defined status: the women were always sexually available, and the men supported them, while remaining free to detach themselves, marry, and procreate legitimate heirs at any time.

Olwen Hufton, discussing prostitution in eighteenth-century Paris, sees the 'kept mistress' at the apex of the profession.[14] She realises that being a kept mistress did not preclude marriage, and, indeed, provides examples of some who married well, but neither in France nor England could such a woman have raised a legal action to transmute the relationship into marriage.

It is worth recollecting that a wife had specific inheritance rights, as did her legitimate children (under Scottish law a man could not disinherit his wife, and a child could be legitimated by a subsequent marriage), which a mistress did not. And Scottish law took a dim view of men making provision for mistresses in their wills. Provisions granted to mistresses or illegitimate children could be contested by surviving relatives on the grounds that they were unlawful because they were granted for an immoral consideration. It is unlikely that such action was often taken, but in 1765 the nephew and heir of Sir James Hamilton of Westport challenged the bonds of annuity granted to his mistress, Mary de Gares, and their daughter. The Court of Session found that the heir did not have to pay the annuity to the mistress, though he did have to pay it to the daughter, who was held to be 'not at fault'.[15]

In view of Scottish marriage law it is not surprising that some mistresses should have tried, after being dumped by their keepers, to improve their position by instigating a declarator action. But very few succeeded.

Notes

1   CC8/6/14. This case is discussed at greater length in Leah Leneman, 'Wives and Mistresses in Eighteenth-Century Scotland', *Women's History Review* (Vol 8 [4], 671–92; 1999).
2   Common soldiers might follow their officers' example. In 1747 William Shaw admitted before Canongate kirk session that he had cohabited with Margaret Baillie for four or five years while he was a soldier, and that she bore a child to him, but denied being married to her. A soldier in the same regiment declared that he always looked on Margaret as William's 'Whore and not his Wife, but owns that the said Baillie during that time, bore Shaw's Name as his Wife to screen her from being drummed out of the Regiment as a Whore'. Leah Leneman and Rosalind Mitchison, *Sin in the City – Sexuality and Social Control in Urban Scotland 1660–1780* (Edinburgh, 1998), 136.
3   CC8/5/24.
4   CC8/5/31.
5   CC8/6/150.
6   CC8/5/6.
7   CC8/5/18. According to the Dictionary of National Biography, David Martin was born in 1737 and died in 1798. He was a pupil of Allan Ramsay and in 1775 was appointed principal painter to the Prince of Wales for Scotland. The DNB also states that he married 'a lady with some property' in London and returned to Edinburgh after her death, but no dates or further details are given for those events.
8   CC8/6/58.
9   CC8/5/11.
10 CC8/6/143.
11 CC8/6/148.
12 CC8/6/148.
13 CC8/6/163.
14 Olwen Hufton, *The Prospect Before Her – A History of Women in Western Europe 1500-1800* (London, 1995), 322–3.
15 Lord McLaren, *The Law of Scotland in Relation to Wills and Succession* (Edinburgh, 1868), Vol 1, 292. I am grateful to Ann McCrum for this reference. The 1765 case is summarised in *Morison's Dictionary of Decisions*, 9471–3. Mary de Gares was a married woman who had left her husband to live with Sir James Hamilton, which may have had a bearing on the decision.

CASE STUDY 8

AIKEN V. BARTHOLOMEW: A GIRL OVER IN EDINBURGH

'IT is not a very probable story that a Gentleman possessed of a pretty Considerable fortune and liberally Educated would treat and Entertain the Chambermaid of an Inn in so familiar a manner or that he would be so very foolish as Choose so amiable a Lady for his wife,' said John Bartholomew Esquire of Baldridge when Margaret Aiken (daughter of a wright near Dunbar) raised a declarator of marriage action against him in 1789. 'She was Content with her Situation as a Chamber maid', she retorted, 'and she never sought to be the Pursuers wife who she reckoned far above her station – Indeed she had no difficulty of Crediting that it was not her high station which enticed the defender to make his addresses to her But the handsomeness of her person and other accomplishments which in many instances over reach equality or superiority of station.' The relationship spanned the years 1782 to 1788, when he married another woman. At that time he granted Peggy, as he always called her, a bond of annuity, and she gave up all claims to him. But when this came to light it did not halt the legal process, because their child George still had an interest in the outcome.

When John appeared in court he testified that he had met her at an inn where she was a chambermaid and took her to 'a house where no questions would be asked … a private Bawdy house'. He next encountered her when he was travelling to England and stopped off at Dunbar; she went to the inn where he was staying and spent the night with him. According to John, 'in the Evening the Landlord came to the Declarant and laughing said "I suppose you are engaged in Some Intrigue" to which the Declarant made answer and said "my Friend Hall what have you to do with that" and spoke in such a way as to Convey the Idea that it was an Intrigue.' After his return to Edinburgh 'the Declarant agreed to take her into keeping at six shillings a week.' He never himself took lodgings for her, but he gave her money to pay for them.

Their child 'was baptised by Mr Moyes one of the Ministers of the English Chapel'. John had gone to Mr Moyes and told him that he had an illegitimate child and that he knew the Church of Scotland would not baptise such a child unless he submitted to censure before the congregation, 'to which he was very little Inclined That as he knew that the Church to which Mr Moyes belonged possessed more liberal Sentiments he desired to know if Mr Moyes would baptize his natural Child and to this Mr Moyes Consented and in presence of Margaret Aiken and her Sister Recorded a Certificate of his having baptised the declarants natural Child'. (Mr Moyes produced in court his book of baptisms in which an 'N' was entered for 'natural child'; he used 'L' for 'legitimate child'.) After she bore a second child 'her Sister who knew very well that the Declarant kept her as a Mistress at six shillings a week came to him and represented that her sister was an honest mans daughter and that the declarant ought not to treat her in that manner but acknowledge her as his wife to which he answered that he Spurned at the Idea of Marrying a Woman who had been Chamber maid in an Inn and who had acknowledged that she had been debauched before he knew her.'

Peggy lived in two different neighbourhoods during the years he kept her, and witnesses from both appeared. They had all been surprised that she kept her own name, being known as Mistress Aiken, but she told them that the marriage had to be kept a secret because of expectations John had from his father. They heard him call her 'my Peggy' and 'my dear' – but never 'my wife', and they found it odd that he often visited her and spent whole days and nights with her yet did not live with her. The landlord, when asked if this did not make him suspicious, replied that 'if he had Entertained any Such Suspicion it was more than overballanced by his coming so pointedly at the times Margaret Aiken said she expected him and his behaviour being so agreeable and peaceable … and he so far Considered them as Married Persons that if he had not received them in that light he would not have allowed them to have staid in his house.'

Other neighbours remembered particular remarks inferring marriage. Nineteen year-old Ann Murray recalled that one day when coming into the room where they were 'Mr Bartholomew jokingly said to the deponent "Annie would you not wish to be as happily Married as Peggy is".' And 41 year-old Janet Nicol remembered that once when Margaret was ill Mr Bartholomew 'funningly or in a funning way said to the Deponent "if any thing should ail Peggy the Deponent would be his Second wife as she knew the temper of George"' (their child). Margaret Darling was convinced because Peggy's 'behaviour was so decent' – and Peggy had told her that 'Principal Robertson' had married them and there were four witnesses who could prove it.

Mary Lindsay, who had been told by Peggy that she was secretly married to John, 'observed to her that it was strange that she should keep at such a distance from a Man whom she Called her husband That she herself should always be Confined to Town when her husband was in the Country and that she should be so ill Supplied with Country fare such as Poultry and to which Margaret Aiken answered that Mr Bartholomew was obliged to be in the Country and was also often obliged to be at London on business, that he had for a Servant an old woman who was obliged to give him an account of every article or provision about the house and therefore he could send nothing to Edinburgh without her knowledge.' Suspicions, however, were growing, and one day a neighbour, a wright's wife, said to another 'that she was surprised to see her so Intimate with Margaret Aiken who passed for a kept Mistress', and thereby provoked a quarrel with Peggy.

The wright's wife, Christian Gibson, appeared as a witness for John and testified about hearing reports that Peggy 'was of a Suspicious Character and a kept Mistress, and that the Taylors wife had been blamed by the Neighbours for walking out and keeping Company with this woman'. John also produced as witness Robert Welwood of Garveck, a friend and neighbour in the country, who testified that between 1787 and 1789 'he had heard Mr Bartholomew say he kept a Mistress That one day the Defender and Deponent being together the deponent was Jokeing him about the Girls at Baldridge and in the Neighbourhood, upon which he declared he had no Connection with them and gave as his reason for having none that he had a Girl over in Edinburgh.'

However, the very fact that as a condition of giving her the bond of annuity John demanded that Peggy renounce any claim she or her child might have on him shows that he was unsure of his ground. Magdalene Murray, a neighbour, testified that when Peggy heard of his marriage to another woman she appeared 'to be in a very distracted situation'. When Magdalene told John of this he asked her 'to go to her and endeavour to reconcile her to what had happened meaning his marriage with Miss Turnbull and Deponed that the deponent said to Mr Bartholomew that he should give Margaret Aiken a handsome Settlement and he answered that he would do so'.

A few days later John called many of the neighbours to a meeting 'relative to Margaret Aikens alledging that she was Married with Mr Bartholomew'. According to Magdalene, when Peggy was asked on this occasion whether she was actually married to John she 'answered that she was not married, but that he had promised to marry her after his father's death and had given her lines under his hand to that purpose'. When John asked where they were, 'she answered that God and his own Conscience knew'. Magdalene told John she thought as Peggy 'had born him Children he ought to have married her'.

John Murray, a 61 year-old plasterer, was also there and testified that Peggy said that there had been promises between them and 'lost her humour or temper'. Murray gathered that if things had turned out differently John might indeed have married her. And he heard Peggy say that John 'had given her a line that he was to Marry her That Mr Bartholomew asked her where it was and she answered "John You know you took it out of my Chest."' Margaret Darling testified that at the meeting 'Mr Bartholomew seemed to be of a feeling spirit and Margaret Aiken was in great grief.' Margaret could not resist saying to Peggy that it seemed what she had said about having been married by Principal Robertson was not true. Peggy, she said, did not answer her 'but looked at the Defender saying "you said you would do it."' Asked in court if there had ever been any talk of Peggy having been with another man before John, Margaret said there hadn't 'but that at the meeting in the deponents house Mr Bartholomew said that if he had taken Margaret Aiken from the paths of virtue he would have thought himself bound to do more for her'. Margaret then felt herself called upon to defend Peggy and said that 'Margaret Aiken had behaved herself well and was come of Creditable people That Mr Bartholomew upon that occasion said that the man with whom Margaret Aiken had been Connected was a Shoemaker and was then in the Kings life Guards.' The witness 'did not remember Margaret Aiken making any answer to this but she seemed to be much overwhelmed with Grief during the whole Conversation'.

The clinching evidence was his letters to her. 'Dearest Girl', he wrote in June 1785, 'I beg my dear you'l take particular care of yourself and of my favorite boy, I intend to see you by the 26 Instant I hope you'l not be inconstant in my absence, you can never be happy if you are. I am to have a house keeper with me till I go to England so it will be impossible for me to see you sooner, I shall however always think of you and that in the tenderest manner. I beg you'll keep a clean handsome house you know I like every thing in that style you know how much I like you Dearest Girl Your real Friend.' In another letter he referred to her as his 'Pretty Lass' and wrote, 'Remember to be cheerful affable and gay sing laugh and be in good humour think I am constantly thinking on you and in hopes of a happy meeting by the end of the month. Do not write me as I have at present a house keeper, Give my best Compliments to the Boy, take great care of his health and your own, I am much Interested in your and his Prosperity remember to stroak his head every night, but be cautious not to ruffle his hair leave that to your beloved.'

The line between wife and mistress shows up particularly clearly in this case. The neighbours thought that a mistress would be some kind of brazen hussy, so when faced with an ordinary quiet young woman they were inclined to believe her story of a secret marriage. To what extent John made his mistress believe that he really would marry her, and whether he ever seriously entertained the thought, can never be known. But Peggy, though financially secure, ended up on the wrong side of the dividing line.

CC8/5/20

CASE STUDY 9

WELSH V. FRASER: CALL ME MRS

THE pattern of the relationship of Charlotte Welsh (the daughter of a deceased corn merchant) and James Fraser Esquire was not one of cohabitation in one place but of constant movement, though by the time the action was raised in 1817 she had borne him three children, two of whom were still alive.

According to Charlotte, they accepted one another as husband and wife in 1807 and lodged with Dr and Mrs Ruxton in Edinburgh for nine months; then she went to lodgings in Rose Street for three or four months, and he sometimes slept there too; then she spent four months in lodgings 'at the foot of the Fish market Close Edinburgh' and he occasionally slept with her there; then they took lodgings together 'in the House of James McIntosh in Richmond Street' and cohabited there for about nine months, when their daughter Elizabeth was born. Then they went 'to a house Mr MacIntosh had taken in Buccleuch Street where they occupied a Dining Room and Bed room'. Then they went back to Rose Street, taking a house 'which they furnished and hired a Servant and in which they lived and cohabited as man and Wife for about twelve months'. After that they 'took lodgings in Leith for the benefit of Sea bathing', where she remained for about four months and he occasionally cohabited with her. Then they lived in North Richmond Street for a few months until their daughter Sarah was born. Soon after that he 'joined the Regiment of Edinburgh Militia as Ensign and afterwards marched with the Regiment into England'. She took a small house 'where she resided with her Children for about two years and while resident in that House she paid a visit to the Defender at Seton Camp in England where he was stationed with his Regiment and where the Pursuer remained in the neighbourhood for four days and Slept with the Defender one night in a Public House as his wife and then returned to Edinburgh'. But then he refused to acknowledge her as his wife.

James responded that he met her in 'a house of bad fame in Shakespear Square and the Pursuer was known by the name of Charlotte Bloss or Bleis'. The thought of marriage would never have occurred to him, 'who tho' imprudent never would have degraded himself so much, as to marry a common prostitute'. She was his kept mistress, and he never acknowledged her as Mrs Fraser, nor the children as his lawful children. He did not lodge with her at the various lodgings, indeed while she was at the Rose Street lodgings, a circumstance occurred 'which she cannot have forgot, namely, that when it was discovered what she was, and that the Defender visited her as his kept mistress, she was turned out of the house'. Later, in the Rose Street house where she had claimed continuous cohabitation with him, she acted as his servant, 'and all the neighbours knew or considered that she was his kept mistress'. He was greatly displeased when she came to England 'and by no means received or acknowledged her as his wife – Indeed at this time it would have been the height of folly to have done so, as the Pursuer was then with child to a Gentleman who she said intended to marry her.' She afterwards bore this child, who was still alive, and never even pretended that James was the father. 'In these circumstances, besides being entirely groundless, this action appears to have been a very foolish attempt on the part of this woman to attain the status of the Defenders wife, as supposing she was successful in this Declarator of Marriage, he would be at no difficulty to obtain a Divorce against her for adultery.'

Rather unusually, in this case it was the woman rather than the man who was interrogated in court. She declared that at the time she met James 'her name was then Charlotte Bloss at least she at that time assumed that name. Declares that her christened name is Charlotte Welsh and that she sometimes took liberties in assuming other names.' Asked about Mrs Quin's house, where she first met James, she declared that 'Mrs Quins house was a house in which Gentlemen and Ladies met with each other.' But she insisted that the first time she met James he asked her 'to go home with him to be his wife'. He conducted her home to her lodgings every night, and he 'was the only person with whom she went home to her Lodgings at that time'. This went on for about five weeks, and he went to bed with her every night 'after he had conducted her from Mrs Quins to her the Declarants Lodgings'. After that he took her to reside in Dr Ruxton's house – as his wife, she insisted, though she had to admit that he had his own separate lodgings. She had had to leave the Rose Street lodging only because James got behind with the rent. The reason for separate lodgings after that was the bad state of James's health. This also explained why they 'neither paid visits to nor were visited by any persons as husband and wife because the Defender wished to postpone introducing her as his wife till he should recover his health'.

Charlotte's witnesses were mostly Edinburgh landladies who naturally testified that they called her Mrs Fraser and considered them to be married. But one of them, Margaret Chalmers, was more frank and when asked 'Did you understand him to be her husband?' answered 'I never put the question nor did any person tell me – it was my own thought that he looked more genteel than the Pursuer' – but she hardly spoke to them. Pressed on this point Margaret Chalmers said, 'they seemed very agreeable with each other and treated each other as husband and wife and I had no business to enquire while they behaved properly in my house but I did think that he was genteeler and might naturally have chosen a person more like his own manners and station.' Margaret Angus, the midwife, also called Charlotte 'Mrs Fraser' but was another who had avoided enquiring too closely: 'it is not very becoming to deliver any person who is not called Mrs – I often call a servant girl Mrs on such an occasion.' And when asked 'whether the impression on her mind at the time she attended the Pursuer was that she was the Defenders kept Mistress,' she answered, 'Something like that.'

With such witnesses appearing on the pursuer's side, the defender did not have too much to do, but he did bring witnesses who had visited him in his own lodgings and never saw a woman there. Archibald Torry visited him at the Rose Street house and, seeing Charlotte there, he assumed she was his servant. Being a close friend, he asked James about her, and James acknowledged that 'the girl was kept by him – that she had been extremely attentive to him during his illness and that he found it less expensive to keep a girl in that kind of way than to keep a servant and go other ways.'

The commissaries found that Charlotte had 'compleatly failed in proving her allegations of marriage with the Defender' and assoilzied him from the conclusions of marriage and seduction. 'Habit and repute' could establish a marriage, but just being called 'Mrs' was far from that.

CC8/6/112

CHAPTER 5

NEITHER WIFE NOR MISTRESS

THE last chapter described cases in which the woman who raised the action was concluded to have been the man's mistress. In earlier chapters we saw women proving themselves to be wives. But the majority of contested cases did not end up with either of those clear-cut conclusions. The women failed to have their relationships declared to be marriage, but this may have had as much to do with the proof available to them as with the nature of the relationship. Also, intentions change, and memories of what occurred, and not every relationship can be neatly pigeonholed. As will be seen in this chapter, some were complicated and messy, eluding easy categorisation.

Outright fraud on the part of the woman was rare but not unknown, and some instances are given in the first part of the chapter. The remainder is about cases where the woman had a genuine case but was unable to provide sufficient proof for the commissaries to declare the couple married.

Fraud

The 1753 case of Elizabeth Benstead against James Adams, mason late of St Mary le bone, London, now marble cutter in Abbeyhill, Edinburgh appears to have been one of outright fraud.[1]

Elizabeth claimed to have been married to James in London in 1738, and those names were indeed found in a marriage register there, but he alleged that she told him that she had been married to a *different* James Adams who had died 'either at Carthagena or in his passage there', and that her claiming James as her husband was a plot of William Coleburn's, a rival marble cutter in Edinburgh, who had persuaded her to come from London and 'ruin' James. Although he had lived in London at one time, he had never been a mason, he said. Elizabeth said that it was true that Coleburn had coaxed her to Edinburgh, but only by telling her that 'her husband was living in flourishing Circumstances as to his worldly affairs but with another wife and two Children.' However, James Graham, a witness, testified that at the time of the alleged marriage he and James Adams were travelling from London to Newcastle and then to Leith, and furthermore that he heard Elizabeth 'say several times that she had been married to a James Adams, a mason who had gone abroad and died', and that she 'had been brought down from England by one Coleburn to claim this defender as her husband Whom she had never seen before And the pursuer at the same time Damn'd the said Coleburn for a Villain for having done so.' The commissaries accepted James's alibi, and assoilzied him.

In 1781 Mary McLauchlan painted a vivid picture of herself as a victim of Archibald McDonald, advocate, whose servant she had been. He had locked the door, she said, thrown her on the floor and raped her, but subsequently he promised to marry her and gave her a written acknowledgement certifying that she was his wife and the daughter she bore him a lawful child. When she learned that he was to marry another woman she tried to stop the marriage, and in response two gentleman, an advocate and a lawyer, called on her and, having asked to see the written acknowledgement, took it away with them. They also 'swore and threatened that they would put her in the Tolbooth and hang her directly if she did not give up her pretensions and write a line to the Reverend Mr Thomas Spankie Minister of the Gospel at Falkirk Contradicting a Notice formerly sent him not to marry the said Archibald McDonald to the said Miss Thomson'. Very touching, but Archibald had witnesses to his version of the story. When the two legal gentlemen called on Mary she admitted that she was not married to Archibald and said she had sent a second letter to this effect to the minister, and when they saw the document it was obviously 'an Absolute forgery' and they told her so. She or her advisers then concocted the story that the men had appropriated it so she would not have to produce it. She was unable to bring any proof, and the commissaries found the action 'groundless vexatious and Calumnious' and assoilzied him.[2]

In the 1792 case of Martha Hutchison against John Brand, in Dumfriesshire, the woman's story was credible.[3] She was his father's servant, he promised her marriage but begged her 'to Conceal their Marriage until the death of a Baillie Brand from whom the said John Brand said he had expectations of succeeding to a Considerable fortune'. She did so, even after becoming pregnant and bearing his child, but when the baillie died and John succeeded to the fortune he denied being married to her. As evidence she produced three letters to her, signed by him 'your most loving husband', which would normally have been sufficient evidence of a marriage. But the letters, though in his handwriting, were signed with a different name.

John advised the court that Martha had previously borne another illegitimate child when she told the kirk session that she was raped by an unknown man. Kirk sessions were very sceptical of 'unknown man' stories (usually with good reason),[4] and Martha had been treated as an adulteress. He admitted having had sex with her, 'But upon none of these Occasions did he ever once think of making her any kind of promise of Marriage whatever Indeed it is Impossible to be Conceived that such an Idea could have entered into his head as making proposals of that nature to a woman so notorious as she was.'

In response Martha stood by her original story of having been forced by an unknown man, and said that since that occurrence – 16 years earlier! – 'her Character has not only been free from Censure, but has in every respect been unblemished and unimpeachable.' When she became pregnant this time she told the kirk session that she was married but refused to reveal the name of her husband. This, she said to the Commissary Court, was perfectly consistent with her assertion that the marriage was to be kept secret. Between that appearance before the kirk session and the next one – when she declared that John Brand was her husband – his uncle had died and left John a fortune: 'his ambition now began to soar a little higher than the humble walk of the Pursuer who was before in the same rank with himself and in every respect a suitable wife to him.' Was there any truth in all this? And what about the letters?

John appeared in court and declared that he had given Martha money 'every time he had Carnal dealings of her Body'. He had not had sex with her at the time her child must have been conceived so he knew he could not be the father (and she did not accuse him of this until a year after it was born). His uncle died in January 1792 but John 'was not a legatee of the said James Brands Testament'. His explanation of the letters was that when she was summoned before the kirk session she came to him in great distress and said she was afraid that the Church would be as severe on her as it had been previously and begged for his help. She knew of a girl who 'had been saved from doing penance by producing a Letter from some person who had left the Country bearing that the said person was Married to her', and she asked John to write her such letters under the name James Thorburn, and swore that she would never reveal who really wrote them.

Feeling sympathy for her, he did as she asked, and the letters were indeed signed 'James Thorburn', though she had tried to deface the signature. It is likely that Martha really did intend the letters to shield her from church discipline, but the kirk session did not believe they were genuine. No doubt someone subsequently advised her that with them she could prove a marriage. She failed.

In 1793 Charles Irvine Esquire (late of the Island of Tobago, then in Queen Street, New Town, Edinburgh) was astonished when his landlady, Catharine Campbell, raised a declarator of marriage action against him, because as far as he was concerned he had had an affair with a married woman. A few months earlier she had even appeared before the sheriff court and acknowledged that she was John Campbell's wife, 'from whom she had separated for private reasons, and who at that time, went to America to follow the business of a joiner, to which he had been bred, leaving her and a daughter behind him in Edinburgh'. Catharine's tale was that when she 'opened furnished lodgings, she judged it prudent as she was a young woman, unprotected by a husband, to put the name of John Campbell Junior one of her Brothers, upon her door, that she might pass for a married person'. Her other reason for doing so was that she had borne an illegitimate child, who was still alive, and she 'supposed it was absolutely necessary for her to represent herself a married person, in order to hide her misfortune, and the better to secure her success in the business upon which she had entered'. It was necessary to carry this deception on when she appeared before the sheriff court, but Charles, she alleged, knew perfectly well that she was not married to anyone else. Catharine managed to drag the case out for a long time, but she was unable to disprove her previous marriage, and Charles was therefore assoilzied.[5]

In June 1796 John Philp, journeyman wright in Kirkcaldy, was no less surprised when Mary Carmichael raised such an action against him. She was old enough to be his mother, he said, and when he lodged with her he 'never had Carnal Knowledge of her Body'. The marriage alleged by her was said to have taken place two years earlier, but no such claim had been made until he was about to marry another woman. Although Mary produced written evidence, John swore in court that he never gave her any promise of marriage and never signed the documents she produced; she was unable to provide any proof, and he was assoilzied.[6]

The above cases appear to have been try-ons. Far more complex are those which follow.

Insufficient Proof

If there is one thing that reveals the difficulty of deciding whether a marriage existed or not it is finding courts coming to different conclusions.[7] The 1763 case (which did not end until 1766) of Margaret Barr, daughter of a mason in Rutherglen, against John Fairlie (or Fairrie), sometime smith now coalmaster there, was one such.[8] Margaret alleged that in December 1759 'they were married in the fields near Rutherglen by a person who called himself a minister and officiated as such and said his name was Mr John Smith.' Actually there was at least one celebrator going by that name around Glasgow at the time,[9] so her story was plausible. She bore Fairlie's child and claimed to be married when cited before various church courts, though she admitted that she had no witnesses, and her 'marriage lines' were apparently forged (though it was never proved by whom).

But John was proving slippery, and in desperation she and her sister stationed witnesses in the house to overhear a conversation while the couple were in bed, when John allegedly said, 'Mary, I never will deny you to be my wife, have a Little patience Make yourself Easy, you have a good house to Live in want for nothing, for what is mine is yours.' John's side spent time discrediting those witnesses and argued that she was trying to prove that she was his wife, 'not openly and avowedly given in presence of any persons of character or credit but by some of her associates placed as spies without the Door to overhear and Testify what expressions she might extract from the Defender when the pursuer and he are said to have been in the room together in bed'. If this was 'to be allowed all the whores in Scotland would soon provide themselves with Husbands of the first charracter and rank'.

The evidence was contradictory, some witnesses testifying that Margaret herself had denied being married, but the commissaries found the marriage proven. However, the Court of Session had already sustained John's objections to one of Margaret's proposed witnesses and on appeal reversed the judgment and found no marriage proven.

Some men initially intended marriage and then changed their minds; the question to be decided was how far matters had proceeded before that change of mind. In 1769 James Pasley of Craig, Esquire, aged 75 (a widower, twice married before), fell passionately in love with Mary Johnstone, aged 22, and asked her to marry him immediately.[10] She said that she felt obliged to tell her relations first. During her ten-day absence in Annandale his grown-up daughters persuaded him that she was not a fit wife for him, and he subsequently wrote a letter to a friend of hers, stating that he was constantly hearing about Mary's 'light Carriage with the Servants and others in the Neighbourhood .... If she behave so now what will she do afterwards .... I wish I may be preserved from danger at this time of life and not be made a speak to the whole Country.'

So when Mary returned home she found not only that the marriage was broken off, but also that aspersions had been cast on her character. Her action was for declarator of marriage with an alternative of damages for slander. His lawyer argued that a proposal of marriage did not legally oblige a man to solemnise the marriage, and that the alternative conclusion was equally irrelevant. The commissaries assoilzied James from the conclusion for marriage but found that she was 'wronged and injured' by his breaking off the engagement settled between them and by his writing the letter, so that he was liable for damages.

In another case of the same year (1769), that of Isobel Brown against James Braidon (or Brydon), farmer at Liberton, it was the woman who changed her mind – too late. James had already married someone else when Isobel raised her action, and he was supporting Isobel's child as his illegitimate son. James had known Isobel for twelve years (they were second cousins), and he testified that he had indeed proposed marriage to her, more than once, but she always turned him down, 'saying that she would not marry this declarant or any man to have his friends look down upon her'. On one of those occasions he 'did insist to have the use of the Pursuers body which she agreed to.' He accepted that she 'yielded to him upon the honourable and honest view of being his wife and not his whore, And believes she would not have yielded had it not been for his previous courtships and sollicitations for marriage.' That was the only time he had sex with her, and even after she was pregnant she continued to refuse to marry him, saying when he told her of his intention of marrying another woman that she had no objections and 'he might marry whom he pleased'. He called her bluff, and it was only after he actually did so that she realised her mistake. As there had never been mutual consent to a marriage her action failed.[11]

Jean Lawrie and James Primrose, clerk to the collector of the customs at Leith, had a turbulent relationship.[12] They met in 1774 through a mutual acquaintance, and in 1775 her brother George 'was at the Dancing School' with James who sometimes visited the family. In 1779 they first had sex, and in March 1781 she bore him a son. Her brother told James that she was pregnant, insisted that he marry her, and threatened violence if he refused. James 'in order to Abate the Violence of the pursuers brother, said that he would think of it', but a few days later he refused to do so, though he agreed to support the child. In October 1781 Jean 'made a great noise and gathered a Mob And threatned to blow out the declarants brains'. Subsequently he was warned that she 'had been practising the firing of Pistols', so he agreed to see her but still refused to marry her. Yet from the end of 1782 James again 'had Enjoyment of the pursuers person'. He declared in court that he never asked her to come and live with him, but that she herself 'offered or rather threatned to come to his house and dwell whether he would or not without asking Marriage'.

In September 1783, according to her version of events, after repeating his promise of marriage she let him into her bed, where he was found by her father the next morning. After expressing 'great sorrow for what had happened' he told Jean and her father that he would marry her publicly, adding 'give me Pen, Ink and paper and go for two Witnesses, and I will give a line acknowledging her to be my Wife, and will declare her to be such openly'. When her father went for witnesses

the said James Primrose took the Opportunity to go Away, half undressed, and being met at the foot of the stair by the Complainers father, and some others, he made a great Noise, altho no Violence was offered to him, Calling out, that he had behaved in a shocking manner, and desiring the Complainers Father to kill him, drown him or knock out his Brains, and then taking to his heels, he run thro' the Town of Leith without shoes or stockings and did not stop till he Came to the Links.

James's version of the scene was that he called on her late one night when he had been out drinking and she invited him into her bed. He was awakened the next morning by her father's voice, and he 'suspected this to have been a Snare laid for him'. James 'thought his life in danger As the pursuers father was a Stronger Man than the Declarant, that the Declarant for that reason thought to sooth him, that he might get safely away'. He had no memory of asking for pen, paper and ink, but he did accede to the father's suggestion that he go for witnesses, 'Intending to take the advantage of his Absence, to Make his Escape'. So, as soon as the father had gone he

Instantly used that opportunity And In spite of the pursuer and her Mother who both held by the Declarant he got to the street, Where by their Cries, the pursuers father met the Declarant And with them used him very Coarsely, Endeavouring to force him back into the house, That the Declarant then Called out for help which made some people come, but by that time a Strong Vest the Declarant had on was torn And great part of the Skin rubbed off his Wrists in the Struggle, but upon two Men coming from Leith the Declarant got away.

Jean was unable to bring any proof of a marriage, and James was assoilzied. (For another attempt at duress see Case Study 10.)

In the 1789 case of Margaret Dalziel (daughter of one of Lord Somerville's shepherds) against John Richmond, son of a 'seedsman' in Edinburgh, it is difficult to work out who was lying.[13] Margaret alleged a ceremony (in 1785) by Mr James Wilson, and produced a certificate, after which – she said – John was sent to England by his parents. On his return he denied the marriage.

After Mary raised her action John denied not only the marriage and paternity of her child, but even 'having ever had any intercourse whatever with her farther than speaking to her when necessary in the same manner that he did to the rest of his Fathers Servants'. He was only 16 or 17 at the time and she 'was at least double that age.' He said that she repeatedly told him that she would abandon the action if he would acknowledge her child as his bastard and provide for it, but he refused. When he appeared in court John again denied everything and said that he went to England 'in order to get Instruction as a Gardner and cannot recollect any other reason or Motive he had for going except to get such Instruction'.

Was he lying? The celebrator testified to performing the ceremony between a woman who said she was Margaret Dalziel and a man who said he was John Richmond, and both he and a witness to the marriage said that the certificate was genuine. None of the witnesses was able to identify the couple in court, but after several years that was hardly surprising. The commissaries did not find a marriage proven and assoilzied John. Margaret appealed to the Court of Session, after which John was again cited to appear before the commissaries for another examination. Again he denied ever courting Margaret, being in James Wilson's house, or even seeing the certificate before he was shown it in court, and the commissaries reaffirmed their original decreet. A puzzling case.

One would not normally have expected the family of a man to show great friendship to a woman who had borne his child without being married to him, so in a 1799 case Ann Lauder used the care and concern exhibited to her by the sisters and brother-in-law of John Dun, surgeon in Glasgow, as evidence that she was his wife.[14] Ann was 'childs maid' to a sister of John's, who moved back to the parental home when she was widowed. John was at that time a medical student; according to Ann they were about the same age, but according to John he was only 16 and she was about twice that age. She said that they accepted each other as man and wife so she went to bed with him; when she became pregnant it was agreed that she should go to his brother's house for awhile, and that John should go to the West Indies until his father died. She 'became extremely anxious to have her marriage publicly announced before his departure' but then discovered that he had already set sail. The shock of this, she said, brought on her labour, and she bore a daughter in May 1790. His sisters and brother-in-law all called on her during his absence and treated her as his wife. His father died soon after that and when he returned to Scotland their connection was renewed and in July 1797 a son was born. But after that he refused to acknowledge her as his wife.

When John (now described as 'Ensign and assistant Surgeon in the 11th West India Regiment') appeared in court he denied any promise of marriage and also insisted that the second child was not his, as the last time he saw her before the birth was two years earlier. He tried to stop her citing members of his family as witnesses, on the grounds that how she was treated by them while he was absent was irrelevant, but the commissaries did not accept this. The key witness was Mrs Isobel Dun or Carrick, John's sister and Ann's former employer.

At the time Ann looked after her children Isobel 'observed an attachment and intimacy' between her brother and Ann. When Ann became pregnant John acknowledged himself the father, and before his departure for the West Indies 'he anxiously recommended the pursuer to her care and still appeared much attached to her.' At the time of Ann's 'inlying and afterwards', Isobel visited her, and Ann was invited by Isobel 'to come and stay with her at her Fathers house where she was about the time of his death'. When her brother returned from Jamaica he appeared to Isobel 'to be still attached' to Ann, and Ann 'at different times visited both the deponent and her sister Mrs Gray'. After the birth of the second child John continued to write frequently to her. Ann often came to visit Isobel 'and was invited to do so as she appeared destitute and often in want of necessaries'. She 'brought her Children alongst with her'. While John resided with Isobel, Ann 'frequently came to her house seeking him and the pursuer and defender had there many private Meetings and conversations together'. Ann 'on different occasions was entrusted by the deponent with the management of her house, and believes that on some of these occasions the defender was then residing in said house'.

So the 40 year-old widow of a clergyman was countenancing this relationship and even giving Ann the charge of her household, yet she never heard her brother acknowledge Ann as his wife. Isobel said that 'he sometimes treated the pursuer better and sometimes worse, but the deponent does not think he treated her as his Wife'. She and his other relations

wished that the connection between the pursuer and defender should be brought to an end one way or another and that it should either be given up or that the pursuer should be made his Wife, That the deponent allways had a good opinion of the pursuer, and would have been very well Satisfied that she had been her brothers Wife, but did not consider her as Such; That the deponent expressed a wish to her Brother that if he had made any promises to the pursuer he should fullfill them, and was told by him that he had made no promises to the pursuer . . . . Interrogated whether she would have kept up the above mentioned correspondence with the pursuer, had she not believed that her Brother was to marry her or that she was her Brothers Wife? Depones that she did not believe that the defender would Marry her and frequently said this to the pursuer herself and desired her by no means to depend on him.

Ann could not prove a marriage, but her story reveals again that – in the eighteenth century at least – even amongst the professional classes a mother who was not a wife was not necessarily beyond the pale.

This was also true in a nineteenth-century case (though in a rather lower ranking group), that of Christian Anderson, daughter of a weaver in Dunfermline, against William Cant.[15] In 1823 William got the lease of a tollbar in Fife and asked Christian to live with him and help him out – as a wife, she said; as a servant, he said. Subsequently he moved to another place, accompanied by Christian, who had one child that died and was pregnant again when she raised her action in 1826. Her first witness was a 66 year-old carter who saw her in the tollhouse: 'she was a servant in the house and she seemed to have more power than ordinary servants, and she used me very well, and I thought in my own mind he should make her Mrs Cant and I called her Mrs Cant to the Defender, and he never gave me an answer.' The witness was asked how many beds there were in the house, and replied, 'I saw but one bed and as they were young folks I dare say they made it serve them both.' He also visited them at the next house, and when asked 'If they were cohabiting together, and habit and repute husband and wife', he replied, 'They were living together – and I thought if he did not make her his wife he should have done it.' Her other witnesses were no more helpful, and the commissaries assoilzied him.

Christian petitioned to have William examined in court, but when he appeared he declared, 'I never promised to marry her all the days of my life,' so the commissaries reaffirmed their decreet. Christian would not have been so keen for him to appear in court if she was not herself convinced that he had promised to marry her before she went to live with him, but his denial robbed her of any chance of this being declared a marriage.

As can be seen from the variety of cases in this chapter, there was really no such thing as a 'typical' declarator of marriage case, but that of Elizabeth Cameron (and her daughters, Elizabeth and Agnes) against Allan Cameron, wright and spirit dealer in the Gorbals, Glasgow, was more unusual than most.[16] The action was raised in 1828, when Allan said that Elizabeth was in her fifties. She had been married to a private in the army, he said, and when her husband was absent in India she 'maintained herself by keeping a small Lodginghouse'. In 1814, when Allan was 17 and Elizabeth was 40, he and his three brothers came to lodge in her house. 'One Evening upon his return from School he found that his Bed had been let by the Pursuer to another Lodger,' and she offered him a share of hers. He accepted, 'and from this time an illicit intercourse was continued between the parties'. But no one knew of their relationship or that he was the father of her children, and during that whole period of about seven years Elizabeth continued to correspond with her husband in India.

In 1824 Allan began to work as a wright on his own account, and Elizabeth sometimes went to his warehouse to see to the delivery of items he had ordered, 'and upon these occasions the Pursuer, when enquired at, represented the Defender to be her Son; and she was known to have a Son of his age and appearance – but who had enlisted sometime before this'. At Whitsunday 1825 he 'opened a Shop or furniture Warehouse in his own name in Glasgow – and as he could not entrust the management of it to his Apprentices, the Pursuer was in use to take charge of it when he happened to be absent'. For three-quarters of a year all went well, but then she

> *began to acquire dissipated habits: She did not account for the money she collected: She was frequently in a state of intoxication, and formed acquaintances with women of loose character: and in consequence of this conduct on her part the Defenders affairs became embarrassed, and his whole Effects were taken by his Landlord in payment of the rent.*

During all that time he never acknowledged her as his wife, and though they both slept in the shop, it was in separate beds. At Whitsunday 1826 he 'entered into partnership with his Brother as Spirit Dealer, and slept from that period with him in a room fitted up for that Purpose in their premises'. But he did not immediately give up the furniture shop, and Elizabeth could not have been as useless as he represented her, for she 'attended it in his absence, and he came several times daily to see what was doing'. Despite such a long enduring relationship Elizabeth was unable to bring any proof of a marriage (or even of her first husband's death).

In the last chapter it seemed that a woman was either a wife or a mistress, but in this one (and the attendant case studies) we see that relationships between men and women could be far more complex than that.

Notes

1 CC8/6/20.
2 CC8/6/40.
3 CC8/5/21.
4 See Leah Leneman and Rosalind Mitchison, *Sin in the City – Sexuality and Social Control in Urban Scotland 1660–1780* (Edinburgh, 1998), 109–11.
5 CC8/5/23.
6 CC8/6/84.
7 This also occurred in one of Lawrence Stone's case studies in *Uncertain Unions – Marriage in England 1660–1753* (Oxford, 1992), 173–4, where the Court of Common Pleas (a secular court) found a marriage proven and the man liable to the woman for subsistence, while the London Consistory Court (an ecclesiastical court) upheld the man's case for jacitation

(freedom) on the grounds of insufficient proof of a marriage. At least in Scotland the final decreet of the Commissary Court was binding.

8   CC8/5/11.
9   Leah Leneman and Rosalind Mitchison, 'Clandestine Marriage in the Scottish Cities 1660–1780', *Journal of Social History* Vol 26, No 4, 852.
10   CC8/6/27.
11   CC8/6/27.
12   CC8/6/44.
13   CC8/6/55.
14   CC8/6/67.
15   CC8/6/158.
16   CC8/6/156.

CASE STUDY 10

McINNES V. MORE: A NARROW ESCAPE

TWO classic scenarios, that of a scheming older woman, and that of an attempted 'shotgun wedding', appear in the 1781 case of Janet McInnes against Alexander More. She was 36, the daughter of a minister of the gospel and widow of an army captain; he was 24, son of a merchant in Aberdeen. Janet seemed to have a good case, for she was able to produce a letter, dated May 1780, in which Alexander acknowledged her as his lawful wife. And in December, she said, while on his merchandising rounds, he also acknowledged his marriage to her brother and a friend, and proposed returning to Aberdeen to tell his father, but relations of his turned up and took him under their custody, and had since kept him confined in his father's house.

According to Alexander's statement in court, after Janet came to Aberdeen she used to call on his sisters, and he began to visit her and go on walks with her. One day in February 1780, after drinking tea at a neighbour's, he 'attended her to her own Lodgings', but before they got there she 'led him into an empty house [ie flat] which was immediately below her own where he had enjoyment of her Person for [the] first time'. He 'had been using some freedoms with her upon the stair', and 'she showed some reluctance and appeared to dislike the freedoms used with her but afterwards led him into the Empty house … and after she was in the House yielded to his desires without reluctance' (the flat was 'unfurnished and tradesmen working in it'). She then 'proposed to him that they should both go to her own house' and 'carried him to her own house up stairs to her own bed room on the head of the stair … when he had again enjoyment of her Person'. From that day until about the end of November 'he had frequently enjoyment of the Pursuers person in her own house and in a Back garden of a House belonging to the Declarants father.' But marriage was never mentioned between them.

In July she told him that she was pregnant, and in November she 'proposed to go to Edinburgh where she had some acquaintance upon whose secrecy she could rely', and he gave her money for the journey and inlying. But the following day she told him that she had advised a family friend, John Grant of Repachie, of the plan and he had disapproved, and suggested that she get Alexander to copy out a letter acknowledging her as his wife, 'and in that case he Mr Grant would go along with her to her Brothers to be Privately Brought to bed there'. And 'if her Brother did not agree to her staying at his house she might still at any rate go to Edinburgh upon her Brothers Sanction and under pretence of Being on Business.' She assured him that 'the said Letter should never be any ways Binding upon him so as to make a marriage which she could never suppose nor did ever she expect after the connection the Declarant had with her so long,' and she also threatened that if he did not do as she asked she would make sure his father heard all about this. At the time 'he had been at Variance with his father on account of the money matters and was particularly anxious to conceal from him his connection with the Pursuer.' She prevailed, and he copied the letter. The next day she asked him for another letter, specifically addressed to her brother, which he refused to give her, and she said that her brother would not therefore allow her to stay with him. She got more money off him, but she did not go to Edinburgh.

A few days later Alexander, on foot, was about 20 miles from Aberdeen collecting knitwear from country weavers when Janet's brother turned up. He said he had been to various houses, asking for Alexander, and 'wished to know the intentions of the Declarant and whether he had sent his sister to his house as his wife or his whore'. Her family friend, John Grant, also came running up, and Alexander 'answered that the intentions of men were not generally known or gave some evasive Answer of a like nature'. His 'reason for answering in this manner was that he apprehended That Mr McInnes and Mr Grant had formed a Plot to carry him by force to Aberdeen'. McInnes had already 'told him that he had brought a chaise with him from Aberdeen', and Alexander 'was surprized and alarmed at the manner in which these two Gentlemen made their appearance'. McInnes 'arrived first riding at full speed on one of the chaise Horses and about half an hour afterwards Mr Grant came running in his Boots having left the chaise at two miles distance on the top of a Hill', and Alexander 'apprehended that these Gentlemen had a design to ensnare him into some passionate and unguarded expressions in order to afford them a pretence of treating him with rigour and Cruelty'. They asked him 'to go with them in their Chaise to Aberdeen', but he suspected a trap and refused.

The two gentlemen then treated him 'with Politeness and civility and seemed desireous to impress him with an idea that they were doing him a favour when they Proposed to carry him to Aberdeen in the Chaise'. But they went with him to another house where he took in stockings and then on to Udny where 'they dined together and drank half a mutchken of Whisky in Punch'. Alexander 'was very anxious to get away and be clear of this Company' but had no idea how to escape. However, 'just after dinner was finished and before they had drank out the punch he heard the trampling of a Horse and imagining either that some person had come to his assistance or that his Lad had wanted him upon business he went [out] of the House where he found his Lad who told him that a Chaise and four was waiting for him at the foot of the road.' He 'immediately took the hat from the servants head mounted his horse and rode full speed to the chaise'. When 'he arrived there he found his Brother and Mr Black his old acquaintance who told him that having heard of Mr McInnes were [sic] in search of him and meant to carry him by force to the Pursuers room and there to have a Minister ready to celibrate a marriage and that they had come to assist him in getting away'. As soon as he got into the chaise 'he gave orders to the Postillions to Drive with the outmost speed and offerred them a reward of a Guinea each if they would reach Aberdeen in an Hour.' He 'also told them that a chaise was coming up behind and that if this chaise was allowed to Overtake them he would not give them a farthing and also that if any of the Horses should be Hurt he would pay the loss'.

Alexander made his escape, and he was not 'confined' in his father's house, as she had alleged. He realised that his abductors might try again, and heard that a minister was kept in waiting at Janet's house 'ready to celebrate a mock marriage', so he 'judged it prudent not to stirr from home under cloud of night but it is known to the whole inhabitants of the City of Aberdeen that he appeared every day upon the Change at Business hours and transacted his affairs as usual without restraint from his father or any of his other friends'.

The rhetoric used on both sides is fascinating, if not always to the point. His lawyer argued that 'The disparity of age Between the parties renders the Proposed conjunction most preposterous', and that her character was 'fraught with design Finesse and Cunning', while his appeared 'artless and unsuspecting'. It would 'be totally inverting the design and intention' of Scottish marriage law 'if artfull Women who had in the first place prostituted their persons and afterwards by their address and cunning entraped unwary Young men into an acknowledgment of a marriage', which had never 'been so much as dreamed of by the partys at the Commencement of their amour', 'should be rewarded for their Crime with the Possession of a Husband whom they had otherwise no title to expect.'

Her side argued that the age gap was of no consequence. In warmer countries 'women of Forty it is well known usually hold the first rank in licentious Society, There is no reason therefore to suppose that a woman of Thirty six years has lost her attractions in Aberdeenshire,' and their year-long amour was 'abundant evidence that the Pursuer was young enough to inspire the defender with a strong personal attachment'. ('...women of Thirty Six often in Polite life retain many of the graces of youth tempered and even some times embellished by that correct taste which the Habits of Cultivated Society conferr'.)

But the letter was crucial, and because Alexander had not alleged that 'he was either concussed to grant the Letter or acknowledgement lybelled on or was under any incapacity to grant the same,' the commissaries found the marriage proven. He appealed to the Court of Session, which upheld the decision. He then appealed to the House of Lords, which reversed it. In the course of the action it had been shown that the letter, although dated May, had actually been granted in November, so it had not predated their sexual intercourse. It also appeared that the acknowledgement 'was not given by the defender or accepted by the Pursuer or understood by either as a declaration of the Truth but merely as a Colour to serve in the other and different purpose which had been mutually concerted between them', and therefore it could not prove a marriage. Janet fought on, but in June 1783 Alexander was finally assoilzied from her claim.

CC8/5/17

CASE STUDY 11

BAIRD V. CAMPBELL: NOT FOR WANT OF TRYING

DUGALL Campbell, accountant in Edinburgh, provided the court with a frank description of his relationship with Nancy Baird. She was only 17 and a servant in his household in 1825 (he was 28 at the time), and with her libel she produced the following in writing: 'Dear Nancy – According to your desire I give you this promise to marry you.' There was no pregnancy or child, and Dugall denied ever having sex with her, let alone promising to marry her.

His examination in court started with the period when Nancy was in his mother's service. He was asked if he 'was in the custom of holding conversations with her and speaking with her apart from the other members of the family' and replied, 'Occasionally I did'. Asked if he paid particular attention to her or courted her during that period' he answered, 'She gave me encouragement to pay attention to her.' Was he in 'the custom of using freedom with her person in any way?' 'Merely in the way of saluting her or kissing her.' Did he use terms of endearment 'such as my Dear'? 'Probably'. Was he 'ever alone with her either in her bedroom or his'? Yes, once in his bedroom 'and once in the place where she slept which was in a concealed bed off the kitchen'.

On the first occasion, he said, 'she came to my bedroom uninvited – It might be about midnight and I was myself in bed at the time … she came up to the bed side and took me by the hand which wakened me I then took her round the neck and kissed her and took her into the bed.' But, he said, he did not have carnal connection with her that night – 'I had not time, and there was a private reason that prevented me, which was that not knowing she was to come I was not prepared to receive her.' What did this mean?, wondered the court. He explained: 'I had been in company with a female immediately preceding and found myself incapable of attempting to have connexion with her.'

But they agreed that she would come to his room another night. She failed to do so, having fallen asleep, so he went to her bed and 'awoke her and prevailed upon her to come with him to his own bed room'. Unfortunately, as they were tiptoeing down the passage a cat knocked over some crockery in the kitchen and woke the household, so they scurried back to their own beds.

Dugall continued to meet Nancy after she left his mother's service. He declared that the first time they met afterwards he spent about an hour with her in his business partner's house but had no sex with her, although this had been his motive in arranging the rendezvous: 'she refused to allow me, because I would not take lodgings for her and take her into keeping.' He went on, 'I put my hand round her neck and kissed her and carried her into another room where there was a bed, and had got her down upon it, but as I could not accomplish it but by force, and as I did not wish to force any woman I let her away.' The same thing happened on two subsequent occasions, he said, and because he was 'always in the way of making her presents of a little money every time I met with her, and I had given her sometime before this after her leaving my mothers house, a pelisse and about two pounds in money, and she probably was in hopes that this was a kind of earnest of my agreeing to take her into keeping which was her object all along – I had refused to give her a promise to do so but I told her that if ever I had it in my power I would agree to do it.'

So how did the written promise of marriage come about? Dugall said that Nancy's father had discovered he was seeing her and would not let them meet any more. Nancy was so upset that at her request he scribbled a few lines, which she was to show her father and no one else; she snatched it off him when he showed it to her, and that was the last time he saw her until she raised her action of declarator. Dugall now petitioned that Nancy appear in court. When she did so she admitted that 'Mr Campbell failed in his purpose'. Asked whether she meant to say that 'on no occasion he had had connection with her', she declared that she did mean this and that 'he tried to have connection with her more than once but always failed.'

Consummation was not necessary to constitute a marriage in Scotland, but there was nothing else in this case to imply a marriage, so Dugall was assoilzied.

CC8/6/157

CHAPTER 6

SEDUCTION

WOMEN who were unsure if they could prove a marriage could ask for an alternative conclusion of damages for seduction, and 25 of them did obtain damages.[1] (There was also just one case in which a woman claimed and won such damages without seeking a declarator of marriage.)[2] The Scottish law granting women damages for seduction pre-dated the Reformation,[3] and in the early examples the women had not specifically sought them, but the commissaries decided that the woman had been deceived by the man.[4]

Two such decreets were issued in 1706. The first was in the case of Margaret Pursell, a farmer's widow, against George Paterson, jeweller in Edinburgh who, she said, had courted her for over two years and once said in public that he would fight any man who tried to take her from him and that none should have him as his wife 'but the said George himself', after which she went to bed with him and ended up pregnant. The commissaries did not find a marriage proven but awarded her £1200 Scots (£100 sterling) damages. As her libel was for declarator of marriage only, Paterson's lawyer twice appealed against the decision, without success. The word 'seduction' was not mentioned, but the commissaries declared that they were allowing her damages and expenses because of his 'fraudulent abusing her', as proven by witnesses.[5]

The second case, that of Janet Stirling against John Hamilton of Grange, raised in 1703, was unusual in two ways. First, at the time Janet raised the process he was cohabiting with another woman whom he claimed as his wife, and secondly, he died a month later, so that the case was fought by his brother and by the woman whom the commissaries in the end found to be his lawful widow. He was found guilty of 'fraudulent abusing' Janet, and his heirs and representatives had to pay her damages and expenses.[6]

The same term was used ten years later in 1716 after Andrew Agnew of Seuchan swore under oath that he had not promised to marry Elizabeth Castlelaw, his housekeeper. After the commissaries assoilzied him Elizabeth raised a new action, for damages for seduction, and won.[7] The 'alternative conclusion' was sought from time to time as the century went on, and from the 1780s onward it became routine in cases where there was doubt about whether a marriage could be proven. Lawyers for the men sometimes argued that this showed the woman knew perfectly well she was not a wife, but in fact the clause did not prejudice the action for declarator of marriage, because if there was no written evidence and the man was prepared to deny a promise of marriage under oath, then it might be impossible to prove a marriage yet feasible to prove deception.

Typically in such cases the couple belonged to the middle ranks of society, the relationship had lasted for some time, the woman was pregnant or had recently borne a child, and the case dragged on for years. Certain themes emerge most strongly. In theory, a woman could not expect a man to marry her if she was not his equal in social rank, so the man might try to prove that the woman was so much his inferior that she could not have realistically done so. The woman, on her part, would try to prove not only that she was of equal rank, but that an open courtship had taken place. Finally, a woman was entitled to damages only if the man had 'corrupted' her, so she would bring evidence of her good character and virtue, while the man would try and blacken her character.

Rank

Logically, the emphasis on equality of rank was nonsense. As Francis Macnab's lawyer put it in the 1780s, 'It does not appear to the Defender that any circumstances in the pursuers situation could have much effect on the merits of this question for one Man may have an intrigue with a woman of his own Station and another may marry a woman much beneath it.' But in fact the question of rank was expressly disputed in this case of Janet or Jenny Buchanan against Francis Macnab.[8]

According to Jenny, after her father's death she 'was brought up and liberally educated both in Stirling and Glasgow' by an uncle, who bequeathed to her and two sisters a farm in Glasgow that produced £50 per annum. After her uncle's death she lived chiefly with her brother, 'and had occasion to visit Mrs Buchanan, Lady Arnprior and her sister Lady Torry'. Lady Macnab of Macnab was a sister of Francis Buchanan of Arnprior, so Jenny 'became acquainted with that family and particularly with Miss Peggy Macnab of Macnab'. In June 1781 she met Peggy at the church in Killin, and Peggy invited her to stay at the house of Kinnell, where she lived with her mother and brother, Francis. It was during that stay at Kinnell that Jenny alleged he seduced her by claiming that they would thereby be married.

Francis asserted that her father was for many years a livery servant in his uncle's house, 'and she herself was till within these few years a maid servant receiving wages in the house of Thomas Buchanan of Leny'. At Kinnell 'she was very far from being put on the footing of a friend and companion to Miss Macnab, on the contrary she was employed to oversee the Servants and to make Gowns and Capes for Miss Mcnab.' In view of 'her humble situation', 'it ought to be presumed more likely that the defender would form with her and she submit to a transient amorous connection than that she should expect or he think of making a proposal of Marriage.'

Her lawyer denied that her father was ever a servant:'he possessed two considerable farms under the late Arnprior.' After her parents' death Mr Buchanan of Leny offered to take Jenny 'to his house at Glasgow for some time that she might have the advantage of the Schoolls in that place'. While she resided there 'she was treated not in a servile or dependant line but on a footing with the rest of the family.' She then apprenticed herself 'to a thread maker in Glasgow and having served out her time she carried on that business on her own account for about twelve months till falling into bad health she found it necessary for her recovery to go to the Country among her relations for some time'. The fact that her circumstances were 'inferior' to his 'might prevent her from thinking of a marriage with him unless the first advances came on his side yet she must say that her circumstances as well as her principles and spirit placed her many degrees above being connected with on any other footing'. As for her status at Kinnell, 'altho the defender has in his Judicial declaration been pleased with a view to degrade the pursuer to say that she was brought there for the purpose of making some gowns and Capes yet the length of time she remained in the family is sufficient of itself to disprove that alledgance ... and the defender knows that her leaving it was only in order to conceal her pregnancy for which he was exceedingly anxious.'

The case turned on written evidence. Jenny produced a document in which Macnab acknowledged her as his wife, but which Macnab claimed was a forgery (as it almost certainly was). However, the contents of letters used to demonstrate Macnab's handwriting emerged as key evidence to show that he did not regard her in the same light as the mistresses who had borne his illegitimate children. At the same time, though, as they were signed 'your most ashoured [sic] friend', they also revealed that he had never considered himself married to her.

So had he seduced her? Initially the commissaries did not think so, nor did the Court of Session on first appeal, but after a second appeal she was awarded £200. The raking up of family background was not the decisive point, but it shows the importance it had in the eyes of the litigants and of the law. Both sides stretched the truth. At one point Francis declared that 'to induce her to comply with his desires' he used the same methods as with his previous mistresses, 'such as kissing and clapping and giving silk handkerchieffs and ribbons'. This, her lawyer said, was going too far,

> For whatever effect silk handkerchieffs and ribbons may have upon the lowest class of young women ... it is out of all sight to believe that he could be so very gross in his Courtship as to think of plying one of the pursuers Station Character and Education with such perswasions or to believe that she would be induced to yeild her virtue by paltry presents of that kind. The manner in which he himself talks of her in his Letters and the

fondness and respect he there expresses are sufficient prooff that he never considered her in so low and despicable a light.

Jenny Buchanan might have been considered 'beneath' him, but she was a woman of substance who could not be bought, or afterwards bought off, as he had clearly done with other women before her.

In a case that ran from December 1791 to January 1798, that of Grace McGowan against Peter Fisher, the commissaries also in the first instance did not award damages, and it was only after an appeal to the Court of Session that she succeeded.[9] Grace described herself as the youngest daughter of a late baillie of, and merchant in, Rothesay. Peter claimed that she was trying to impress the commissaries

with an Idea that she is a person somewhat above the common rank by designing her father in the Lybell 'late Baillie and Merchant in Rothesay' This however is a mere deception – It is no doubt true that he was a Baillie there about 40 years ago but it is equally true, to be then a Baillie of that Burgh conferred no great respect owing to the poverty and paucity of the Inhabitants and so far as the Defender understands her Father never was a Merchant nor has he for many years carried on any business whatever His only Means of Support arose from one of the Meanest Offices about the Custom house of Rothsay, namely that of a Tidesman which is well known to be neither a post of honour nor great emolument.

Grace, he stated, had been a menial servant, 'after which she came to be a Labourer and derived much of her Support from wages earned at the Cotton Mill of Rothsay in consequence of which she had frequent occasion to See the Defender, and in this Manner he became Acquainted with her.' Peter was a partner in the Rothesay cotton mill, so this social disparity meant that she could never have believed he meant to marry her. But, of course, her version was very different. She was

his equal at least in point of Rank, Education, and Virtuous example in every respect. Her assendants in the male line for several Generations, have been Burgesses Merchants and Heritors in the Ancient Royal Borough of Rothesay; Her connections both by Father and Mother have also long been real Freeholders and Voters in the County of Bute; Her father was one of the Magistrates of Rothesay, and above Twenty years a Counsellor there. It is true that by a course of misfortunes he fell back in his circumstances, But what Merchant or Manufacturer is secure against such a reverse? .... It was from want of influence not defect of Rank that he did not procure a higher office than the one he now holds.

She received a gentlewoman's education, she said, and was never a menial servant. Nor had she ever been a labourer in his mill; it was a type of needlework she did, learned from a 'gentlewoman', to 'keep her in pocket money, and to be an amusement', and she 'was so employed in her father's house by the Managers of the Miln, long before the defender came to the place'.

Her lawyer's rhetorical question stressed the relevance of social equality: 'Could seduction be expressed in more explicit terms, than by taking advantage of opportunities to use freedoms with a young female his own equal in order to induce her to comply with his wishes?'

The relationship between Jean Farquharson and Alexander Anderson of Candacraig lasted for some years before she became pregnant and raised her action against him in 1794 (he clearly had intended to marry her and then changed his mind); the decreet was not issued for another ten years.[10] Jean's lawyer raised the issue of rank at an early stage. She was the daughter of 'a Gentleman of a respectable family and moderate estate in the County of Aberdeen', received 'an education suitable to her rank in life which altho' it perhaps did not extend to some of the most elegant accomplishments, was well calculated to have made her a good wife to any Country Gentleman of the Defenders station'; and her father had left her 'a very competent fortune'. Alexander 'was the natural son of the late Mr Anderson of Candacraig, who originally intended him for the Church, but afterwards having no lawfull issue, left the defender his Heir in the Estate of Candacraig'. His father and her family were related, and she 'had every right to consider herself as the defender's equal in every respect, and consequently had ever reason to look upon any advances or addresses which he made to her as of an honourable nature and with a view of Marriage'.

He mocked this, pointing to her sister's marriage to 'a small farmer in that corner, a widow[er] advanced in life and deformed in his person and bankrupt in his circumstances'. But a witness testified that this sister 'was Married to Robert Gordon Farmer in Clashmore who was then a Respectable farmer and reputed to be in good circumstances, but afterwards became bankrupt in consequence with [sic] his connection with a Mr Mcpherson a Drover who had failled', and that 'Mr Gordons first Wife was the Daughter of as good a Gentleman as was in the Country.' All the witnesses agreed that pursuer and defender were of equal rank in society.

In 1819 Marion Meikle's lawyer, in her suit against Robert Mcghie of Trows, thought 'It would not be disputed by the Defender that in point of Rank and Station his family and the Pursuers stood upon an equal footing and in questions of this sort this circumstance was of some importance.'[11] Amongst others a neighbouring gentleman, John McKirdy Esquire of Birkwood, testified that 'from report and common estimation so far as the deponent could judge, the family of the Pursuer and the family of the Defender are much upon a footing in the society of that neighbourhood and the deponent is not aware that there was any irregularity between the Pursuer and Defender in rank or station.'

Robert would get nowhere by claiming social disparity, so his lawyer tried a different tack:

Let the Pursuer take what advantage she could of her respectability in life it did not follow that no woman in such a station could have a child without being so seduced as would found her in an action of damages on account of Seduction. That class of society was not protected from the influence of strong passion and indeed that very rank to which the Pursuer belonged was one in which Women were more likely to yield themselves without Seduction than almost any other. They were not kept down by indifferent food and hard labour, but they lived well, they had leisure to pursue their own gratifications without having that refinement and those habits of delicacy which were peculiar to a class still higher.

But this nonsense got him nowhere either.

Ranks could also be stressed in an urban context, as in the 1823 case of Anne Turphy against Nicholas McCandie.[12] Ann's parents died when she was young, and she was brought up by her aunt and uncle who kept an inn in Edinburgh. Nicholas was a medical student there and for about three years was a constant visitor. The picture his lawyer painted was of

a Young man attending his Education. Being quite simple inexperienced and at a distance from his Friends, he was, like every Young person similarly situated, exposed to the intrigues of the designing; Like others, at his time of life, he would frequently, of an evening, have sauntered into a Coffee house or Tavern, and among others he happened occasionally to go into Scotts Tavern in Leith Street where the Pursuer assisted in the House.

After he got to know her she 'insinuated herself into his good graces and he was unfortunately, or rather Sillily, led into an Illicit connection with her'. Apart from there having been no promise of marriage, 'No person in her rank of life ever thinks of claiming or is allowed to claim damages on account of Seduction.'

This version of her status was disputed. Her aunt and uncle were both now deceased, but 'so far from their House being a Coffee house or Tavern the resort of all and sundry – and to the service of which, as is farther insinuated, the Pursuer devoted herself – the fact is that it was exclusively resorted to by Travellers, and the Pursuer never served any Company in it in her life'. Nicholas's lawyer then said that Nicholas was a Highlander, and

he and some of his Companions, from the North, were in the habit at times of having dances in which the Gentlemen appeared habitated with kilts – For as much as that dress may be admired in the North it is only in parties of the first respectability that our Lowland Ladies are fond of joining when it is used – The consequence was that the

Defender and his young friends often felt themselves at a loss for females at their Dances, and they had no other resort but to take girls from Taverns snuff shops or the like where they could best be got.

But her lawyer was able to trump this, for Ann had learned from Nicholas himself 'that he had no higher pretensions than that of being the natural [ie bastard] son of a Captain McCandie, who was for some time in his Majesty's service; and therefore your Lordships will scarcely suppose that there was any such unequality as at once to open the eyes of the respondent, to shew her that his object was seduction, and not marriage.' In fact, he was clearly treated almost as a member of the family (even attending her aunt on her death bed), only to try to avoid marriage when she became pregnant, so that claims of a huge social gulf could never have prevailed. But, once again, the detail is crucial: the niece of an innkeeper was of an entirely different rank from a girl who served in an inn. Nicholas likewise failed to show that Highland balls were only attended by low, lewd women when witnesses declared that the balls 'were very respectably attended and rather small and select parties'.

Courtship

Lawrence Stone writes that 'among the middling and lower gentry social classes, unmarried English women enjoyed what was by European standards a quite exceptional freedom to conduct their own courtship rituals'.[13] The 'freedom' was as great in eighteenth-century Scotland as England, but the word 'rituals' is misleading because 'courtship' by then was so informal and undefinable that women had great difficulty in providing evidence of it.[14] As Jean White's lawyer put it in her 1808 suit against John Dickson, 'It must at once occur to the Commissaries that what is called a Courtship or marked attentions are terms very vague and undefinable.'[15]

Because the relationship between Jean Farquharson and Alexander Anderson of Candacraig (discussed in the section above) had lasted for several years, Jean was able to produce a number of witnesses to what they perceived as a courtship for marriage.[16] For example, Isobel McConnoch had 'seen them walking together by themselves like Sweethearts', and 'the behaviour of the defender had the appearance as if he wished to gain the love of the pursuer'. Mr Andrew Marshall, minister of the gospel, testified that Alexander showed particular marks of attention to Jean, which made the witness conclude that he was courting her for marriage. When asked to be specific the best he could do was that they were much the same as he had paid his wife when courting her.

However, another minister, Mr George Forbes, could recall the defining moment. He was riding with Alexander and when they saw some women winnowing corn, one of them, Jean Farquharson, immediately came to join them. Anderson remained on his horse, and Forbes noted 'the partys having one of each of their hands clasped together and they continued in this posture till they came to the Close of Allargue'. Forbes ascribed Anderson's not alighting from his horse 'to the very particular Intimacy which subsisted betwixt him and the pursuer'. They all went into the house of Allargue where they remained some hours, and while they were there Anderson 'sat Closs by Miss Farquharson, with one hand leaning on the back of her Chair and the other clasped in hers'. He saw the parallel with his courtship of his own wife.

In an urban milieu some specifics emerged in the case of Ann Turphy against Nicholas McCandie during the 1820s in Edinburgh (also discussed above). Ann's cousin, Mrs Anne Drysdale, was often at the same parties and balls, and testified that Nicholas's attention to Ann 'was upon all of these occasions both marked and particular – That she was very often his partner at these dances, and that he seemed to pay her every attention'. Furthermore, he was 'displeased on occasion of any particular attention being paid to the Pursuer by any other Gentleman than himself'. Mrs Drysdale recollected 'in particular of his being visibly displeased at such attention having been paid to her by a Captain Douglas a Master and Owner of a Ship … he showed this displeasure by looking very sulky at the Captain and sometimes intruding himself between them when they were sitting together'.

In many cases a courtship was said to be the 'common report of the country', but the difficulty lay in pinning this down to specifics. Without objective external signs of courtship, this could be discounted on the man's side as idle gossip. The case would then turn on the beliefs and intentions of the parties.

Virtue and Character

Even if it were proven that a woman had had intercourse with a man because she believed that he meant to marry her, she could not claim that she had thereby lost her virtue, reputation, and future chances of happiness unless she was pure and chaste before the man 'seduced' her. Inevitably, therefore, men tried to blacken the character of their accusers. One way was to brand her a whore, a second was to portray her as the seductress, and a third was to blame her for not resisting. All three emerge in our cases.

In the first case in which damages were awarded (1705) George Paterson claimed that Margaret Pursell was 'a person whose Character is pretty well known both in Town and Countrey: for it is notour that in her first husbands time her Carriage was so publickly light, that she was Convened befor the West Kirk Session, where several Acts of Levity and misdemeanours were made appear which was imputed to be the Cause of her husband's Death'. Furthermore, the occasion when she alleged that Paterson referred publicly to marrying her was irrelevant for 'she had yeilded her body in Carnal dealing a long time befor, for the space of several Moneths, so that it will thence appear she was an accustomed prostitute'. Her lawyer treated all this with the contempt it deserved, referring to Paterson's 'injurious and calumnious Reflections', which did 'but furder evidence the Defender's Unmanliness and Baseness'.[17]

In 1747 Alexander Hamilton younger of Gilskercleugh claimed that Elizabeth Lining (daughter of a minister of the gospel) 'Indulged him in the most wanton and Lascivious freedoms, Which were too strong temptations for one of the Memorialists Age, and at last Provoked him to ask what he ought not to have asked, and far less any Woman ought to have granted'. He admitted that she had initially resisted unless he promised to marry her, but although he refused to do so she finally came to his 'Appartment when He was Lying abed, And Satt down by him, When Both their Bloods Being heated And their Passions high, she readily consented and suffered the Memorialist to Enjoy her'. Furthermore, she could not 'Plead youth and Unexperience Which sometimes may expose a young Girl to Fall into snares That may be laid for her, She was come to full years Being about Thirty one'.[18]

Similarly, in 1779, George Nicoll (a farmer's son) claimed of Elizabeth Black (daughter of a neighbouring farmer) that 'whatever other Intimacy or Criminal Correspondence was betwixt them the same proceeded from the Pursuer by her sending Messages to him to come and speak to her at all times in the night and even coming herself to him at midnight to the room in his Father's house where he slept'. And in 1819 Robert Mcghie said of Marion Meikle that 'he had heard and was very soon satisfied by experience that she was of easy virtue'.[19]

To rebut such arguments the women needed character witnesses to demonstrate their virtuous character before being 'corrupted'. Elizabeth Black was able to produce a witness who declared that he 'never heard any thing laid to the Charge of the pursuer but that she had always a very good Character'. Jenny Buchanan, in her suit against Francis Macnab, produced certificates 'from every person with whom she lived or with whom she had occasion to be more intimately connected in the town of Glasgow certifying in the strongest terms her blameless and irreproachable behaviour'. Her lawyer could then argue that as her 'character was Spotless when she came to Kinnell the Commissaries will not readily believe that she was brought to submit to the defenders embraces without being seduced by promises and expectations on which to her loss she now finds she has too much relied'.[20]

In the case of Margaret Cameron against Alexander Cameron, for which decreet was issued in March 1814, witnesses were convinced that he had promised to marry her and only reneged because of his father's opposition (though he denied this under oath). For example, one said that at the time Alexander was reneging on his promise 'it had been much observed, that she [Margaret] was extremely cast down'. This witness had not then realised that she was pregnant, for 'her character was then such, that nobody could suspect her of unchastity'. Another witness declared that 'she never saw any young woman behave better than the pursuer had always done, so far as the deponent could perceive, till this discovery; and she was the last person she would have suspected of such misconduct.' The importance of such testimony is explicit in the commissaries's finding that 'the defender openly paid his addresses to her in the way of honourable courtship; that, until it was discovered that she had fallen with child to the defender, her character had been irreproachable; and that her conduct in all other aspects, excepting this connection, appears to have been blameless.'[21]

The most extreme case of character blackening – and vindication – was that of Jean Farquharson and Alexander Anderson of Candacraig (discussed in the two sections above).[22] According to Alexander, Jean was a woman 'of loose morals' whose child had, in fact, been fathered by another man, a labourer named Alexander Milne. Therefore, as well as recruiting witnesses to her own good character, Jean had to rebut this tale about 'Saundy' Milne.

Apparently Alexander had offered Milne four good horses to sign a letter stating that he was the father of Jean's child. After doing so he was seized with remorse and was seen by one witness 'even Shedding tears'. Milne himself was traced and appeared in court. From his own testimony it is clear that he was attracted to Jean and would have married her given half a chance but knew that this was unrealistic as she was 'above his degree'. Just such a half chance, rather than the four horses, seems to have been the bait that Anderson laid for him. So he signed, and immediately repented, but it was too late, for the document had been whipped away. 'The letter', he told the court, 'was false in the date as in every thing else, to the witness's sad regret.'

The commissaries were incensed. While they did not find a marriage proven they did find

> a publick Courtship ... established by clear and unexceptional evidence. Find that during the course of this Courtship which it was impossible for the pursuer to consider in any other light than as honourable on the part of Alexander Anderson of Candacraig defender, She was prevailed upon to yield to his embraces, Find the facts form a case of flagrant Seduction which entitle the pursuer to Damages, Find that the original injury of Seduction has been highly aggravated by the attacks which in the course of the process the defender has most improperly made upon the pursuers character, as well as by the improper practices employed on his part appearing from the proof.

In view of this they awarded punitive damages of £2,000. However, the Court of Session ruled that damages should reflect the man's circumstances, not a perceived aggravation of the injury. The higher court instructed the commissaries to tone down the wording of the decreet to a simple finding that the charge of seduction was proved, and lowered the amount to £750.

Seduction not Proven

In her libel of 1796 Elizabeth White alleged that when she refused John Law, a watchmaker in Edinburgh, 'the privileges of a husband' he said that 'a man might make use of his wife as he pleased', and as she 'was now his own, he was entitled to use her as his wife', whereupon she yielded to him.[23] His lawyer retorted that such a 'hasty and Strange Courtship', could only have angered any virtuous woman. John's story was that she made all the running, and he produced several letters of hers which bore this out. He confessed that 'having fallen in with her one evening when heated with liquor he indulged in those freedoms which she evidently wished for and desired, and the result of their intercourse was that she proved with Child'. (The infant died, and he paid the funeral expenses.) He never gave her 'the least reason to think that he was to Marry her, but on the contrary had always told her that from his Situation in life he being Journeyman to a Watchmaker he could not Marry either herself or any other woman whatever'.

After John swore under oath that he had never promised to marry Elizabeth he was assoilzied from the conclusion of marriage, but Elizabeth was given the chance to prove seduction. She claimed that he courted her while she was a servant in the Dewars' household, 'in consequence of which he was allowed to come into the house, having been considered by Mrs Dewar and all the other persons in the family as the man to whom she was about to be married'. John denied this. Whatever she may have told Mrs Dewar to make her believe there was a courtship between them was irrelevant, for he himself never 'did or said any thing that could lead Mrs Dewar or any other person to consider him as addressing the pursuer for marriage'. The commissaries assoilzied him from the conclusions for damages.

In the 1797 case of Margaret McNeill against Robert Wilson, merchant and cooper in Greenock, Robert lodged in her aunt's house and stated that

> *Miss McNeil was by no means guarded in her conduct ... when at Mrs Crutchfields, she had allowed the Gentlemen who boarded in the house to use such liberties with her, as would not be permitted by any woman of virtue ... she seemed to pay no respect to the ordinary rules of decorum or that appearance of modesty which every one in her situation ought to cherish and possess – Thus she permitted the Gentlemen, who lived in the house, to visit her in her bed room in the morning while she was in bed, to pull the bed cloaths off her and use very unbecoming and indecent freedoms without any resistance on her part.*[24]

She was the one who seduced him, he insisted, and though he gave her money for her inlying and promised to take care of the child he swore under oath that he had never promised her marriage. The commissaries assoilzied him from the conclusion of marriage, 'and In respect that an award for damages does not necessarily follow in every case of an illicit connection betwixt a Man and a Woman, but that to entitle her to recover them, She must condescend upon and prove something of the Nature of deception or fraud', they assoilzied him also from that conclusion. However, after appealing to the Court of Session she was allowed to bring proof to support her accusation of seduction.

Robert was again questioned and repeated that 'Miss McNeil laid herself open to Freedoms from the Declarant and all the other Lodgers' (he defined those 'freedoms' as 'putting his Hand on her bosom'). Margaret then produced a list of witnesses, and Robert expressed himself as very surprised at this as he had a letter from her dated 9 January 1799 in which she wrote that she relinquished the process and all claims against him. Her response was that he had persuaded her to write the letter by saying that he would do more for her 'than any Court of law could compel him to do', by which she thought he meant that he was going to marry her. After discovering that he meant no such thing she expressed her determination to continue the action. The commissaries allowed her to do so, but nothing else happened. Either she knew that she had no realistic chance of winning her case, or else she came to an out of court settlement with Robert.

In 1819 Catherine Glen lost her case against Robert Gentle, cattle dealer and butcher in Dunfermline, in spite of universal attestations to her good character before she became pregnant, because her witnesses did not bear out her version of the nature of the relationship. Mary Anne Ross admitted that Robert paid 'assiduous attentions' to Catherine, but when asked if it appeared that he was courting her for marriage, she replied, 'It never struck me so.' Thomas Inglis, manufacturer in Dunfermline, in response to the same question, replied, 'I never thought so.' Colin Lennox, slater, responded: 'I really could not say – they were intimate enough – they were neighbours and often out and in together but I could not say from what I saw what his intentions were'.[25]

In the 1823 case of Helen Lindsay against David Sellers, student of medicine in Dundee, it appeared until the very end (in December 1827) that she would win.[26] David ('a young man of colour') was a minor at the time the action was raised, having been sent from his home in Tobago to receive a medical education in Scotland. He met Helen in Dundee, where he had relations, and wrote to her from Edinburgh where he went for his studies. As soon as he returned to Dundee, a year and a half later, 'he took advantage of the tenderness excited by his return after a long absence, and the sentiments of unabated kindness which he expressed towards her, to urge his wishes.' She yielded to him, and he abandoned her when she became pregnant. His judicial declaration contained many equivocations, but he firmly denied any promise of marriage, so he was assoilzied from that conclusion. After various appeals Helen was allowed to bring proof of seduction.[27]

Helen brought convincing evidence of David having had 'honourable' intentions toward her. One witness declared that an uncle of David's had told him more than once that David was courting Helen, and that he 'would be a damned scoundrel if he did not fulfil his engagements with the Pursuer and marry her, after he had gone such lengths with her'. Another witness said that 'they appeared to be fond of each other, and to be courting for marriage'. However, David was able to blacken her character. At the time of the alleged seduction he was only 17 and she was 24; she had slept with other men before him and had borne a bastard child prior to his, and she had been afflicted with venereal disease at the time she slept with him. Her lawyer protested, but the commissaries allowed him to bring proof of his allegations. David was able to back up his claims with witnesses who testified to having had intercourse with her, and a surgeon who had treated her for venereal disease. The commissaries assoilzied him from the conclusion for damages.

A woman who did not win her case in court did not necessarily end up with nothing. Some won settlements out of court, such as Christian Smith against James Grierson, merchant in Brechin. This case dragged on from 1752 to 1757, when he paid her £270. In the 1766 case of Helen Moffat against Hugh Dalrymple Esquire of Craig (discussed in Chapter 4, as she was alleged to be his kept mistress), 'with respect to any claim of damages he had fully satisfied her and had instantly paid to her the expence of said Process Therefore she thereby not only past from and renounced any such claim of Marriage declaring that he never made any such promise to her' but also quitted her claim for damages. And the 1807 case of Jean Cameron against John Gillies ('one of the Contractors for the Caledonian Canal and tenant in Kinloch Morar') was settled before the man responded to his citation to be examined in court.[28]

A final point brought out by two unsuccessful cases concerns the future prospects of women in such a situation. The rationale for damages for seduction was that a woman in the middling ranks of society who lost her virginity and bore a child out of wedlock was stigmatised and had no hope of a respectable marriage afterwards.

Janet Cameron, eldest lawful daughter of John Cameron of Collart Esquire, raised an action against her second cousin, Ensign Angus Cameron, in December 1787. Her lawyers were certain that the commissaries could not 'suppose that a Young Lady, of birth, Education and fortune would form a connection with him on any other footing, than that of marriage'. But John declared in court that when he stayed at her home she would come to his bedchamber, when she 'permitted him to kiss and toy with her' and finally 'allowed him the last favour without any solicitation upon his part'. Marriage was never discussed. After she became pregnant her relatives tried to persuade him to marry her, which he refused, and then tried to get him to pay something to avoid a legal action, but the sum they demanded was too high. The commissaries found her case not proven and in June 1788 assoilzied John completely. Janet meanwhile had married a Mr Gray and obviously gave up her action for marriage but continued to seek damages 'on account of the impropriety of the defender's conduct'. The commissaries were having none of this and reaffirmed their decreet.[29] It certainly did not take long for Janet (undeniably a member of at least the lesser gentry class) to find another husband in spite of her previous conduct (and she was advanced in pregnancy when her action was raised).

In response to the action for declarator of freedom raised by John Dalziel, writer (lawyer) in Wigtown in 1788, Eleonora Hannay raised an action for declarator of marriage, with the alternative conclusion of damages for seduction.[30] John had married another woman in March 1787 and was angry that Eleonora was claiming that he was her husband and their daughter a lawful child. The action dragged on, and in the course of it Eleonora, realising that there was not enough evidence to win her declarator case, married 'Alexander Turnbull Carpenter and Mariner in Wigton a husband much inferior to her station and expectation in life'. This social relegation was part of her claim for damages. Witnesses confirmed that she was of at least equal rank (if anything, higher) than John Dalziel. But they also testified that at an earlier date Eleonora had eloped with a soldier. Apparently she was brought back before losing her virginity to him, but 'it was talked of in the neighbourhood and considered as a most imprudent step'. She had also carried on with other men, and the commissaries found that Eleonora had 'failled in proving that she was seduced by the Defender' and therefore assoilzied him. Eleonora might have had to marry 'beneath' her, but given that her record was far from virtuous, she had no problem finding a husband (who also took on her daughter).

After Hardwicke's Act of 1753 banned irregular marriage in England a Scottish woman was certainly in a stronger position legally than her English counterpart, for not only was it possible to prove that she was a married woman if the man had promised marriage before they had intercourse, she also had the back-up claim of damages for seduction. In England a woman did not have this option, though her father could demand compensation for the loss of his daughter's domestic services as a result of her impregnation. By the 1820s, noted Lawrence Stone, when such cases became increasingly common, this was a mere legal fiction, abandoned, 'and one lawyer openly admitted that the suit was to uphold public morality as well as for compensation to the father because "his hearth and household had been dishonoured".'[31] English women could, of course, sue for breach of promise – but then, Scottish women had *that* option as well.[32]

Notes

1 A summary of all the successful cases appears in Leah Leneman, 'Seduction in Eighteenth and Early Nineteenth-Century Scotland', *Scottish Historical Review* (1999), Vol 78, 39–49. Much of the material in this chapter also appears in that article.
2 Jean White against John Dickson, 1809, CC8/5/30.
3 Patrick Fraser, *Treatise on the Law of Scotland as applicable to the Personal and Domestic Relations* (Edinburgh, 1846), Vol I, 198.
4 A case sometimes cited later in the eighteenth century was actually decided by the Court of Session rather than the Commissary Court. In 1696 Isobel Hislop alleged that Walter Ker persuaded her 'by false and flattering insinuations, to grant him the use of her body', got her pregnant, and then married someone else. Because 'such debauchery and fraudulent designs ought not to pass undiscouraged', the court granted her damages. James Fergusson, *Treatise on the Present State of Consistorial Law in Scotland* (Edinburgh, 1829), Reports, 128–9.

5   CC8/5/1.
6   Ibid.
7   CC8/5/2.
8   CC8/5/18.
9   CC8/6/65.
10 CC8/6/57.
11 CC8/5/40.
12 CC8/6/164.
13 Lawrence Stone, *Uncertain Unions – Marriage in England 1660-1753* (Oxford, 1992), 8.
14 One 'ritual' is emphatically denied here. Stone writes: 'It has long been known that bundling was common in Wales and Scotland, as well as New England and Scandinavia. It is now certain that it was also very common throughout England in the seventeenth and eighteenth centuries.' He describes the practice as a courting couple being allowed to stay up together all night, without fully undressing but with the man permitted to fondle the woman's breasts and belly, often with a sister, maid, or mother looking on. Ibid, 9, 66. In fact, such a practice would not for one moment have been countenanced in eighteenth-century Scotland. See Rosalind Mitchison and Leah Leneman, *Girls in Trouble – Sexuality and Social Control in Rural Scotland 1660–1780* (Edinburgh, 1998), 92. No witness in a declarator of marriage case ever described such a thing.
15 CC8/5/30.
16 CC8/6/57.
17 CC8/5/1.
18 CC8/6/15.
19 CC8/6/38; CC8/5/40.
20 CC8/6/38; CC8/5/18.
21 Papers for this case do not appear to have survived either in the Commissary Court records or Session Papers. Fortunately details are given, including witnesses' testimony, in Fergusson, *Treatise*, Reports, 139-55.
22 CC8/6/57.
23 CC8/6/61.
24 CC8/6/63.
25 CC8/6/119.
26 CC8/6/154.
27 The complicating feature was that she had first erroneously raised an action for breach of promise before the magistrates of Dundee.
28 CC8/6/19; CC8/5/11; CC8/5/29/3.
29 CC8/5/19.
30 The papers for his action are in CC8/6/50; the decreet for her action is in CC8/5/20.
31 Lawrence Stone, *Road to Divorce – England 1530–1987* (Oxford, 1992), 83–5. This type of legal action is also discussed in Susan Staves, 'British Seduced Maidens', *Eighteenth Century Studies* 14 (1980–1), 109–34. In spite of the title of her paper, the author had no inkling that Scottish law differed from English. I am grateful to Anne Lawrence for this reference.
32 Breach of promise cases would be heard by local courts rather than the Commissary Court and therefore do not form part of this study.

CASE STUDY 12

KENNEDY V. McDOWALL: AN INCREDIBLE INFLUENCE

'I LOVE you a thousand times more than life and esteem the smallest proof of tenderness from you more than all the good things this world ever bestowed on its most favoured Daughters', wrote Margaret Kennedy to her lover, Andrew McDowall.

This was not a typical seduction case. Indeed, it is not typical of any other case in the records, but the extraordinary relationship it depicts is worth recounting. To sum up: Margaret Kennedy, eldest lawful daughter of the deceased Robert Kennedy Esquire of Dalgarroch, lost her virginity at the age of 16 to Andrew McDowall Esquire of Logan (Member of Parliament for the county of Wigton and a Lieutenant Colonel), who was 24 at the time. For ten years after that she was in utter thrall to him, had sex with him whenever possible, and would have done anything for him. No one else knew. Between meetings they corresponded, in terms apparently so indecent that the bulk of the letters could not be produced in the process. At one point Margaret had a miscarriage but managed to keep even that a secret. In January 1794 she bore a daughter, and the secret was out. Andrew refused to marry her, and an action of declarator of marriage, with the alternative conclusion of damages for seduction, was raised in March. A year later Margaret was dead of consumption, but her relatives fought the case on behalf of her infant daughter, Helen.

During his first examination in court Andrew was disparaging about Margaret. He admitted that she was of equal birth, and 'in his opinion she possesst a considerable share of personal beauty … but he did not think that she received the Education or acquired the accomplishments which a Young Lady ought to possess … she had indulged herself too much in reading novels which had become her favourite study'. Perhaps it was these that gave her romantic notions. In any case, before they became lovers he was aware that 'whenever he left the room she was sure to follow him, and when he was in a room by himself to join him'. One night, toward the end of 1784, when they were both staying at Lochnaw, he went to her bedroom; he said he would not stay, but 'she got up from her chair, and they embraced to bid good night, her arms round the declarant, having a Candle in one hand which the Declarant happening to look at, she drew away suddenly and the Declarant understood what she expected, and of course put it out and laid her down on the bed, where he found no resistance.' He declared that there was very little conversation before this happened, 'what was, was on the subject of being heard by the Young Lady in the next room'.

What happened afterwards he described on three separate occasions in court, but only in the last did he tell the whole truth: 'in bed after the first Copula ... he remembers her clinging round him and crying and sobbing that she was ruined, and pressing him to promise to marry her which he evaded as much as possible, but that she still continued her Complaints louder and alarmed him very much from the fear of her being heard by the persons in the other room, and while he was endeavouring to quiet her as much as he could, That he is satisfied in his own mind that he did say he would marry her if she was with Child, That she still continued her entreaties and sobbing, to which he put a stop by repeating the copula and then left her.'

Her own state of mind that night she described in letters, though they were written some years later. In September 1788 she wrote, 'could I have got you out of the room that night at L— dearly as I love you you should never have had it in your power to accomplish your purpose again for till that time I never suspected what you meant or thought further than that your attentions were highly agreeable to me.' In another letter she wrote that the first time 'I cannot say I found when you succeeded so much pleasure as I did pain and yet it was most pleasing pain I ever felt I forgot that I ought to be angry when after I rose we sat on the bed side and I was taking off my cloathes I did feel vexed but your breath upon my cheek as my head leaned on your shoulder and your arm round my waist made it a pleasing sorrow the second time made me more at peace with myself and had you staid sometime longer I had been quite reconciled but after you left me I shall make a pass over of my feelings.' But in February 1790 she described what those feelings had been when she reflected on 'what a great change you have made in my sentiments since that night I thought my self perfectly ruined and had I been possessed of any laudanum I should have been mad enough to have rendered repetition of the crime impossible I even went to the window after I had bolted the door and if I could have got it opened I am not certain what madness would not have led me to do &c But I have now come to a wiser way of thinking Whether I am right or wrong God knows, but I think myself not more guilty than If I were realy your wife.'

The next time they met her courage failed her until he got impatient, but when she got her 'arms round your neck then your kisses your every thing you did in short was so charming I was in extacy and blessed you in my heart for what had passed at L— as it paved the way for what I then enjoyed ... I am more than half afraid you will not like me so well for telling you so much truth and being so excessive free but remember it was your own desire or I would never have been so That was one of my reasons for being so unwilling to grant you the last favour I feared having been told men never liked women after That you would hate me when it was over but they have either told me a lie or you are a singular instance as you appeared to like me even better after that never to be forgotten night to which I stand indebted for all the happiness I ever enjoyed.'

The sway he held over her is powerfully shown in a letter she wrote to him after her miscarriage:'I am pleased that you in some degree regret my loss Nothing but the terror I was under of who the father was being discovered (which indeed brought on the miscarriage) could have reconciled my mind to the loss of it as every day I found my love for you and fondness for the fruit of our love encreasing ....Were a woman I think even indifferent to a man before her having a Child to him would give her a quite contrary feeling What then would I feel who have loved you more and more every year since I was sensible what the passion was ... tell me does a man like a woman better for having a Child to him. I think they should Why do you now give me such a charming and delightful description of the happiness I would have received from you It makes me regret much more what I have lost ... you say you are happy on my account the affair is ended without being known as it would have been a great risque of my future situation from your not making me your wife. Certainly I would rather be your wife than live with you on other terms partly for the sake of my friends but still more for that of our Child had I kept it ....I have been attached to you almost from a Child for years now my love has been unbounded perhaps had I been a year or two older and been possessed of a little prudence and discretion I might not have fallen into such error (but that is not to be mended now). I am however certain at any time I could never have loved another and as certainly must sometime have either yielded to my love for you one way or other for had I had strength of mind to preserve my virtue I must have lost my life. Since that time we have lived on a footing which the world would condemn me as very criminal for did they know, but as I am under no other engagement and have every reason to believe you unmarried So situated I could appeal to the Judgement of a more perfect being than any of his Creatures who sees the utmost recesses of my heart and is my witness if in my whole life I either ever committed an action inconsistent with my fidelity to you or even the slightest wish for any other man whether I am in fact even half as guilty as if I had married one man and loved another.'

The great shock to Margaret was the letter she received from him two days after she gave birth, when he wrote that it was impossible he could be the father and signed himself 'Madam your humble Servant'. Two days later he ascribed this letter to his state of 'agitation', and wrote, 'I doubt not but I have been too hasty and too short in my answer, you may however rest assured upon every support and protection which I can give you and the unfortunate infant through life. Every reasonable attonement shall be made that I can give with propriety, but that of marriage you must be certain never can take place.' Subsequently he wrote, 'so far different from that hasty Letter I wrote from Logan, which I have long since sincerely regretted, it is my firm resolution to provide for you and your Child liberally, and make you independent of the world.'

Her lawyer argued that 'Even if there had been no previous and positive engagement of marriage, it is believed, that there are few Gentlemen of honour, and of the profession which the Defender hold who would hesitate whether they ought to save from obloquy and disgrace a Young Lady, by birth their equal, if not superior, in age, accomplishments, and situation, in no respect unequal, or, whether when they are overwhelmed with misery, and stamped with disgrace, the unfortunate object of their attachment for years, they will at the same time deeply injure their own character, and the honour of their profession, by a most flagrant violation of the rules of Society.' But Andrew would not marry Margaret, and so the legal action had to be raised.

It was fought on the grounds of his judicial declaration, and of her letters. On her deathbed she declared to her relations that it was her wish that all the letters she wrote to Andrew, in spite of their 'impropriety', be produced. 'As he ruined her peace of mind, and broke her heart', it was 'surely the duty of her friends to comply with her dying request, and shew the just indignation due to the person who destroyed her and brought her to an early grave.' In response to the request it was said that 'almost all of them contain passages referring to the conduct of third parties unconnected with the process in such a manner that the productions might be followed with the utmost mischief – The fact is therefore literally true that he never showed them even to his own Counsel but contented himself with making extracts of such passages as appeared to relate to this cause.'

The commissaries decided on a compromise. The advocates on each side were to read all the letters and report to the court anything they found relevant to the cause. Initially her advocate refused the task, but in the end they agreed. Andrew had destroyed some of Margaret's letters, but 84 survived. The first was dated November 1787, though it was clear that the correspondence had commenced before then. There were only 14 surviving letters from him to her, mostly relating to the introduction of a cypher. 'And it seems proper to observe that the late pursuers Letters produced by the Defender serve to explain the reason of her being possessed of so few of his Letters for it from thence appears that he had taken a promise from her that [she] should destroy his Letters immediately or within a short time after she received them while at the same time he solicited and obtained permission to keep her Letters.'

After reading them the two advocates agreed that 'most of the Letters produced in the packets by the defender are unfit for being produced openly in Court or for being read or looked into further than the ends of Justice necessarily require on account of the many gross indecencies which they contain and some passages also in a few of the Letters may tend to reflect upon third parties.' Furthermore, they might be harmful or hurtful to the child. However, 'in justice to the memory of the Lady', they felt 'bound to observe that she appears to have been taught by the example of the Defender to use the very indecent stile which appears in the Letters and induced to use it by his desire and direction and to please and gratify him who as the Letters show had acquired an almost incredible influence over her by the time the letters that now appear were wrote so that she was ready and even eager to comply with the least hint of his will in every thing'.

At first she found it hard to write as he wished, 'tho' it afterwards became very familiar to her'. In January 1789 she wrote, 'How can you expect so much honesty from a woman as your last demands from me Do you consider that we are bred up with the idea of keeping all our thoughts and feelings within our own breasts not only from the men but even from one another.' She would do her best to 'change the stile of my Epistles' but wished 'you would let me rather come in to your way of writing by degrees Believe me the wish to please you will make me apt scholar.'

When she found herself pregnant the first time she wrote: 'Our connection, the strong love I have for ever felt for you has made me wish to think innocent and if I did not altogether succeed in that I at least persuaded myself that as we were both single I could not be very criminal That it gave much pleasure to ourselves and could be productive of no harm to no person you then also promised that if ever I was with Child you would marry me This assurance as I believed your word made me perfectly easy.' And after her miscarriage she wrote, 'I shall do you every thing I think can afford the smallest gratification Some may I daresay most people would think rather odd as you so lately refused to marry me when I so much required it But I have before said I think differently from others therefore do not in the least degree blame you for not marrying A man ought to have a perfect confidence in the virtue and prudence of the woman he made his wife She was to be the mother of his lawful Children and entrusted with the care of his honour and I own it would be expecting impossibilities to think you could have that opinion of a woman who was with Child to you.'

Even after the birth of her child she admitted to feeling 'a very strong reluctance to urge you to marry me now yet I must once more try it'. She knew she did not have long to live, but 'even tho the infant live which I do not expect she is but a Girl and cannot hurt your making any future marriage nor do I think that any proper thinking woman or one who in my opinion deserved you would be more reluctant to become your wife because you had removed the shame you had brought on an Honourable family or by performing the promises you had on our first connection made given me leave to die in peace.'

There was nothing in any of the letters to suggest that Margaret thought herself married to Andrew, and the commissaries found that there was 'no ground upon which the Legitimacy of the surviving pursuer can be declared' and assoilzied Andrew from that conclusion of the libel. After an appeal from her lawyer they appointed him to appear in court again, and after he admitted (as above) that he had said he would marry her if she proved to be with child it was argued that this promise, followed by a long connection, established a marriage. His lawyer responded that as the promise was not made prior to the first sexual connection, and no claim of marriage was founded on it during all the years of the relationship, it could not constitute a marriage. The commissaries heeded the pursuer's side and altered their decision, declaring a legal marriage.

Andrew appealed to the Court of Session, which reversed that decision, so the commissaries reverted to their original finding.

But there was still the alternative conclusion of damages to be fought for. Andrew offered the family £1,000, an offer which would be retracted if the case was not withdrawn, 'and then the infant pursuer will have those alone acting for her to blame, if in place of having such a liberal provisions she is reduced to such yearly sum for aliment, as the law shall find the Defender liable in'. The offer was refused.

When Margaret was only sixteen, argued the lawyer for her daughter, in the house of 'a widow Lady of the highest respectability and character to whose family during her residence there he becomes the sole male guardian', she was by him 'betrayed and ruined .... In the course of a long correspondence her dependance upon him for the concealment of her shame, and for all her hopes, is used in a manner altogether unprecedented to corrupt her morals and deprave her mind.' Her daughter, Helen, 'is debarred from the rank in Society of a near relation of the noble families of Cassillis and Eglinton and of the Honourable families of Cathcart of Carleton and of many others on her mothers side, and from the respectable claims of birth which she would otherwise have inherited thro' her father'.

In February 1801 the commissaries found her (and hence the child) entitled to damages of £3,000, with interest from March 1794.

CC8/5/25

CHAPTER 7

RIVAL CLAIMS

Most cases in which two women claimed the same man as husband stemmed from bigamy (intentional or unintentional), but there were cases where the man, in order to try and defeat an action for marriage, persuaded another woman to collude with him in claiming a previous marriage. There were two cases in which the rival claimants were men.

Bigamists

The earliest case of two women both claiming the same man as husband ran from 1746 to 1753 and is described in Case Study 13. The complicating factor was that the man was dead. The case having been appealed to the House of Lords, the implications of two women both having a legal right to a man as husband, the decision being only which one had the *stronger* right, was a decisive factor in the English legislating against irregular marriage.[1]

However, a year before the decision in the above case was made final, in which the second irregular marriage followed by open cohabitation was decreed the valid one, the commissaries came to a very different decision in similar circumstances. John Grinton, a farmer in Lasswade parish, proposed marriage to Alison Pennycuik when he was drunk; she agreed, had intercourse with him, and bore a child, but her action against him in 1748 was only for child support and damages for seduction. John declared under oath that his promises of marriage were made 'in liquor', and Alison abandoned the case. In January 1750 John married another woman, Ann Graite (with no objections from Alison), and they lived together and had a child. In January 1751 Alison Pennycuik brought a new action, to establish her prior marriage and the legitimacy of her child, and then to divorce him for his adultery with Ann Graite. Ann Graite raised a counter process, to have *her* marriage declared valid.[2]

Considering that Alison had claimed in her first action that she had been 'debauched', she could hardly have believed herself married. Nevertheless, because John had admitted promising to marry her before they had sex, in January 1752 the commissaries declared Alison's marriage valid. On appeal to the Court of Session that decreet was upheld. And Alison also got her divorce, on the grounds of John's cohabitation with Ann.[3]

In a case that ran from 1760 to 1764 John Elliot younger of Halgreen in Dumfries-shire and clerk to the deceased John Boston, chamberlain to the Duke of Buccleuch, denied his marriage to Charlotte Armstrong, daughter of John Armstrong younger of Sorbie, and affirmed his marriage to Janet Boston (his late employer's daughter), but Charlotte was found to be his legal wife.[4]

According to Charlotte's libel, they accepted each other as husband and wife on 7 March 1758 'in that part of the house of Sorbie possessed by Christean Elliot', and when Christean asked him why he did not marry her regularly he said that 'he was as well married' as if any minister had married them, and he wrote and signed a document acknowledging the marriage. In February 1759 they awoke Charlotte's father and called him to witness a bedding and hear a verbal acknowledgement of the marriage. Some months later John deserted her and went to cohabit with Janet Boston. Janet's story was that they had secretly accepted each other as husband and wife in September 1757 and confessed it publicly when her father died in June 1758, a month before her child was born.

Much of the initial evidence came from the church courts. Charlotte produced a letter that John had written her when they were summoned before the kirk session, in which he wrote: 'you are by no means to go to the session nor you never shall appear before it .... I wonder you know me so little as to think I would be giving every impertinent body the satisfaction of declaring a marriage. To such as deserved such a Condescencion I have freely made it.' But then he denied the marriage to the session, so that the case was referred to the presbytery, when he again denied it. He said that to those he did not think deserved the truth 'he would to get rid of their impertinence have Answered "Married to be sure" or "Do you think I would Marry" just as it struck him without any further thought or design never having the least notion that these Expressions used in manner foresaid were to be brought against him before a Court'. On the night of the alleged bedding, he said, he was drunk and insensible.

Charlotte's father might have been objected to as a witness before the commissary court on the grounds of his close relationship to her, but church courts made no such distinctions, and the written extract was admitted as evidence in this case. He told the presbytery that in March 1758

> *John Elliot Junior in Hallgreen came to me at Hask and asked me if I knew that my daughter Charlotte and he were married I told him I did not upon which he said they were and asked if I was displeased; to which I answered it was no time to ask that. And soon after coming up to Sorby, and meeting with my said daughter asked her if the above was true, she said it was but (as John had said before) said it was not to be made publick till after whitsunday; I think I told her she had done a rash thing but as she never asked my advice in any thing she did, she could blame none but herself.*

Her father also told the presbytery that he had seen the document in which

John acknowledged the marriage. After seeing it her father returned it to her 'and desired her to keep it; but I understood not very long after he by his artifice and Cunning and in a way of diversion got it from her, saying it signified nothing and he would give her something more full'. Armstrong also described the bedding and verbal acknowledgement and said that John was not drunk at that time. The presbytery found that John had owned her as his wife, but because he was living in Edinburgh with another woman as his wife the presbytery referred the case to synod. Charlotte meanwhile appeared before the presbytery, and confessed that she was with child to John, 'but now as he hath most perfidiously deserted me and (as common report is) hath married and cohabited with another I am heartily sorry for my undutifull and disorderly consent to be his wife'. Charlotte and her father also petitioned the sheriff depute of Dumfries for John to be arrested for bigamy. In the commissary court Charlotte was able to produce witnesses who heard John acknowledge her as his wife.

But what about Janet Boston? According to a witness, when she first heard that he was married to Charlotte 'she was like to have fainted'. Janet may have had doubts about the validity of her marriage for she denied her pregnancy to everyone who asked and apparently tried to abort it. The crucial thing was that neither John nor Janet had any proof of a marriage prior to March 1758 whereas Charlotte had plenty of proof of an acknowledgement of marriage in that month. The commissaries found the marriage between John and Charlotte lawful, and they granted her a divorce on the grounds of his adultery with Janet Boston. John also had to pay £100 damages plus child support. Janet's appeal to the Court of Session was unsuccessful, and it was suggested that John Elliot should be criminally prosecuted.

In 1768 Elisabeth Thomson raised a declarator of marriage action against John Barronet in Stirling, but after apparently proving her case, another woman (Ann Gromold) raised a rival action against him.[5] Not all of Elisabeth's witnesses were complimentary. William Christie, in whose house the couple stayed, always called Elisabeth 'Mrs Barronet' without any contradiction and testified that they 'were looked upon as husband and wife by all the neighbours in Stirling, tho some People spoke of her as a mistress only'. Christie, because of John's own acknowledgments, 'had no doubt of the pursuer being his wife tho at the same time he thought the pursuer but a low bred woman'. John Burn, a merchant, was invited to tea when he was introduced to Elisabeth as John's wife, and Burn agreed to be godfather to their child. He once saw Elisabeth 'overseeing some of the Defenders workmen'.

John appears to have been a thoroughly nasty piece of work, for when he wanted to get rid of Elisabeth he asked another William Christie, a gunsmith,

to be witness to a paper which he was to get the pursuer his wife to sign owning herself guilty of being a drunkard a Thief and a whore etc and if she should sign such a *paper before witnesses then he said he would get the Provost to drum her out of Town next Monday But the deponent absolutely refused to witness any such paper tho' the defender offered him what money he choosed to demand if he would do it and soon after this the deponent heard of the pursuers being turned off because she would sign no such paper.*

After Ann Gromold brought proof of an earlier marriage, the commissaries awarded Elisabeth damages for seduction. It is unlikely, however, that she ever saw a penny, for John absconded.

In Chapter 2 we saw that Elizabeth Richardson, a chambermaid, proved by his letters to her that John Irving, writer (lawyer) in Edinburgh, was her lawful husband.[6] The action was raised in April 1783, and after Elizabeth had proved her case and John 'had exhausted every pretence for delay which his ingenuity could suggest', he thought he would 'fight to more advantage under the banners of Jean Crichton, the woman to whom he says he was lately married', and an action for declarator of marriage was raised by, or on behalf of, Jean Crichton. The commissaries were having none of this. The second action was only raised after the proof was concluded in the first, so when they found Elizabeth's marriage proven, they assoilzied John from Jean Crichton's action. Whether Jean Crichton married John Irving in good faith, believing his protests that this chambermaid from his past had no real claim on him, cannot be ascertained. What he could not pretend was that he had married Jean *before* his acknowledgement of marriage to Elizabeth Richardson. Others could, and did, attempt this ploy.

Collusion

These cases are largely a phenomenon of the nineteenth rather than the eighteenth century. A good example is that of Andrew Hamilton, carter in Glasgow, claimed as a husband by Isobel Robertson and Marion Baillie.[7] Isobel initially raised an action before the Commissary of Hamilton and Campsie (in October 1802) rather than before Edinburgh Commissary Court, alleging that she had married Andrew the previous month. This was a mistake on her part, as local commissary courts had no powers in such cases, yet the Commissary heard the evidence and pronounced them married persons. Andrew then insisted that he had married Marion Baillie in January of that year and had granted her a written acknowledgement in June. Marion raised a declarator of marriage action before Edinburgh Commissary Court in March 1804, and Isobel found it necessary to do the same in May 1805.

Isobel's story was that in summer 1802, while she was a servant to a Mr and Mrs Burnside and looking after their children in Airdrie, she met Andrew who courted her assiduously until she agreed to marry him. On 21 September they signed lines acknowledging themselves to be man and wife, and on the following day they appeared before JPs and were fined for marrying irregularly. Then they spent some days together before he deserted her and said he would have nothing more to do with her. During the eight months her action was being heard by the Commissary of Hamilton and Campsie no mention was made of any prior marriage, but once Andrew realised that he would be found liable to her for aliment 'he bethought himself of the device of pretending a prior marriage with Marion Baillie. No such marriage had ever been heard of in Airdrie where the parties resided and the manner in which the allegation was brought forward is of itself sufficient to shew that it was a mere device.'

Initially Andrew's line was that he was 'a young man under twenty years of age' while Isobel was 'an elderly woman who had a bastard child some years ago.' As noted in Chapter 3, he also said that when he appeared before the JPs to acknowledge a marriage he was drunk and had no idea what happened.

After Isobel raised her action the commissaries joined the two processes. Marion needed to prove the veracity of the date on the written acknowledgement, and her claims of being accepted as Andrew's wife by his father and relations. Her story did not stand up, so Isobel's marriage was declared valid, and Andrew had to pay her a weekly aliment.

The 1806 cases of Jean Roxburgh and Elizabeth Templeton against John Thomson, son of Alexander Thomson of Stoneygate, were more complex.[8] Jean Roxburgh stated that on 30 June she and John had gone together to an Ayrshire JP and been fined for irregular marriage. In his defence it was claimed that he was 'a man of a weak and facile temper and very easily imposed on'. He was under promise of marriage to Elizabeth Templeton, 'and the regular celebration of marriage betwixt them had only been postponed untill the parties should be further advanced in years when it was hoped the weakness and imbecility of mind in the Defender might be removed'. Elizabeth had borne his daughter four years ago – but now Jean was also pregnant too. John's lawyer alleged that on 30 June (after she became pregnant) Jean's father, brother and sisters 'compelled him by force and threats to go with them to different Justices of the Peace in the neighbourhood'. They all, knowing his 'weakness and facility of temper, declined to have any thing to do in the business', but eventually a JP was found about eight or nine miles away, who knew nothing about John, and who therefore did fine the couple for an irregular marriage.

Elizabeth's story was that in 1803, while she was a servant in the household, she and John had accepted each other as man and wife but were forced to wait until he became less 'weak and facile'. Jean insisted that Elizabeth had been suborned to bring this case simply to defeat her own claim. For five years Elizabeth had 'lived as an unmarried woman who had born a natural child' to John. John had appeared before the congregation as a fornicator, and Elizabeth had even raised a legal action against him for aliment of her child as a 'natural child', so it was clear that this was a case of 'the most evident Collusion'.

Elizabeth countered by saying that she and John had actually given their names up to have the banns proclaimed when his father stopped them because of his 'weak and facile disposition'. It was her relations who raised the action against him for aliment for the child, and after he appeared before the congregation Elizabeth discovered that he was as fond of her as ever, and

> had merely in this penance affair acted to please his father and that by his renewed protestations and promises, and even acknowledgements of marriage she would be placed publickly on the footing of his wife whenever he was at liberty to declare himself and had obtained the consent and approbation of his relations for so doing.

She was

> most happy in the thoughts that the man who had at first robbed her of her virtue was perfectly disposed to render her justice for so doing and that a subsequent marriage would make every thing right with regard to herself and would also legitimate the child which by the then present conduct of parties behoved to be considered as illegitimate.

It was therefore a great shock to her, she said, when Jean's family kidnapped him and got a JP to fine them for irregular marriage.

Jean reiterated that Elizabeth had never considered herself to be John's wife. Immediately after she bore her child, which she always acknowledged to be illegitimate, she 'entered into Service, and has continued in the Capacity of a Servant ever since without once urging her present pretensions until the marriage between John Thomson and the Objector was completed'. Elizabeth also, not only John, had appeared before the congregation for the sin of fornication. Furthermore, when Elizabeth had become pregnant she was by John's father 'turned out of her Service with disgrace ... and enjoined in the strictest manner never to enter the threshold of his door'. It was only now, years later, that he saw a use for her as wife to his mentally retarded son.

Jean brought so much evidence of all this that there can be no doubt that hers was the true story. But she was obviously paid off, because after various appeals attempting to stop her bringing proof of the alleged collusion, when she was finally allowed to go ahead she failed to do so. She therefore lost her case, and in 1810, after John appeared in court and swore that he had promised to marry Elizabeth and then impregnated her, the court had little option but to find them married persons. This meant that Jean's child was illegitimate, but presumably the pay-off was sufficiently large to make up for that. Why Mr Thomson Senior objected so strenuously to Jean cannot be ascertained, and of course her own family's conduct was hardly praiseworthy either. Mentally deficient John is a shadowy figure in all this; he was unable even to sign his name to his judicial declaration.

A nice simple fraud is found in the 1829 case of Catherine Swan against

Benjamin Galbraith, sometime teacher of mathematics in Edinburgh.[9] Benjamin claimed that he had been married to Ann Tilbury prior to his marriage to Catherine, and a declarator of marriage action was raised on Ann's behalf in 1830. Although the marriage was alleged to have occurred in January 1821, Catherine claimed that Ann had not even met Benjamin until 1827 at the earliest. They

> *did not live with each other as husband and wife nor did they live together or cohabit at all On the Contrary the pursuer down to the year 1828 lived as Mistress with a Gentleman of the name of Clark and as the Respondent rather believes the Defender was not in the habit of visiting her till Mr Clark had abandoned that connexion.*

Ann could produce only one dubious witness, and the commissaries threw out her claim.[10]

Male Rivals

In Chapter 9 we will encounter cases of men claiming marriage to very young girls, and at first glance the 1807 case of John MacLauchlane (residing in Auchindinnan near Dunblane) against Mary Couper (residing in Hutchison town near Glasgow) appears similar. The girl was only 15 and alleged an 'intrigue' on the part of the man and his accomplices, who on 7 March 1806

> *got her prevailed on to go to an Inn and not suspecting they had anything improper in view, she was pressed and induced to take a Glass with them, more than was proper and when it was late in the evening (between 10 and 11 o'Clock so far as she recollects) she was imposed upon when not altogether sensible of what was doing, to sign a paper without being properly informed of its import or the use the Pursuer meant to make of it.*

However, instead of following the line of other teenage pursuers by pleading her youth as a defence, Margaret claimed to have been married to another man, Robert Stark, some months prior to the incident with John MacLauchlane. She bore a son in November 1806, with paternity claimed by both John and Robert.[11]

John described the events of 7 March very precisely. After some months of 'honorable Courtship' Margaret agreed to marry him. John applied to Captain John MacLauchlane of Binnachray, a Justice of the Peace, who agreed to marry them, but when they arrived at the inn they discovered that he had gone to dine with his friend, Mr Thomson of Hillhead. It was agreed that the marriage would take place at that house instead. No alcohol was drunk, and after the ladies 'retired',

> *Captain MacLauchlane put the usual Interrogatories to the pursuer and defender vizt Whether they were unmarried persons? Whether they were willing to take each other for Husband and Wife &c All of which having been Answered in the Affirmative the parties*

were solemnly married & declared married persons in presence of the Gentlemen then assembled in Mr Thomsons house. All of these Gentlemen were men of the most respectable character.

A document was written out by Mr Thomson and signed by the parties and some of the gentlemen as witnesses. At about 10 pm 'they all joined the Ladies in the drawing room and a Glass of wine was there drunk to the happiness of the new married couple.' They then went to John's brother's house where they 'immediately went to bed together as Husband and Wife …. Next morning the defender exhibited to several of her acquaintances the marriage ring which the pursuer had presented to her on the preceding day and told them of her Marriage and used language expressive of her happiness.'

According to John, it was her mother and sister who disapproved of him as a husband and persuaded her to deny her marriage, in spite of her pregnancy. Her child was born nine months later. In the meantime she had eloped with Robert Stark, with whom she was now cohabiting. As soon as John learned of this he took legal action, and obtained custody of the child. But as Mary continued to cohabit with Robert he was forced to raise this declarator of marriage action. Mary did not deny that

the parties met at Glasgow on the 7th of March, and that John McLachlane a man advanced in years had the address and wickedness to betray Mary Couper a young woman of 15 years of age, who might have been his daughter into certain very rash and incautious, tho' by no means criminal proceedings, nor into any proceedings which have the effect of supporting the present action.

She again insisted that she had been drunk on that night and believed 'what took place in the house of Thomson was regarded as a jest by all present'. And after it was over he accompanied her to her sister's house and left her there; she had never had intercourse with him.

The circumstance of the gold ring is clearly of no great importance – The giving a ring is no part of the ceremony of Marriage with us as it is in England; and a young girl of 15 would without suspicion or thinking any thing of the matter receive a bauble of this description from a man advanced in years, whose brother was married to her sister.

Soon after the child was born Robert applied to have it baptised, but the kirk elders, having heard of John's claim, wanted to wait until the matter was cleared up. John 'bribed the Nurse to deliver up the Child, which he instantly carried to the Minister of the Episcopal Chapel at Glasgow … and being a stranger to the parties, and the whole circumstances, he necessarily baptized it under the character in which it was produced to him.'

John insisted that a valid marriage had taken place. 'Young persons,' argued his lawyer

> *are said sometimes to regard marriage as a frolic or as a state in which they are to encounter nothing but pleasure, and that after more mature experience, they consider themselves as having been rashly employed when they engaged in it. But that circumstance cannot alter the Laws of Society or authorise Individuals to violate the most important engagement known in human life. The Defender Mary Couper at the period alluded to, was of an age when she was capable of becoming a Mother, and will not be permitted to say, that when she went into the presence of a Magistrate and of a number of Strangers and solemnly declared herself a wife her intentions were not what they appeared to be.*

Her alleged earlier marriage with Robert Stark, John's lawyer said, was nothing more than a ruse to drag out the case.

The commissaries allowed Robert to raise his own action, alleging a marriage on 24 January 1806, and suspended John's until a decision was reached on the allegedly earlier marriage. John appealed against this to the Court of Session, but that court concurred. But then it appears the case was abandoned and no final decision made.

The only other example of rival male claimants was that of Robert Chapman, dyer, and Alexander Lindsay Junior, farmer, against Catherine Forgan or Patullo, a farmer's widow, in Errol parish.[12] Robert stated that on 8 November 1819 he and Catherine went to Dundee and acknowledged themselves married before witnesses, followed by a bedding. On the 10th – according to him – she wrote to one of the elders of the parish: 'Sir As I have totally changed my mind in respect to Marry Alexander Lindsay I request of you to stop the Proclamation As I am become Robert Chapmans lawful Wife.' Robert raised his action in May 1820, and Alexander raised his in July. In March 1824 the commissaries found that though it was expressly alleged that Catherine and Alexander consummated their marriage, their 'subsequent conduct' appeared 'totally irreconcileable with the fact of sexual intercourse'. The commissaries therefore found that there was no marriage between Catherine and Alexander. Robert continued to press his case and in 1826 he was found entitled to all of the expenses of the conjoined processes. But as late as 1836, 16 years after the original action was raised, and beyond the purview of this study, the case was still dragging on.

The cases of rival claimants, whether male or female, genuine or collusive, serve once again to underline the complexity of relationships between men and women in eighteenth and early nineteenth-century Scotland. Gender relationships were not necessarily any different from those in other parts of the British Isles or western Europe, but the elasticity of Scottish marriage law gave scope to individuals to bring those relationships into court and reveal aspects which would otherwise have remained hidden from history.

Notes

1 See R B Outhwaite, *Clandestine Marriage in England 1500–1850* (London & Rio Grande, 1995), 76.
2 CC8/6/19.
3 The case is also summarised in James Fergusson, *Treatise on the Present State of Consistorial Law in Scotland* (Edinburgh, 1829), 152 and Reports 130–3.
4 CC8/5/11.
5 CC8/5/11. This is the decreet in the seduction action. Process papers do not appear to have survived for either of the declarator cases, but much of the evidence for Elisabeth is repeated.
6 Session Papers, Signet Library, 182;36 (1785).
7 CC8/6/83.
8 CC8/5/31.
9 CC8/6/167.
10 Catherine's case was not resolved before the Commissary Court's functions were transferred to the Court of Session.
11 CC8/6/87.
12 CC8/6/150. Most of the process papers were transferred to the Court of Session in 1836, leaving only a handful with which to reconstruct the story as far as possible.

CASE STUDY 13

CAMPBELL V. COCHRAN: THE DEAD MAN WITH TWO WIVES

THE case began in 1746 after the death of Captain John Campbell of Carrick at the battle of Fontenoy. Although John had been living with Jean Campbell as his wife for some 20 years, Magdalen Cochran laid claim to the widow's pension. Jean Campbell therefore sought a declarator of marriage.

Jean had married John irregularly on 9 December 1725 in Roseneath, Dunbartonshire. She had a certificate of the marriage and an extract from the minutes of the kirk session of Roseneath revealing that John Campbell had acknowledged his irregular marriage to Jean and promised to adhere to her. The couple lived together at Roseneath and had three children, though only one was still alive at his death. He wrote her some 50 letters during that period (addressed to Mistress Campbell of Carrick), and signed two deeds of trust with her as his spouse. They were considered by everyone to be husband and wife.

Magdalen Cochran had been courted by John but married another man, Lewis Kennedy, and was thereafter known as Mistress Kennedy. Lewis died, and according to Magdalen she was irregularly married to John Campbell of Carrick at the Abbey of Paisley on 3 July 1724. She did not have a certificate of this marriage but did have a later document signed by John acknowledging this. He asked her to keep the marriage secret for a while because he was dependent on the Duke of Argyll who would not approve of it. When Magdalen learned of his marriage to Jean he told her that Jean had seduced him when he was drunk and had become pregnant; because she was closely related to the Duke of Argyll he had had no choice but to marry her. In fact, Jean's first child was not born until ten months after their marriage, so this was a lie, but the lie was John's, not Magdalen's. He told Magdalen that he still considered her to be his true wife and begged her to keep the secret. For the next 20 years, whenever he came to Edinburgh, he spent much of his time with her, and he wrote her over a hundred letters.

Jean's lawyer expressed disbelief that any woman would keep quiet while her husband married someone else and set up house with her. But bigamy was a crime. And a letter from John to Magdalen immediately after she learned of his second marriage demonstrates his emotional manipulation: 'My ever Dearest though Cruel, Madie ....You are a stranger to the mighty woe that Surrounds me, And if I have imposed upon you in any one thing, it is in having concealed it from you, and for no other reason but to prevent the Encrease of Your pain. Your Letter lies now before me; I have not words to Express my Agony of Soul upon reading of it. I sunk from my Chair to the floor, void of all manner of sense and when I came to myself there was no body to pity me. Oh had my dearest Madie been there and heard my Groans, I fain would persuade myself she would have behaved with the affection of a tender wife; and even now my spirits fail me, and your cruel Letter has broke my heart. Would to God I had Died many years ago; I have ruined the best of women and the best of wives, and by my own folly have put it out of my power to do my duty to her or relieve her in the terrible Distress she must be in.'

Magdalen believed that she had to protect him, and once locked into a cycle of deceit it became harder and harder for her to extricate herself. In March 1735 he wrote: 'To Mrs Campbell. I conjure you by the most sincere regard and affection ever entered the heart of a husband for the most deserving wife, not to disquiet yourself and Ruin your health .... Nor is it in the power of anything on earth to give me Satisfaction, till I can declare to the world that you are mine and I yours. I do assure you that it was with difficulty, I kept myself from crying when I thought of you and that I must live absent from the person on earth, that honour, Inclination, love, Gratitude, and every thing that can tye one soul to another obliges me most to esteem and regard; And even now when I tell you so the tears are ready to drop; And nothing but the Generous Return I have always met with from the darling of my soul, could have possibly supported me.'

Yet in 1738 John asked the Lord Provost of Edinburgh to invite Mrs Jean Campbell, 'whom he called his wife', and Magdalen, to dine with him 'because that he wanted to have his wife made Acquainted with Mrs Kennedy', after which they also met on other social occasions.

Naturally it became known that John spent a good deal of time with Magdalen, but she was considered to be his mistress. Dame Margaret Dalrymple, spouse of Sir John Schaw of Greenock, sent for Magdalen 'and told her that she was sorry to hear that she kept a Criminal Correspondence with Carrick which was very Disobliging to his Ladys Relations to whom she had been obliged for her pension'. Magdalen swore that 'she had no Correspondence with Carrick furder than a kiss in Civility when he came to Edinburgh or left it' and promised never to see him again, a promise which, of course, she broke. By the time John went abroad Jean herself knew about it. A servant maid saw him burning some letters, which he said 'were that Damned whore Mrs Kennedys Letters'. When the servant admitted that 'she had abstracted two of them he begged of her not to shew them to his Wife ... for that she had gott too much Grief and Trouble by Letters of that kind already'. But the servant 'nevertheless delivered those two Letters to Lady Carrick'.

In fact, shortly before his death John himself knew that if he remained on the scene there would be a reckoning. In June 1744 William Calder, a 'master gunner' whose mother was John's aunt, accompanied Magdalen to Ostend where she cohabited with John. Calder 'asked the said John how he could be so Cruel as to have two marriages upon his hands and conceal them so long ... and John Answered, That before he would go home again He would if the war was ended go serve the Turk'. John's brother and heir, Colin Campbell, was caught in the middle of it because, before leaving, John asked him to treat Magdalen as his sister. It was therefore she whom Colin consoled after the Captain's death; but afterwards he wrote to Jean, denying that he had ever considered anyone but Jean to be his brother's lawful wife.

In spite of Jean's knowledge of a relationship between her husband and the other woman, it must have been a shock when Magdalen claimed a pension before an English court at Canterbury as his widow, for, if upheld, this would not only invalidate her 20-year marriage but also make her daughter illegitimate. (Magdalen had no children by John Campbell.) She therefore immediately raised an action before the Commissary Court, while Magdalen raised a counter-process. Jean had plenty of evidence: the marriage certificate, the trust deeds, the letters, and innumerable witnesses, ranging from servants to gentry, who had known them as husband and wife. On 6 August 1747 the Court found that the marriage had been sufficiently proven and threw out Magdalen Cochran's claim. In legal terms this seems bizarre because none of Jean's evidence disproved a previous marriage. Magdalen, failing to overturn this ruling in the Court of Session, appealed to the House of Lords which, on 6 February 1749, ruled that Magdalen should be allowed to prove her claim.

Jean then rationalised that, although she had initially been persuaded to oppose this, 'Yet upon more mature deliberation, It's considered that this might give a handle to mistres Kennedy to say that she could have proved her marriage had the court allowed her, so to avoid Clamour of this Kind mistres Campbell is willing to allow mistres Kennedy the opportunity of Justiefieing her Character (if she can).'

It was alleged that Magdalen attempted to bribe witnesses, and this was borne out by Jean Auchinloss, wife of a tide waiter in the port of London, who declared that 'the pursuer at Different times within these two years has promised to get her husband a higher post in the Custom house if she would go and speak in the pursuer's favour when she was called.' She believed that the promises were made to her husband 'to Induce her husband to prevail upon her the Deponent to mind or Remember more than she knew And her Reason for this belief is this, that the Deponent would tell the truth without any offer And therefore thinks that the offer was made to Induce her to say more than she knew'.

The strongest witness for Magdalen was John Cunnison, who said that in 1725 John had told him about the marriage and implored him to keep it secret. However, Jean's lawyer destroyed him in court. A letter from a magistrate of Dumbarton stated that 'John Cunnison a native of Kintyre was about Eighteen Years agoe Employed as an officer of Excise … in that office He misbehaved often was several times suspended At Last Discharged as unworthy of that Employment, as to his morals, It was Commonly reported of him, He was a vitious louse person much given to uncleanness, and had a Child or two born to him in Adultery that he was Aiding and Assisting to others in Carrying on their Lewd Intrigues.' And a certificate signed by the minister, kirk session and magistrates of Campbeltown stated that Cunnison was 'a man of a most abandoned wicked and dissolute Life of a Subdolous fraudulent temper Addicted to the basest of vices, particularly Drunkenness and Adultery so infamous was his Character that he would not be admitted sponsor for a Child born him here'. His wife was as bad, and 'their family was such an Emblem of Hell, that they were a pest to every neighbourhood they lived in'. So much for Cunnison's testimony.

Most of Magdalen's evidence comprised witnesses who had been let into the secret. By the early 1740s she was clearly finding the situation intolerable and felt the need to unburden herself, not only to servants but to members of her own class. The Countess of Eglinton was told in April 1743 and when she asked Magdalen 'why she concealed her marriage so long, she answered that it was her tenderness to her husband, and for fear of his utter ruin and Destruction'. That same year Magdalen also told the Duchess of Atholl, showing her the document signed by John, and also saying that she had concealed the marriage for fear of ruining her husband. Lord George Ross declared that when Magdalen told him of the marriage 'she seemed to be in a very doleful Condition and weeped'. His Lordship 'thought this so very odd a story that he does not think he told it to any person, As the Deponent had heard from many persons, that the said John of Carrick Had lived for a considerable time with Mrs Jean Campbell as his wife.' Whether they believed or disbelieved Magdalen, most of those she confided in did not want to know – including one James Smollett, an advocate who subsequently became a judge in the Commissary Court that refused to hear her case until so ordered by the Lords. (He then gave evidence in the case he was judging.)

One witness whose advice she had sought (in 1743) was Mr George Wishart, a minister of the gospel in Edinburgh. He told her that she 'had been in the wrong in concealing her marriage so long if she really was married to Carrick', but as to claiming the marriage at this late date, he 'did at first hesitate on Account of the difficulty and uncommonness of the Case' but in the end gave it as 'his opinion that she should still claim Carrick as her husband in a legal way' (ie by raising a declarator of marriage action). Magdalen would have attracted more sympathy if she had claimed a husband who was still alive; the mercenary motive attributed to her by Jean's lawyer was certainly not her sole reason for waiting for him to die first, but that aspect of the case was unfavourable to her.

On 21 June 1751 the commissaries found that Magdalen had not proved her prior marriage and dismissed her process. She appealed to the Court of Session which upheld the commissaries' decision, so she appealed to the House of Lords, which also upheld the decision.

That final appeal, in January 1753, had an impact well beyond the parties involved, for it prompted the Lords to press for new legislation to prevent clandestine marriages, as Lord Hardwicke had long been urging. Lord

Hardwicke's Act abolished all forms of irregular marriage in England but, though the case that convinced the English of the need for such a law was a Scottish one, the Scots did not follow suit, and the possibility of other rival claims for the same husband (or wife) remained open.

CC8/5/6

• Much of the material in this study previously appeared in 'The Scottish Case that led to Hardwicke's Marriage Act', *Law and History Review* 1999; Vol 17:(1), 161–70.

CHAPTER 8

DEAD BUT WED?

TWENTY-FIVE actions were raised to prove a marriage to a man who was dead (and in one further case the man died during the course of the action). All of them were raised by women whose claims to be the man's widow were disputed by his kin. Seventeen women were successful, but mostly in uncontested cases. Of the 18 contested actions, two were abandoned, and ten were successful.

We have already seen one such claim in Case Study 13. Even in uncontested cases the commissaries demanded evidence of a marriage. In contested cases, because the man could not speak for himself, they demanded a great deal of proof, and such cases often ran for years. They are among the most interesting in the records, because so much detail emerges about the lives of the couple in question.

Uncontested Cases

If a regular marriage had not been celebrated a man's surviving kin might claim that no marriage existed, but once the woman raised a legal action they might concede without a fight. Written evidence could be crucial. After the death of George Kinnaird, a nephew of Lord Kinnaird, in 1734, his children by his first wife, Lady Helen Lyon, disputed the claim of Susana Gordon (daughter of a doctor in Banff) to be his lawful widow.[1] Susana had borne him two children, of whom one survived, and was pregnant a third time when he died. The verbal evidence in this case was discussed in Chapter 2, but Susana was also able to produce a letter from him, dated 24 February 1732: 'my dearest life Since you are curious to have it under my hand declareing our marriage this I grant under my hand declares hereby you to be my lawfull married wife and till death I shall Continue your affectionate husband.' And in December 1733 he wrote that he was 'much perplexed that as yet I have not secured you in ane aliment in case you shall survive me', and he stated precisely the financial provision that should be made for her if he should predecease her. With a document in his own handwriting setting this out in detail, fighting the case was pointless.

In the 1765 case of Ann Neilson against the nieces and nephews of the deceased Mr William Sloan, minister at Dunscore, the crucial letters were written to his wife's relatives.[2] Ann and William married in 1752, but as he was then only a probationer and could not afford to support a wife, it was agreed to keep it secret. In March of that year he wrote to her brother, 'Sir by this missive I acknowledge myself married to Miss Annie Neilson … but as it is not prudent the discovery of it should be made before I am in a settled way of life I depend on your Friendship that it should be a secret till that time'. By summer 1754 he was settled as a minister at Dunscore, and her family were clearly pressing to acknowledge the marriage, for he wrote to her uncle:

> Sir as my marriage with your neice has caused you interest yourself in her behalf I must own myself greatly obliged to you for the moderate and prudent measures which at my desire you have agreed should be followed. My Character as a Clergyman makes a private or Clandestine marriage Fatal, and as before I was ordained a minister it was Absolutely necessary to keep our marriage a secret otherwise I must forever have renounced all hopes of succeeding in that way so now it is Equaly important to Continue the same plan for some time, the same Law which would have prevented me from getting a ministerial Character would deprive me of it, after it is got and I should in all human probability be deposed was our marriage now to be known.

He insisted that after five years had elapsed he would no longer be in any danger, and arranged to pay her uncle a sum of money for her support until he acknowledged her as his wife. But he never did declare the marriage publicly, 'upon a pretence of the insufficiency of his stipend to support the Expence of the marriage state untill he should be transported to a better stipend', and after he died his relations queried the marriage. Despite the lapse of time between the above letters and his death, they clearly established a legal marriage.

In October 1810, when Walter Rule's relations disputed Jean Dickson's marriage, she was able to produce the following letter from him written in January of that year: 'Dear Madam, In consequence of our marriage lines having been lost some considerable time ago I for our mutual satisfaction, hereby acknowledge you as my lawful wife and have to request that you will be careful in preserving this letter – I am, Dear Madam, your affectionate husband.' He must have known that he was seriously ill, for in June he granted and signed a last will and testament, leaving his entire estate to Jean as his lawful wife. She also had witnesses who heard him verbally acknowledge the marriage. The result was a foregone conclusion.[3]

Contested Cases
The relatives of deceased men were not necessarily acting out of spite; some had reason to doubt that a marriage had ever existed. This was particularly likely if the woman had been considered as the deceased's housekeeper-cum-mistress.

In 1758 Jean Ballantyne was housekeeper to Mrs Elizabeth Park in Paisley, when Robert Wallace (a merchant) also lived there.[4] According to Jean, they were married in that year,

> But as Mr Wallace had great Expectations from his Aunt Mrs Park an old Lady possessed of an Ample fortune to whom he was Heir at Land And being apprehensive that she might take offence at his marrying one below his station It was proposed by him and Agreed to by the Complainer that the marriage shoud be kept secret till there shoud be a fit opportunity of discovering it and making it publick.

By the time of Robert's death ten years later this still had not been done, and his brothers (his nearest of kin) 'always understood it to be a Notorious fact, that Jean Ballantyne lived with Robert Wallace in the Capacity of his Servant maid, and that she continued in this Situation to the day of his death'.

The brothers stressed Robert's behaviour to Jean, for, they said,

> sundry times during her Service Mr Wallace discharged her and refused to keep her any longer, and more particularly he did so at periods subsequent to the times of her pretended Marriage – Not only did she act as a servant, but received Fees as such and those who had occasion to dine or sup with Mr Wallace can testify that she did not sit at Table.

The evidence revealed a stormy relationship. Hugh Snodgrass, a 38 year-old weaver, heard rumours of a marriage, but Robert 'said he was surprised how such a story could arise, did any person think he would ever marry his servant, and said that the deponent would never see such a thing as long as his blood was warm'. Snodgrass accompanied a drunken Robert home that night and saw them quarrel and Robert order Jean out of the house, 'and said he would pay her her wages that night or the next day'. But Snodgrass also said that when Robert was drunk and was told off by his aunt for his drunkenness he would sometimes 'order his aunt out of the room'. This was the aunt who Robert was afraid of offending – so similar words to Jean did not preclude his being married to her.

Margaret Wood, who had been asked by the couple to allow them to sleep together in her house

> asked Mr Wallace his Reason for Concealing his marriage to which he made answer it was not on account of his father for he had married his own servant maid without advising him but his aunt had always proved to him as a mother and therefore he did not like to Disoblige her for fear of Vexing her.

There were many more witnesses, giving contradictory evidence, but fortunately for Jean, about a month before he died Robert acknowledged his marriage in the presence of the parish minister and two elders, saying that he had married her about nine years earlier. In August 1770 the commissaries found that they were married persons 'at the time of the said Robert Wallace's decease and for several years before'. His brothers appealed to the Court of Session, but the decision was upheld.

Helen Henderson raised her action against the father, brother, sister, and brother-in-law of John MacLean in 1772, four years after he died, 'leaving behind him a Considerable sum which he made in money and effects'.[5] By this time Helen had remarried, but she fought for the legitimacy of her son and for the sum of about £4,000 which John had left and which his relatives had appropriated. She had letters from him dated 1759, the year they were irregularly married, including one to her father which ended 'Your dutiful son'. But the tone of his letters to her suggests that even at that time he was regretting the marriage.

The defenders stated that when very young John, who was 'originally bred an Engraver', became acquainted with Helen, 'then a Common Servant Maid in Town', and, knowing nothing of her real character, became fond of her. But, of course, they denied that any marriage had ever taken place. John was 'a young man of uncommon parts and an enterprizing Spirit and therefore after having by hard Labour and parsimony gathered a little money he went to the academy at Woolwich and there studied Gunnery and Fortification in order to qualify himself for pursuing his fortune as a military man'. At the end of 1761 he was recommended for service with the East India Company. He got an ensign commission and two years later was made captain.

During the seven years that Captain MacLean was in India the Pursuer does not pretend that he acknowledged her as his wife or kept any Correspondence whatever with her … on the Contrary the Captain in Several Letters he wrote during that period to the Defenders and others expressly disowning for his Wife and regretting his ever having had any Connection with her tho' at the same time as was very natural he signified his desire that proper care should be taken of the Boy.

Before his death John made a will leaving half his estate to his father, and a quarter each to his brother and sister – with no mention of a wife. But Helen argued that there was little or no inequality between them:

Her Father was a respectable farmer in East Lothian and at the time she became acquainted with Mr MacLean she was assistant or directress of a Boarding School in Edinburgh and not a Common Servant as the Defenders have alledged Mr MacLean on the other hand was a Lad who had been bred to the Engraving business and his father kept a little shop in Edinburgh but without either money or credit to carry on business to any extent, so that in point of circumstances the pursuer was in every respect as good a match as Mr Maclean had any title to expect.

More to the point, she could prove an actual marriage and cohabitation.

She acknowledged that after he went to India she did not correspond with him.

> *His relations in this Country … carefully concealled from her all Intelligence concerning her husband so that she was ignorant of his place of residence or situation in Life she had it not in her power to correspond with him. After Mr Maclean found himself rising in the army to a rank much higher than he had reason to expect it is possible he might have wished to get free of his marriage with the pursuer but she cannot believe he would ever seriously deny that a marriage had taken place between them.*

Witnesses from Helen's home parish of Whittingham testified that the couple 'were habite and repute husband and wife by all the neighbourhood', and that John never so much as hinted that Helen was not his wife. He would stay with Helen for a week or more at a time in her father's house and always acknowledged her as his wife, calling Thomas Henderson 'his Goodfather in publick Companies'. After he departed Helen continued to be known as Mrs MacLean.

The defenders had no counter-evidence so Helen won her case, and her son was pronounced their lawful child. The inheritance was still in dispute: under Scottish law a husband could not disinherit his wife, but under English law he could. Her lawyer argued that as both were Scots it was Scottish law that counted, while the defenders argued that the will had been made in India, under English law. The case was therefore transferred to the Court of Session, and the outcome is not known.

Mary Parker was another woman considered beneath the man she claimed as her husband, having entered the service of William Hannay, writer (lawyer) in Maybole, as his housekeeper in 1783, cohabiting with him and bearing his children until his death in February 1814.[6] His kin knew nothing of the private transaction by which their uncle had acknowledged Mary as his wife, and they denied that the couple were habit and repute married persons. They all lived in and around Maybole, 'but they never heard it alleged that their uncle and Mary Parker were married – altho' with others they had often cause to regret that he injured his respectability by retaining in his House a woman of the Pursuers abandoned character'.

Most witnesses were tradesmen and servants. The tradesmen all called Mary 'Mrs Hannay', and when they were offered refreshment Mary 'acted as a wife and gave directions to the servant what to bring'. Three women, who had been servants at different periods, testified that the couple 'slept in the same bed and eat their victuals at the same table and behaved in every respect as man and wife'. Mary 'had the keys of the house and took the sole direction thereof'. And they all called, and referred to, their mistress as 'Mrs Hannay'.

The two crucial witnesses were Thomas McMutrie, a wright, who often did small jobs about the house for them, and Andrew Campbell. Campbell had said to William before the birth of his first child 'that it was improper conduct to have a child with the said Mary Parker without being regularly married to her, to which Mr Hannay answered that if it was a fault he would make amends for it'. But it was not until February 1813, when William was seriously ill, that he took heed, calling McMutrie and Campbell into his bedroom as witnesses. Both men testified that at that time he took Mary's hands in his and declared that he took her, or owned her, as his lawful wife, and that the children were his lawful children. William did not tell his relations about this, but after they heard all the evidence they conceded that Mary was William's 'lawful Relict' and the children legitimate, so all the commissaries had to do was decree accordingly.[7]

Of Unsound Mind?

In four bitterly fought cases of this nature the essence of the defence was that the deceased was not of sound mind when he acknowledged a so-called marriage.

In the 1768 case of Helen (or Nelly) Buchanan against the nephews of the deceased Archibald Buchanan of Balfunning (in the parish of Drymen) Archibald's relations alleged that he fathered a number of illegitimate children, and that he courted Nelly only to shake off those other women.[8] According to the nephews, from 1762 onwards

> *Balfunning, what with Debts he owed, the Processes carried on against him by the Mothers of the Bastards and Processes at the Instance of his Sisters for their Portions, so perplexed and confused him, that all thoughts of Marriage with any person were dissipated, in so much that he lost his Judgment at some times, and particularly within these two or three Years past, he ran through the Country, lodged the original Rights of his Lands in a Moss-hole, threw away his Money in handfuls, and at last his Friends were forced to take him up, and as he was furious to bind him with Ropes, and confine him in his House till he convalesced.*

In December 1767, when he went to Nelly's house and insisted on sleeping with her as his wife, he was – they alleged – in a 'Delirium'. Next day a minister refused his request to marry them regularly, after which he was taken home, 'when he took his Bed; and in a languishing condition continued to the Time of his Death'. Basically, the defenders' case was that the only time their uncle owned himself married to Nelly and signed a declaration to that effect was when 'he was in a Delirium'.

Nelly, on her part, protested 'in the strongest manner that he had his senses and Judgement about him like other men'. It was true that 'he sometimes Drunk freely and was disordered while the effects of Liquor was upon him (which is the only grounds from which the defenders can attempt to inferr that he was out of senses) Yet it is certain that when he was sober he understood his own affairs and managed them perfectly well and was esteem'd to do so by every Body who knew him.' The allegations concerning his madness were 'gross calumnies'.

Nelly produced many witnesses. One declared that about seven or eight years ago, before Archibald's father died, he was asked to deliver a message to the latter, 'that he his son intended to Marry Miss Nelly Buchanan the pursuer, but wanted to do nothing without acquainting his father'. This witness 'did accordingly deliver the said Message Upon which Balfunnings father without expressing either his approbation or disapprobation of the intended Marriage only said, what will he do with all his whores then'. Another, James Buchanan, brewer in Glasgow, testified that about two years earlier he was drinking with Archibald in a public house and asked him 'if he was yet married, And gave for the reason of asking the question, That he would drink his wife's health as a toast To which Archibald Buchanan answered That he was married and was Married to Nelly Buchanan of Bolquhan.' Jean Buchanan, spouse of a grocer in Glasgow, testified that about four years earlier she heard someone say to Archibald, "'I think you might marry that woman by whom you have had the child, for she will make a very good wife," to which he answered "I cannot marry her nor no woman for Nelly Buchanan of Bolquhan is my married wife"'. Mary Mackay, servant to Mrs Buchanan of Bolquhan, testified that about a fortnight before his death she heard Archibald acknowledge his marriage in the presence of two kirk elders and a number of other witnesses, and said that he had been married to her for six years. One of those then present declared that 'Balfunning appeared that night to be in his ordinary way and no ways intoxicated, That Balfunning in his ordinary way of speaking spoke both loud and fast.' Some of Nelly's witnesses had heard stories of Archibald being 'disordered in his senses' but had never observed this themselves.

However, the nephews continued to harp on the theme of Archibald's 'madness'. None of their evidence amounted to much. For example, Archibald's servant, Daniel Fisher, testified that on the night Archibald went off to go to bed with Nelly, he 'appeared to be somewhat disordered', and Archibald did act a bit odd during the last days of his life. But Fisher also said that when the minister called and asked Archibald if he was married to Nelly, after returning several evasive answers he finally 'called out aloud in the presence of all that were in the Room, Mr Gourlay, You shall see that I mean what is honourable'. And 'at this time, Balfunning did not appear to be intoxicated or disordered in his Judgement.' The commissaries concluded that from the date of the written declaration in December 1767, and at the time of his death, Archibald Buchanan of Balfunning and Helen Buchanan were married persons.

The sister and brother-in-law of the deceased Robert Gourlay, merchant in Edinburgh, had a stronger defence of unsound mind when Christian Callman and her daughter raised an action, since Robert hanged himself just over a fortnight after privately declaring a marriage.[9]

Christian had become Robert's servant in 1786, but when her child was born a year later his relations strenuously objected to his keeping her in his house, so that he had to take other accommodation for her. On 3 August 1793 he sent her the following letter: 'My Dear As Mr and Mrs Jack is to drink tea with me to morrow afternoon will you come and bring my bony [sic] Jessie along with you will drink tea betwixt five and six o'clock I am my Dear Your most affectionate husband.' She went to his house and

> *they drank tea with the said Mr and Mrs Jack persons of Character and where he explicitly and seriously acknowledged the pursuers as his lawful wife and Child and soon after tea he made a small quantity of Toddy and drank to the pursuer Christian Callman saying 'My Dear your good Health' and then added to the other pursuer his Daughter 'My Dear Jessie You will be called no more a merry begotten'.*

The defenders alleged that on that day, and right up to his death on 19 August, Robert 'was in a state of mental derangement and incapacity which rendered him totally incapable of deliberately adhibiting any consent'. They stated that for some months before his death Robert 'was often in the greatest distress of mind, and seemed completely unhappy and melancholly That he appeared at same time to have taken a suspicion against all mankind'. Furthermore, during those months he 'was in the habit of taking considerable quantities of laudanum'. They described odd behaviour by him and said that for two or three months before his death his memory appeared

> *to be very much impaired, and that his looks particularly his eyes had something very uncommon and allarming in their appearance ... that a female shop keeper was often afraid to stay in the shop with him, when the other servants were out, as he frequently walked about the shop muttering to himself wringing his hands, and the sweat standing like pease upon his face, and his eyes staring in his head, that she was often afraid to look at him.*

The pursuers retorted that his relations' throwing them (mother and child) out of Robert's house 'may have contributed to sink his Spirits, and the acrimony and severity of their expostulations by which he was compelled to adopt a measure so disagreeable to him, could not fail to sour his temper'. Also, at that time he had lost a great deal of money through the failure of his bank (Bertram Gardner and Company). And

> *altho the Coroner's Jury in England are in the practice of adopting a very useful fiction of law, and uniformly imputing suicide to insanity and altho such depression of spirits as produces suicide may be construed into a momentary insanity, yet the Respondents do not conceive that it will be received by the Commissaries in the light of that sort of permanent insanity or imbecility which ought to hinder a man from having the management of his own affairs ....That he was often unhappy and melancholy evidently is nothing to the purpose. That he became suspicious, was circumstance by no means*

unnatural, when he found himself deceived, where he had thought his money most secure; and still more when he found his nearest relations resolutely bent to prevent him from legitimating the Child whom his affections were set upon, in order as he naturally would conclude, to secure his succession to themselves. Any man in this situation, in proportion as his heart had formerly been open and his affections warm, is in the same proportion disposed to fly into the other extreme and to become misanthropical and suspicious of all mankind.

As for the 'alarming expression' which his servants and shop assistant were alleged to have seen, those were 'very easily to be accounted for from the laudanum', as were the drowsiness and excessive sweating.

The defenders called many witnesses in their attempt to prove Robert Gourlay insane, though not all served their purposes. A surgeon, John Rae, agreed that Robert was depressed for about six months before his death, but the surgeon 'was rather inclined to attribute Mr Gourlays low spirits to an anxiety about his worldly affairs, than to any infirmity of body or mind'. Robert's shop keeper, Amelia Fauchney, testified to his sweating fits and that his eyes became 'wild and staring from the time that he first began to be troubled with his sweating fits', but she was never really afraid of being alone with him. His clerk observed an alteration in Robert Gourlay's behaviour after he met with several losses, for 'he became extremely suspicious and acted in such a way as if he did not believe there was such a thing as honesty among mankind'. Many other witnesses testified to his depression and odd behaviour during those months.

Christian had her own parade of witnesses ready to confirm that Robert was sound in mind, albeit depressed about his business losses. The commissaries were soon satisfied on that score and moved on to the marriage itself. Mr and Mrs Jack testified in detail to the occasion on which Robert said to them, 'I want you to know that this (pointing to Christian Callman) is my wife', and the Jacks drank to them as a married couple. Robert asked them to keep this a secret for the time being, and 'seemed to be perfectly in his sound mind and Judgement'. He was also described as dotingly fond of the child. Witnesses confirmed that the handwriting on the letter asking her to come to tea with the Jacks and signed 'Your most affectionate husband' was Robert Gourlay's. The commissaries found the defence of insanity not proven and the marriage 'sufficiently instructed', and the child lawful and capable of succeeding to his estate.

Another suicide and alleged insanity was that of the deceased Quintin Macadam of Craigingillan (Ayrshire), in 1805.[10] Quintin was claimed as husband by Elizabeth Walker, the daughter of a tenant on the Earl of Cassilis' neighbouring estate, who came to live with him in 1800, when she was eighteen. By 1805 she had borne him two children and was pregnant with a third, whose tutors and curators (two of them baronets) were also pursuers in the case. Fighting the case was Alexander Macadam of Grimmet, Quintin's first cousin. The pursuers admitted that the relationship was originally illicit but said that 'it became the source of strong and fixed attachment on both sides, and that the wish and intention of Mr Macadam to convert this original connection with a permanent and legal union was not at last suddenly taken up, but had been long in his serious contemplation.' Indeed, a letter was produced quite late on in the case in which Quintin had written (in February 1800) to Elizabeth's brother:

Dear James, you will be surprised when I tell you, your Sister is come to live with me, But I hope you will not be angry when I tell you I mean to behave to her in the most honourable manner, I have already settled Sixty Guineas on her yearly during her life. I have made her no promise of marriage, but it is very probable it will end in that.

John Ballantine Esquire, banker in Ayr, testified that whereas in the presence of his mother and sister Quintin would speak 'in a manner improper, and too freely for modest women's Company', he never did so in Elizabeth's presence: 'in the company of this young woman, he was very guarded and paid her great attention, and showed that he wished the company to pay her attention, by asking the deponent and others to sit beside her, and to drink wine with her, from all which the deponent thought there was something in the report, of his having given her an assurance of marriage.' David Limond, town clerk of Ayr, said that Quintin behaved to Elizabeth 'in a very polite manner, as if she had been the first lady in the land.'

On the morning of 21 March 1805 Quintin went to David Woodburn, his factor, said that he wished to acknowledge Elizabeth as his wife, and asked Woodburn to write out a contract. Woodburn did not feel himself capable of writing out such a document, so Quintin wrote to Thomas Smith, his agent: 'Dear Sir As I intend to marry Miss Walker immediately, come out as soon as you receive this and bring stamped paper to write the contract.' He then called three of his servants into the dining room as witnesses. He asked Elizabeth 'to rise, which she did, and having given her hand to the said Quintin Macadam, he, holding it said "I take you three to witness that this is my lawful married wife, and the children by her are my lawful children."' He then sent for the housekeeper, as an additional witness, and repeated the same words. (The servants later testified to the solemnity with which all this was carried out.) En route back to his own house in the afternoon he stopped at his factor's and told him about the marriage. He proceeded home, went upstairs and shot himself.[11]

Alexander, the defender, claimed that Quintin had been 'periodically affected with insanity', at which times 'his eye had a particular appearance which is only remarked in persons who are insane'. His worst attack was in spring 1803, when he went completely berserk.

Alexander could not find any witnesses to corroborate this picture. Certainly Quintin was a hard drinker, and when asked if he 'was naturally of a hot or cool temper', John Dick, a neighbouring tenant who often dined, walked and hunted with Quintin, replied that 'he was hot enough if he was crossed by any person who did any thing to displease him: That on these occasions he might express himself passionately, but the deponent believes not more so than is usual with many other country gentlemen.' However, Quintin had a stomach complaint (perhaps an ulcer?) which came upon him periodically, rendering sleep almost impossible and shortening his already short temper. Most of the servants (even the housekeeper) fell out with their master on at least one occasion, and one said that when Quintin was ill his face had 'a discontented and unsatisfied appearance', but the servant could not honestly say 'that his eye had any particular look at these times; but when one is out of humour, it is to be seen from the looks'. Quintin once threw a parcel at him, and 'once threatened to knock him down with a bottle, and some such silly threats,' but they were not taken seriously.

As for the occasion in 1803 when he went on the rampage, his factor testified that he saw Quintin that night 'making a great noise and speaking nonsense', and the next morning Quintin said, 'I have been playing the very devil and have been drunk almost ever since I left home.' Doctors bore out this version of events, and other witnesses testified that he tempered his drinking habits afterwards.

The commissaries concluded that Quintin made Elizabeth his wife, 'by joining his hands with those of the Pursuer and declaring her to be his wife, and her children his lawful children, in presence of several persons whom he had called up to his Dining room to be witnesses to this Declaration', which was 'made in the most Solemn serious and deliberate manner', and that he was 'in his perfect sound mind'. By this declaration 'the Status of the Pursuer as his wife and of her children as his lawful children was fixed, and could not be affected by any subsequent act of Mr Macadam.' The claim of insanity they rejected. Alexander appealed to the Court of Session but his appeal was refused.[12]

In the 1807 case of Agnes Ferguson against James Logan Esquire of Westsidewood, brother of the deceased John Logan of Woodend, lawyer, James alleged that John's 'propensity to dissipation carried him away from his proper pursuits', and that 'the constant practice of drinking to excess when in Company succeeded by the still more destructive indulgence in the use of spirituous liquors in private, and at all times in the day at length so far debilitated both his body and mind that he became quite incapable of looking after his own affairs and totally neglected those of his clients.'[13] He became bankrupt and took refuge in the Abbey of Holyroodhouse, where his creditors could not pursue him, and 'resided for many months in the most degraded state of continual intoxication'. It was during that period that he acknowledged Agnes, his servant, as his wife. Not long afterwards he died. Agnes's lawyer responded:

the Defender has been pleased very little to his honour to indulge himself in a variety of abusive reflections against the memory of his deceased brother …. But this is the mode almost uniformly resorted to in cases of the present nature where the friends of any person find themselves likely to be disappointed of an expected succession by a marriage as to which they were not consulted and as to which had they been consulted they would have endeavoured to have prevented. In such a Case the defunct is always represented as a Drunkard a fool or a mad man and sometimes as combining all these in one character. But such representations have never yet had the effect to mislead the Commissaries from the true point at issue.

Agnes's witnesses included the widow of George Shaw Esquire of Kernie Bank, who testified that about a year earlier John came to her house with Agnes one evening when she was drinking tea with her sister, and said, 'Mrs Shaw this is my wife will you shake hands with her,' which Mrs Shaw had no objection to, and invited them in for tea. Robert Miller and his wife were also introduced to Agnes as John's wife, and Miller said that 'he paid her the attention a husband ought to pay to his wife.' When asked for the defender 'if on these occasions when he has heard Mr Logan call the Pursuer his wife he was entirely free from liquor,' Miller replied, 'Oh yes.' James had some witnesses to testify that his brother had been a heavy drinker, but so what? The commissaries found that Agnes was his lawful widow.[14]

All of the cases in this chapter so far have been successful ones, as are Case Studies 14 and 15; those were in the majority. But the chapter will conclude with two cases (and Case Study 16) in which a woman failed to prove herself a widow.

Unsuccessful Cases
We have seen cases in this chapter of a man who waited until the approach of death before declaring that the woman who had been his housekeeper or kept mistress for many years was his wife. Unfortunately for Jean Anderson (in 1792), George Fullarton, collector of the customs at Leith, hedged his bets to such an extent that she was unable to establish herself his widow.[15]

George had married two other women who had both died before Jean entered his service as housekeeper in 1768, and it was the daughters of those women and their husbands (one of whom was Henry Erskine, Dean of the Faculty of Advocates) who contested Jean's claim. She lived with him for 23 years and bore him children, of whom three daughters survived. According to her libel, she acted as

sole manager of the family, hiring and directing the servants, paying them their wages, sitting at table with Mr Fullarton, receiving and entertaining his company, and, in every respect, conducting herself as his wife; excepting that she did not assume the name, a false pride, as he himself has said, rendering him unwilling openly to declare a marriage.

The children were brought up at home and known as the Miss Fullartons, and he provided liberally for them. Finally Jean persuaded him that some written evidence of a marriage was required, and on 16 April 1791 he wrote the following:

> *My Dear Jean Anderson, As you and I have cohabited together, as man and wife, for upwards of twenty years, although pride and connexions prevented me declaring to the world, that you was my wife; yet, on account of your unspeakable attention to my health and interest in my family affairs, and above all, the love I bear to you and the three children you have born to me, viz. Margaret, Jean and Maria Fullartons, your and my daughters, I think it a duty incumbent on me to subscribe what I truly am, Your affectionate husband. (Signed) George Fullarton.*

Jean was satisfied with this, and the document was locked away in George's repository. Three days later he became ill, and two days after that he died. The document was found amongst his belongings, but her status as his widow was not accepted, and in February 1792 she was forced to raise a declarator of marriage action. In May 1793, after a bitter fight, the commissaries found a marriage proven, but after the defenders appealed they reversed this decision.[16]

Jean produced witnesses to the relationship, but they were ambivalent. Mrs Turrup testified that she had seen Jean 'riding in the coach with Collector Fullarton, and sitting in the parlour with him, which she thought more like a lady, than a servant'. But when asked if she 'on these occasions understood, and believed her to be his wife?' she replied, 'that she did not: That she thought it was something like it, and was sure he would make her his wife, before he died.' Why? Because of 'the family he had by her, and the kindness he had always shewn to her'. Another witness, Mrs Shearer, believed the children to be lawful, because of his love for them, 'their sitting at the table with him, being in the carriage with him, and other such marks of attention paid to them, together with the regard and respect which he showed to their mother'.

George's brother, interestingly enough, was on Jean's side, and had talked to him the winter before his death 'relative to the legitimating his children'. In court he declared unprompted that 'he would look upon the pursuer as his brother's widow as long as he lived, and the children as his lawful children, and countenance them as such.' When George died Jean told John Pattison, town clerk of Leith, who sealed up the deceased's repositories, that she and he were married and told Pattison where in the repository he would find the written proof, thereby bearing out her story of the events on the night in question.

Why, then, did she lose her case? According to the defenders, the question was

> *Whether a letter, left by a deceased person in his repositories, undelivered, declaring a certain person to be his wife, but who was never acknowledged in that character, during his life, can have the effect of establishing a marriage by the law of Scotland?*

The defence was that it did not, and they had the Dean of the Faculty of Advocates on their side. Jean herself had admitted that she had never been acknowledged as George's wife during the twenty-plus years they lived together, and the children were born long before his letter was written. The letter might state that 'the parties had cohabited as man and wife for more than twenty years; yet this, in the legal sense of these terms, was confessedly not the case.' And George had not delivered the letter, but kept it in his repositories:

> *During his life, he seems at all events to have resolved, that neither the pursuer, nor any other person, should have it in their power to consider him as married … while it remained in his repositories, it was just the same as if the intention had remained in his own breast, as it cannot be supposed to have been communicated to any other person; and even if it had been his intention that it should have effect after his death, when his repositories came to be opened, yet this was altogether impossible, as this would be creating a post obit marriage, which was not to take place until after his death, which is perfectly absurd, and altogether inconsistent with the very nature of marriage.*

If a marriage could be constituted by writing such a letter, which was then tucked away out of sight, then 'any person, by this simple expedient, might marry whom they chose, without even the consent and knowledge of the other party.' As for George's kindness to Jean:

> *the propriety of Mr Fullerton's conduct does not afford the least presumption that he ever entertained the most distant intention of marrying her. Indeed, his conduct in this respect, if it can have any weight in forming a conjecture concerning his intention, must rather have the contrary tendency. A man, who for a long course of years has shown that decent attention to a woman of inferior rank, placed in the situation in which the pursuer stood, with regard to him, affords a strong presumption that he would not form any other connection than what had for so long a time taken place.*

Those were clever legal arguments, and really George Fullerton tried to have it both ways, by not 'lowering' himself to marry his servant while trying to have his daughters considered legitimate after his death. Had he acknowledged a marriage to even one person before he died he would have assured Jean's position as his widow, but his written acknowledgment failed to have that effect.

Another unsuccessful pursuer, Ann Sutherland, raised an action against the daughter of the deceased William Yeats, sometime merchant in Airdrie, in 1826. When William died in May 1825 he was over 80 and Ann was less than half his age. After he retired from business William used to go to Leith once a year, and stayed in lodgings kept by Ann. In 1824 she accompanied him on an excursion to the west of Scotland, where they stayed in inns or furnished lodgings, 'never remaining above a few days in the same place; and never going near Airdrie where

Mr Yeats was best known'. After a few weeks they went to furnished lodgings in Edinburgh, and then they travelled to London and Brighton where Ann's son was born. As soon as William died she 'took possession of his effects and money and of the title deeds and vouchers of his property, and of every thing else belonging to him on which she could lay her hands'. William had not introduced Ann to any of his numerous friends in Airdrie or Glasgow, and in Edinburgh when spoken to by his friends 'regarding the connection with the pursuer, he uniformly denied any thing of a matrimonial connection, and was ashamed of his criminal connection'. Ann was unable to bring any proof of a marriage. [17]

The one thing all of the cases (and the case studies which follow) have in common with each other, and with most cases in earlier chapters, is that they were raised by women. The next chapter will look at the reverse side of the coin.

Notes

1   CC8/5/4.
2   CC8/5/11.
3   CC8/5/31.
4   CC8/6/29.
5   CC8/5/15.
6   C8/6/100.
7   Mary then petitioned for damages and expenses, on the grounds that the defenders 'cannot be permitted to say that they were ignorant of all the facts which have been proved and which were so notorious they living in the Town and neighbourhood of Maybole. They were therefore *in male fide*, when they stated in their Defences, that they had no knowledge of the transactions stated in the lybel, and denying that Mr Hannay and the pursuer were habite and repute married persons, and that the other pursuers were his lawful children .... They conclude their Defences by saying that the pursuer was a woman of abandoned character.' But the petition was refused.
8   CC8/6/27.
9   CC8/5/22.
10 CC8/5/21/1.
11 The servant who found his master with half his head blown off, and the housekeeper, tried to keep Elizabeth from seeing the corpse, particularly as she was far advanced in pregnancy, but they did not succeed, and she 'threw herself upon the body'. Although witnesses testified to Quintin's discussing future events on his way home, George James Campbell Esquire of Treesbank reported an earlier conversation in which Quintin had said that his cousins would not get a shilling of his, 'as marriage could always take place on death bed; by all which the deponent understood Mr. Macadam to mean, that it was in his power to marry Miss Walker on death bed'. It therefore seems likely that Quintin's public declaration to legitimate his children was part of his preparation for suicide.
12 Elizabeth's answers to a second appeal were printed and can also be found in Session Papers, Signet Library, 473; 43.
13 CC8/5/29/4.
14 James appealed against liability for expenses to the Court of Session. Agnes's lawyer pointed out all the expensive delaying tactics he had used, his 'aspersions on the character of the Respondent and the most unfeeling attempts to traduce the memory of his brother. To all these reasons for finding Expences may be added that unless they are found the

Respondent will truly have lost her cause. For though she may have vindicated her character there is much reason to fear that she may be involved in embarrassments from which she may never [be] relieved.' His appeal was refused, so he had to pay expenses.

15 No papers appear to have survived for this case amongst the Commissary Court records, but the case can be reconstructed from Session Papers, Signet Library, 199; 16 (1795).

16 Jean then appealed to the Court of Session, and it was as a result of that appeal that the above was printed. The decision of the Court of Session is not noted, but it seems safe to assume that they upheld the commissaries' decision.

17 CC8/6/155.

CASE STUDY 14

GUY V. OSBURN: LOST AT SEA

IN 1733 James Osburn, 'a young man about nineteen or twenty years of age of low stature and pretty much pockfretten', told the master of the sloop he was serving on as a common sailor that he was 'the son of a minister in Scotland', and that 'he had been a wild young man and had disoblidged his parents'. James had left his home in Fintry, Aberdeenshire, and run away to sea. In 1734 he fetched up in Philadelphia, in the colony of Pennsylvania, and courted Mary Guy, marrying her in September of that year. He then heard that his father had died, so he sailed to Aberdeen to claim his inheritance, but he died at sea. Their son was born in June 1735, and in March 1737 Mary sailed across the Atlantic to raise a declarator of marriage action. James's only sister, and her husband and child, knowing nothing of any marriage, had claimed the inheritance.

Mary's tale was that she first met James in summer 1734 in Philadelphia at the house of a friend, a shoemaker, when he bought his shoes. She saw him frequently after that, and only two or three weeks later he proposed marriage to her. She did not give him an 'answer at that time (tho' he pressed much to have the marriage solemnized before he went to Antigua which he then intended)'. She 'saw no more of Mr Osburns condition than that he was a common Sailor before the Mast nor did he ever in the conversation between themselves give himself out to be of a better rank untill after their marriage'. Mary (who could not write) and her sister had come from Dublin about ten years earlier and were employed as domestic servants.

James then sailed to Antigua for two months, and on his return Mary married him. She had a marriage certificate and witnesses. Charles Steedman, second mate on the ship St Andrew in October 1734, testified that he had reproved James for staying ashore at night, when James confessed that 'he was married and went on shore nightly to his wife and asked the deponents permission so to do till the ship should sail and obtained the same promising at the same time that he would always attend his duty on board early in the morning.' Steedman 'had several times heard the said James Osburn own and acknowledge the said Mary Guy to have been his wife'.

This next voyage was across the Atlantic, to Rotterdam, and James intended to make his way to Aberdeenshire to claim his inheritance. As the ship proceeded, Steedman, 'taking notice that the said James Osburn kept a Journal and could take an observation, took opportunity to converse with him, being desireous to know something more of his character and circumstances: And the said James Osburn in conversation told the deponent that he the said James was the only son of one Mr

William Osburn minister at Fintry near Aberdeen, and that he the said James Osburn had only one sister, and that his father being lately dead something considerable would fall to him, for which reason he intended to go to Scotland as soon as possibly he could.'

James asked Steedman 'to help him to obtain his discharge at Cowes in England when the ship should arrive there'. But when they got to Cowes the commander of the ship refused to discharge him, and on 24 February James and another man 'being on the small Bower Anchor fixing a Runner and tackle the said James Osburn was by the spray of a sea washed off and notwithstanding all endeavours to save him he was drowned'.

Many witnesses appeared, some in Philadelphia. The defenders tried calumny, producing two sailors who claimed that 'the woman who pretended to be married to him, bore in Philadelphia the character of a common whore And they doubted much of the truth of his being married with her.' But Mary's witnesses said that she 'was always reputed a virtuous woman'. The defenders then argued that there was no proof that the man who had married Mary in Philadelphia was the James Osburn who had left Aberdeenshire.

Actually, there was plenty of evidence. Ralph Leys, who had heard Mary and James avow their marriage, and had seen their marriage lines, said that in the witness's 'Judgment and apprehension he appeared to have a better Education than common Sailors usually have'. John Falconer, another witness, testified that James 'wore dark blue gray cloaths trimmed with black which the said James said was second mourning for his father and complained … that his sister had been extravagant in laying out too much money in mourning cloaths'. James also told him 'that he intended to get to Scotland as soon as he could, for he should be of age by the time he arrived there and had about seven hundred pounds sterling whereof he could take possession and wherewith he proposed to come over to Philadelphia to build a ship and that he did not doubt that some gentleman in Aberdeen would be concerned with him therein.'

Yet even in his last letter to his uncle, from the Isle of Wight, James made no mention of being married. It was not until a year later, when a ship came from Philadelphia, that the uncle first heard it said that his nephew had been married, and he did not believe it. Mary, however, had plenty of proof, and in February 1740 she was declared to be James Osburn's lawful widow, and their child a legitimate son.

CC8/5/6

CASE STUDY 15

CAMPBELL V. CAMPBELL: SEPARATE LIVES

IN 1813 James Campbell, brother to the deceased Archibald Campbell, sometime farmer and afterwards feuar on the island of Bute, was infuriated when Ann Campbell claimed Archibald as her husband and their daughter Mary as a lawful child. James insisted that her story of a marriage in 1794 was 'most completely, and distinctly *contradicted and disproved by every circumstance* in the life and conduct of the parties for the whole period of 25 years, which interveened betwixt the date of their connection and the death of Archibald Campbell.' She had had several bastard children, he alleged, only some of whom were said to belong to Archibald, the rest being supported by other men. Nor was Archibald any better, for he 'was famous in the Country, as a Votary of Venus, and his connections were widely extended, and he [was] reputed as the Father of a numerous Offspring, by a variety of Venters'. 'He was well educated, of a good address, had some property, and it was general matter of observation, that if instead of following the illicit intercourse, in which he indulged, he had married, he would have been highly respectable.'

James knew of three different women whom Archibald had courted during those years, though all broke off with him (one of them 'was so hurt at the Libertinism of her Lover, that she would not have him'). Ann and her daughter by Archibald had been living on their own in Glasgow for some years, 'keeping a Bread Shop, or more properly a Stall, in one of the Wynds of that City'. In February 1813 Archibald went to Glasgow, almost immediately fell seriously ill, and soon after died.

Ann's version of events was that he married her secretly because of his family's opposition and never told them of this, 'and the same cause of course had prevented him from taking the Pursuer to reside with him in Rothesay – He however availed himself of every opportunity to come to Glasgow to visit his wife, and was never above five or six months absent from her at a time during the whole period which elapsed from his marriage till his death.' This way of life suited them so well that even when his financial situation improved they continued to pursue it. She 'found more scope for her industry in Glasgow, and in exerting herself there for the support of herself and her family, she felt more satisfaction than she probably would have experienced had she been introduced among her husband's relations as his wife'. Even if the allegations of intercourse with other men on her part or with other women on his were true, that would simply have been adultery.

On his last visit he knew he had consumption and might not survive, so he sent for his man of business and told him of 'his intention of leaving to them his whole property – The only difficulty of course which stood in the way of their succeeding to this property on his death without any dispute was the circumstance of his wife not having resided constantly with him. To obviate this difficulty the deceased was advised to join with the Pursuer in subscribing a writing declaring that they had been lawfully married ... and that the child surviving of their marriage was their lawful daughter.' He died a fortnight later.

James said that the reason given for not cohabiting was nonsense: 'Archibald Campbell was at all times totally independent of his relations and did not regard their opinions or those of any other person'. Not only was there no cohabitation 'but during the whole period of Twenty five years that Archibald Campbell lived in Bute and the Pursuer in Glasgow, he never wrote her a single Letter or scrape of paper in which he acknowledged and addressed her as his wife.' His conduct in proposing marriage to other women proved that he did not consider himself to be married to Ann. And whereas adulterous married women conceal their affairs, Ann had compelled the other men in her life to support their illegitimate children.

However, the only point which the commissaries considered relevant was the declaration of marriage made a fortnight before his death. They found it was deliberate, solemn, well witnessed and unambiguous, and that Archibald was of sound mind when he made it.

The key witnesses were two surgeons (James Stelle and Ebenezer Hislop), a lawyer, and a fourth man who were all present when the written declaration was read out three times at Archibald's request, 'and at each time Mr Campbell the Patient was asked if he was pleased with it or if that was his wife, and each time he answered that it was just what he wanted or just the truth'. Archibald said that he had been married to Ann for 16 or 18 years, and both of them seemed 'to be perfectly distinct collected and sober during the whole of this interview and the business was gone thro' deliberately leisurly and gravely by all concerned'. Because this was all done on a Sunday, Archibald then had misgivings about its legality, and the whole performance was gone through again, with a new written declaration, a couple of days later.

James had already appealed against the commissaries' decision that the only thing that mattered was the verbal declaration, for Archibald's will had divided his entire property between Alexander Cameron and Mary Campbell, as his natural children by different mothers, with no mention at all of Ann. James might, therefore, have appealed to a higher court, but a settlement was reached with James who conceded the case as long as he did not have to pay expenses, and the commissaries upheld the marriage. Whatever the truth of this relationship in the intervening years, at the end of his life Archibald made sure that the daughter born of it was legitimate.

CC8/6/99

CASE STUDY 16

McGREGOR V. CAMPBELL: AN UNEQUAL RELATIONSHIP

THIS case dragged on from 1792 to 1799 because the relationship was so vaguely defined that persuasive testimonies could be brought for both sides. The deceased, Lieutenant Duncan Campbell, was a gentleman, and the woman, Catharine McGregor, was his servant. They lived near Comrie, Perthshire. Catharine claimed that in August 1790 they went to Kinghorn in Fife, took the ferry to Edinburgh, and were married in Leith. But she was unable to name the minister, or produce marriage lines or witnesses to the marriage.

Duncan's brother, Patrick Campbell of Edurchip, and his sisters, argued that their relationship was anything but conjugal, for 'the deceast often turned the pursuer out of doors when she acted improperly and that she as often returned without making any Complaint such as a wife would have done'. When he died she 'delivered up her Charge in the house', and then left, 'carrying with her the whole of her clothes and demanded her livery meal or board wages as a Servant for her maintenance from that time till the term of Whitsunday the time of her engagement which was accordingly given her'. Furthermore, when she was cited before the kirk session after her pregnancy was discovered, she confessed to fornication.

Catharine's lawyer painted a picture of a rustic innocent, much wronged, her claims of marriage ignored: 'alas the plain and unvarnished tale of the pursuer an innocent country Girl of parentage obscure, was not to be hearkened to or regarded by these defenders or their Mother who pretended to be Campbells of a superior rank and therefore the pursuer so far from being justly dealt with as is alledged in receiving wages and board wages she was by their order forcibly turned out of Doors without her clothes or wearing apparell and sent to the house of her father friendless and unsupported where for some time she experienced the severest and most cruel treatment that the violence of this family could invent and besides reviling the memory of the Defunct in terms very unbecoming on account of his having married the pursuer they tried by every means to disqualify her from prosecuting her just claims and this they were for some time successfull in untill the pursuer got a state of her cause made out and transmitted to Edinburgh where she obtained the benefit of the poors roll of this court.'

In court Catharine explained that when she met Duncan she lived with her father at Cathaladow, where he 'rented a small pendicle of land of about half an acre'. He 'had formerly been a shoemaker but on account of ill health had given up that business and then subsisted chiefly by the earnings of his children', and Catharine 'employed herself in Spinning lint and wool'.

Dundurn, where Duncan came to live about seven years before his death, was across the water from Cathaladow. He hired Catharine first as a harvest shearer, and then as his housekeeper, when she was about 23.

She told the story of a marriage ceremony but, not knowing Edinburgh, could not say where they were married or who the minister or witnesses were. (But she was able to describe the fabrics that Duncan bought for her in remarkable detail: 'there was about a yard and a half of Muslin between Eleven and twelve yards of printed Cotton all of one pattern black silk for a bonnet and cloak Nine or ten yards of red and white stripped Muslin for a gown and petticoat and ribbons for two Sashes' – but 'no silk for gowns'.)

Catharine could not 'read write' or write herself, but even so her story of what happened to the marriage certificate seems a bit unlikely. She 'kept it Loose in her pocket for about six months', she said, until 'one night about the end of that period Lieutenant Campbell being ill', she 'rose to light a candle and took said piece of paper out of her pocket being the first she laid her hands on and lighted the candle therewith, That after lighting the candle she threw the paper on the hearth stone and trod out the flame'. Next morning 'Lieutenant Campbell found the remainder of the paper and tore it all to pieces and threw it in the fire because the declarant had been so silly as to light the candle with it.' He 'was in a great passion at the declarant and did not speak to her again that day'. Some time after that he told her that 'he would give her no more writing but that when he got time he would go to Perth and make out a writing which would serve the declarant in its stead,' but he 'never was at Perth afterwards'. While she still had it she never showed the certificate to anyone 'lest their marriage should be discovered by Lieutenant Campbells mother who is a bold boistrous woman and who always disowned Lieutenant Campbell on account of his not setting the declarant away from his house'.

She denied ever being dismissed or turned out of the house by him. And she denied confessing to the kirk session that her child had been begotten in fornication. One day as she was coming out of church 'one of the elders in presence of the minister told her that she must declare who was the father of her child to which the declarant answered that they needed not to enquire for all the country round knew who was the father of her child.'

The Defence tried to stop Catharine even being allowed to prove her case unless she could come up with a more cogent account of events. They had located kirk session minutes that revealed that she had admitted fornication before that court. She had claimed to have been introduced to neighbours as Duncan's wife, yet she also said she had not shown the certificate to anyone for fear of his mother's finding out. She had also insisted that there were no gentry in the neighbourhood, which was false for there were 'a great many respectable families in the neighbourhood of Wester Dundurn to none of whom the pursuer paid visits with Lieutenant Campbell'.

In August 1793, because Catharine could not come up with witnesses to the alleged marriage celebration, and because of her contradictory stories, the commissaries dismissed the process. Her lawyer appealed: it would be hard on Catharine and her son to have their case thrown out just because she was forgetful when interrogated. 'Her appearance before the Commissaries being the first Instance she ever was in a Court of Justice she naturally felt embarrassed and express[ed] herself defectively and probably incorrectly. The judge examinator will recollect with what innocence and simplicity she delivered her unvarnished tale and how unequal she was to the cross examination she underwent.' It was the rights of the young child that changed the commissaries' minds, and they altered their decision and allowed her to bring proof.

Catharine's first witness was Ensign Murray Drummond, who had lived about twelve miles from Dundurn and was an intimate friend of Duncan's. Drummond testified that on one occasion, several months before his death, Duncan introduced Catharine as his wife to him, and that when Drummond dined at Dundurn Catharine sat at the table with them. Duncan's family had not visited him for some years because they were angry at him keeping Catharine. According to Drummond, it was 'a current report' that they were married, and though people still called her Kate or Catharine, it was 'common there for the Country people even to call married Persons simply by their Christian names'. By 'Country people' he meant 'small farmers and Cottars and that the generality of the farmers there are small ones'. During that period 'the manners and stile of Living assumed by Lieutenant Campbell were in general like to those of the farms in the neighbourhood'. Drummond's wife, Mary Robertson, 'had never any reason to know or suspect that the pursuer had not been Lieutenant Campbell's wife'. Catharine was always referred to by the Lieutenant as Mrs Campbell, 'except when he spoke to her as another man would do to his wife by the name of My Dear Katy and the like'.

Betty Mcilwhanel (spouse of a wright in Comrie) was a more equivocal witness. After the couple returned from Edinburgh Betty met them at Comrie fair and Duncan told the landlady of the inn that Catharine was his wife, but that was the only occasion she could recall when Catharine was called Mrs Campbell. One day she called at Dundurn, and Catharine's sister, who was a servant there, 'bade the witness stay and rest her and Kattie would rise and speak to her'. The court was so surprised at a servant referring to a married mistress in that way she was asked if she was certain that that was the answer given to her, and said it was. Catharine's lawyer helped to repair the damage, asking 'if it is not a common practice in that part of the country to call married women by their maiden name Depones that is according to their station that the wives of the best farmers get the name of Mrs but that the witness having been Long upon an intimate footing with the pursuer Used the freedom to call her by her maiden name and the sister (the servant) knew this well. That she knew the pursuer ought to have got the name of Mrs Campbell but that she the witness being so Intimate with the pursuer gave her the name of Kathy McGregor both when she spoke of her and spoke to her.'

Other neighbours testified – some in Gaelic, via interpreters – to their certainty that the couple were married. For instance, Grizel Drummond remembered her husband sitting by Catharine when Duncan said, 'you may take a kiss of my wife and you will allow me to take a kiss of yours'. (Grizel did not recall 'whether the kisses were exchanged'.) She testified that 'the behaviour and conduct of Lieutenant Campbell and the pursuer was such as made the neighbourhood consider them to be man and wife.' She could not think of further specifics, 'as it was not the Business of the witness to make enquiries but seeing them keeping Company as before deponed to like man and wife she considered them as married persons'.

We then get a glimpse of what the defenders' lawyer had been up to, for the judge examinator at this point 'in order to cut short the immoderate length of Cross Interrogatorys most of which seem solely calculated to perplex the witnesses and to prevent the pursuer from bringing her proof to a conclusion', directed the interpreter 'to allow no cross Interrogatory to be put which does not immediately arise from and is explanatory of the answer to the Interrogatory on the part of the pursuer and in particular to reject all Interrogatorys which go to hearsay from a person who has already been examined as a witness for the pursuer or who is to be adduced as a witness or those which have no other tendancy than to make one witness contradict and discredit another.'

Alexander McIsack, a farmer and distiller and in the parish, testified that once after their return from Kinghorn, he 'happened to be riding in Company with Lieutenant Campbell on the road … and being Intimately acquainted with Lieutenant Campbell as a Country man and as a Gentleman Introduced a conversation with regard to being married or not being married and the witness expressed a wish that the Lieutenant should take a Lady to which the Lieutenant answered "Saunders do you doubt that I am not married If you doubt it I am as sure married as you are".'

James McIsack, a 29 year-old labourer, was also told by Duncan that he was married to Catharine. After their return the witness saw Catharine riding behind Duncan on horseback, which he had not seen before they went away, and also afterwards he saw them 'going both to church and market in a cart together', adding that it was 'a usual thing for people a little above the lowest rank to travel in this manner husband and wife together in a Cart'. But inevitably he had to admit that unmarried people might share a horse or ride in a cart together. He also admitted that 'the wives of Gentlemen in that Country are always called by the names of their husbands'.

Another neighbour, John Drummond, was told off by Duncan 'for quarelling his wife and the deponent is perfectly certain that in speaking of the pursuer on that occasion he called her distinctly his wife'. Drummond 'was in some measure surprised to hear the Lieutenant acknowledge the marriage as the deponent thought it was improper for him to marry so mean a woman', but 'in other respects the deponent was not surprised as they had lived together for some time on the footing of husband and wife as the deponent thought.' John Orr, jeweller in Greenock, was in a public house when Duncan introduced Catherine as his wife. Orr was not inclined to take this seriously but Duncan 'said "By God Mr Orr I take it very ill that you do not salute my Wife".' Orr 'asked him if he was serious Lieutenant Campbell assur'd him he was the deponent asked him if she was his wife to which he answered "Yes by God She is my lawfull wife".'

Then it was time for Duncan's side. Alexander McArthur, ploughman at Dundurn, testified that Catharine behaved and was treated as a servant as much after their return from Kinghorn as before, and she would occasionally come and stay with them for a few hours saying that she had been turned away by her master. After Duncan's death she asked him 'to apply to the Deceased's mother and Brother to be allowed her meal like the other servants and to take it to her fathers house'. McArthur heard Duncan call her Catharine 'and sometimes call her brodie a sort of bye name which the deponent supposes might have been given her from her thickness' – but never Mrs Campbell. James McGrigor, shepherd in Wester Dundurn, testified that Duncan 'used to call her Kate Dochart and Dochart is a name given to a branch of the family of McGregor, That he frequently heard him call her Kate Breddie which means thick or fat But he never heard him call her Mrs Campbell'. When he asked the Lieutenant about rumours of marriage he replied that 'he neither was nor ever would be married to her'. Archibald Dewar, a neighbouring tenant, testified that Duncan had denied any marriage to him, and after Duncan's death 'he saw nothing in the pursuers behaviour like a person mourning for the death of her husband or different from the rest of the servants.' Duncan, he said, 'was very easy and familiar in his manners and used frequently to enter into Conversation with people of the deponents station as easily as with his equals'.

When the defenders sought to examine witnesses locally rather than in Edinburgh, the pursuer's lawyer argued that 'the defenders are people of great opulence and power in that part of the highlands where they reside and where the proof would fall to be taken That influence might be made use of to the purpose of Concussing or overawing the witnesses proposed by them to be adduced.' The petition was refused, but they still had plenty of witnesses. John Ferguson, the schoolmaster, had also asked Duncan if he was married, which he denied. About a year before the death the schoolmaster asked Catharine 'whether she was married to the Lieutenant that he might respect her accordingly and she answered that she was not but that the Lieutenant was only her master'. Others testified along the same lines.

And what about the kirk session? The elder who had allegedly asked Catharine about the father of her child testified that after Duncan's death Catharine asked to have the child baptised. 'She was not asked whether She was married to Lieutenant Campbell nor did She say any thing upon that subject' and 'she was not reproved before the Congregation nor in the Kirk Session.' But her 'application to the session did not look like that of a married woman and he never knew a married woman apply in such way.' This looks like a craven kirk session studiously ignoring the misdemeanours of a powerful local family. But subsequently the minister testified that Catharine 'was rebuked in the ordinary way as for fornication'.

The case dragged on. Catharine petitioned for money as she and her son were in desperate 'want of food and raiment'. The commissaries ordered the defenders to pay £10 'to be applied for his Colin Campbells behoof principally for bringing this cause to an end'. The defenders appealed to the Court of Session which instructed that the decreet be reversed, but after an appeal by Catharine's lawyer the child Colin was found entitled to interim aliment of £5 a year since the time of his birth.

More witnesses appeared for both sides. James Drummond alias McGregor in Meikle port, a widower in his eighties, went to Dundurn in about 1791 and asked Duncan for permission 'to get corns grinded at the Mill'. Catharine passed by while the two men were talking and James, who 'had not seen her from the time she went to live there and wishing to give her a taunt and noticing that she was better dressed than before said to her Catharine you look as if you was Gude Wife of the house Upon which Lieutenant Campbell said she was not only Gudewife of the house but of the toun which expression on the part of Mr Campbell the deponent considered as made in joke for he was a very joking man.' Alexander Comrie in Dalginross testified that Katharine 'has behaved soberly and decently ever since his death as well as before it'. The witness had seen her 'wearing black ribbons on her head' and heard her 'lament that Lieutenant Campbells death was the hardest thing she ever met with'.

In the end the commissaries decreed that there was insufficient evidence to establish a marriage.

Duncan had left his options open: he introduced Catharine as his wife to some people and denied a marriage to others. Had he lived beyond the birth of his son he might have wished to legitimate him – but perhaps not. Duncan was Catharine's social superior and her master, whether married or not married, and because he clearly felt more at ease with men of lower rank and was not bothered by an estrangement from his family there was no pressure on him to formalise the relationship. It suited him fine as it was.

CC8/5/24

CHAPTER 9

SUBVERTING THE NATURAL ORDER

FOR a woman to raise a declarator of marriage action against an errant husband seemed entirely reasonable to her contemporaries. For a man to claim as a wife someone who said she had never married him seemed perverse. In the 1824 case of Francis Humbieston Mackenzie against Maria Mackenzie, Maria's lawyer stated:

> For the most part, the pursuer in such cases is a seduced and injured female struggling for a status, which alone can retrieve her character, and restore her to society, and where success is almost indispensable to make even life itself desirable. But, in the present instance, the pursuer ... is not the seduced, but the seducer; and his sole object seems to be, by ruining the peace of mind and the reputation of his victim, to deprive her of the sympathy of her friends, and so to drive her of necessity into the snare which, for his own interested purposes, he has so unfeelingly and dishonourably laid for her.[1]

As noted in Chapter 1, only 46 of the 417 declarator of marriage cases were raised by men, and of the 28 male-initiated cases that reached a conclusion only 8 were successful. Male-initiated cases are, therefore, atypical, but they are also fascinating and informative, for they shed light on expectations of the marital relationship from a very different angle. We begin with some unsuccessful cases in which the men may have genuinely believed themselves to be married, and then move on to those in which fraud or force of some kind was employed. Finally we look at instances where the man successfully proved a marriage.

Convinced She Loved Him

The 1763 case of Archibald Malcolm against Anna Murray foreshadows modern cases of stalkers who convince themselves that the object of their affections returns their regard. Archibald said that he had courted Anna for five years, and 'relinquished all thoughts of looking out for a female partner for life elsewhere', and that he had given her valuable presents. But now she was married to another man.[2]

Anna stated that she had 'for sometime past had the misfortune, to be pestered with the solicitations and importunitys of Archibald Malcolm Surgeon in Dalkeith'. She thought the fact that she had been orphaned very young encouraged him in his 'Wrongheaded Scheme' of importuning her by letters and 'of forcing his company upon her', in the expectation of her running away with him. When word of this reached one of her guardians he 'thought it his duty to expostulate with Mr Malcolm on this frantick Scheme, and threatned him that the proper legal means should be used for his confinement'. Archibald, however, 'wildly avowed' that he was certain Anna 'was so fond of him, that if he Could but obtain an Interview, she would Consent to marry him'. Though her guardian, Mr McDonald, 'well knew the direct contrary to be true ... in order to Cure his diseased imagination the guardian agreed to give him an interview with her at his house, where he should have a fair opportunity of fully knowing her sentiments upon that subject.' So they met at McDonald's, and Anna

in plain and Strong terms expressed her aversion at said Malcolm as well as loudly complained of the bad usage she had met with from him by frequently haunting her Company in the houses of third partys, where she could not presume to be so rude to him, as his conduct deserved. Mr Malcolm however still persisted in his folly, and behaved in the most extravagant manner in so much that Mr McDonald was obliged to turn him down stairs and renew the threatnings he had formerly used to him.

But Archibald's 'wild fancys still continued to work upon his imagination'.

As for presents, 'she remembers to have received in an unsigned anonymous letter, wrote in a disguised hand, a thing of very small value, but as the letter came by post, and she did not know by whom it was wrote, she could not get any opportunity to return it.' At that time Archibald's wife was still alive, so Anna 'had no reason to suspect it came from him, And Could scarce have thought he would have had the impudence now to acknowledge it did'. Some miniature pictures he had sent her were three times returned to him. Anna declared in court that she never promised to marry him or gave him any encouragement.

A more convincing case was that of Patrick Taylor against Agnes Kello in the 1780s.[3] Agnes was the daughter of a miller at Skirling Mill, Peebles-shire, 'who had saved a Sum of Money, considerable for a Person in his Sphere of Life, to which ... his only Daughter, succeeded at his Death'. Patrick's home was near Bathgate, West Lothian. They met at Skirling fair in 1777 when she was 22 and were immediately attracted to one another. After that he visited her several times at her home, and she fell in love with him. Because he came from a different part of the country her relatives knew nothing about him. They subsequently learned that he had become bankrupt in 1773, inherited a landed property, managed again to squander everything so that it had to be sold in 1778, and in 1780 became bankrupt a second time. His version of events was that he was very young and inexperienced when his father died, and 'he became a Prey to designing People', so that he ended up in debt. The property he inherited from his uncle he used to pay off those debts, and he became surety for the debts of his relations, 'by which Means this Succession was exhausted'.

Agnes's relations' picture of Patrick as 'idle and dissipated' appears to be borne out by his own words in court:

> *Declares, That the Declarant has resided for some Years past with his Mother in the Town of Bathgate; That his sole Occupation during that period has been to go in and out to his Cousin James Taylor's Farmer at Boghead, within a Quarter of a Mile of the Town of Bathgate, and there to do any Thing for his own Amusement, or to serve the said James Taylor, as was most agreeable to the Declarant himself.*

According to Patrick, Mrs Kello's opposition to him did not initially reflect his financial circumstances but 'the Influence of her Pastor, a Gentleman who holds the strictest Tenets of any of the dissenting Congregations from the Church of Scotland', who wanted Agnes to marry someone of his own communion. At one point, in March 1780, her mother actually agreed to the marriage, and the banns were proclaimed, but then the impending bankruptcy was discovered, and Agnes was forbidden to have anything more to do with him.

However, a year earlier, in February 1779, Patrick had persuaded Agnes to exchange mutual written declarations of marriage. Agnes threw hers in the fire when her mother discovered it (or, in a different version, her mother threw it in), but Patrick kept his, and after she was proclaimed for marriage with another man in summer 1784 he founded on it for his declarator of marriage action. A few months after granting him the written declaration Agnes had written him a long letter begging him to return it to her; he refused to do so, but then he left her alone for a couple of years and she thought she was safe. Indeed, when Patrick first heard of her being proclaimed with the other man he came to her and wished her happiness, which was certainly one factor that eventually lost him the case. But on 28 March 1785 the commissaries ruled

> *in respect it appears that the Defender, when arrived at an Age when, by the Law of Scotland, she was deemed capable of Consent, voluntarily and deliberately granted to the Pursuer the Declaration libelled on, and received from him a Counter Declaration of the same Import: Find the mutual Obligations relevant to infer Marriage between the Parties*

and declared them married persons.

Apparently this was not a unanimous decision. Two of the judges disagreed, and had all four been present when the judgment was pronounced, Agnes would have been assoilzied, 'the Rule of the Court being, that when the Judges are equally divided, Judgment goes for the Defender.' But it so happened that three only were present, two of whom were against her. An appeal to the Court of Session was unsuccessful, but then the case was appealed to the House of Lords.

The main argument was that nothing in writing could ipso facto make a marriage, and the behaviour of the parties afterwards showed that there had been no serious intention of marriage. Although Patrick had alleged consummation (and even a miscarriage) Agnes denied ever having sex with him. He insisted that he did not visit her for a year and a half only because her mother was so implacably opposed to him, but consoled himself 'with absolute Confidence in her Protestations of Constancy and Affection'. Her agreeing to marry another man he explained by the pressures exerted on her by her family (when that man was told of Patrick's prior claim he 'instantly broke off all Connection' with Agnes.)

However, on 16 February 1787 the House of Lords declared that the letters when exchanged had not been intended by either party to constitute a marriage, in fact it had been agreed between them that 'the purpose they were Calculated to serve proving Unattainable', the letters would be returned. That agreement was 'further proved by the whole and uniform subsequent Conduct of both parties'. The Lords therefore instructed that the commissaries' decision be reversed and Agnes be assoilzied from the conclusion of marriage.

In a 1789 case the woman – Isabella Beveridge – also gave the man – Samuel Colvin in Dumfries-shire – a written declaration of marriage and then changed her mind.[4] On 29 September 1788 she wrote that she bound herself to him: 'that I shall have no other man for my lawful husban but you'. However, on the back of the paper was a written note by her acknowledging that that was the document that 'I tore my name from and desired Mr Smith to take up as I've altered my mind and declines ever having any Conniction with Samuel Colvin'.

Isabella's story was that Samuel courted her secretly and persuaded her to exchange marriage declarations. She told him that she would never consider herself married to him unless a ceremony took place, and he convinced her to go to Dumfries and stay overnight with relations of his. But in the early hours of the morning, 'reflecting seriously on the rash and imprudent step she had made', she panicked, went to her brother-in-law's house and asked him to get her out of it. When she appeared in court she declared that she had never acknowledged Samuel to be her husband and never had carnal knowledge of him. About a year later Samuel suddenly appeared, 'took hold of her and wanted to carry her away by force but the Declarant resisted and cryed out'. Samuel was unable to prove her consent, and Isabella was assoilzied.

In the above cases the men exerted undue influence but at least were acting under the impression that the women loved them and were prepared to marry them. And indeed some women did, albeit briefly; later examples will show that women who changed their minds could not always get out of a marriage. But in the cases below the element of fraud or force was at the very heart of the case.

Force and Fraud

The 1751 case of Thomas Gray, merchant in Edinburgh, against Jacobina Moir (daughter of the deceased James Moir of Earnslaw) is the only one in which an abduction was carried out.[5] An accomplice of Thomas, Christian Duncan, persuaded Jacobina's mother to let Jacobina accompany her in a coach to Leith, though the mother insisted on a maid going along as well.[6] We know nothing of Jacobina's age or the relationship between her and Thomas, but when they stopped at a house in Leith, and Thomas appeared, Jacobina created a fuss and demanded to be taken back to her mother. Christian pretended to agree, but in fact she, Thomas, and another accomplice, James Syme, told the coachman to drive to Musselburgh. When Jacobina protested at the route they were taking, Christian said that 'by Reason of the badness of the direct Road to Cannonmills, the coach had been in danger of Overturning ... and that therefor the Coachman had Chosen to go by the Stage Coach Road to Edinburgh'.

After going along the coast for some time, Jacobina again became uneasy but was told they were going by Jock's Lodge, a good road into Edinburgh. But they continued driving along the sands until Gray and Syme came up on horseback and stopped the coach. They dismounted, 'and both stepped into the Coach, the said Christian Duncan having at their Desire opened the Door thereof'. Thomas then told Jacobina he was resolved to marry her that very night. When the maid started crying Thomas threatened to turn her out of the coach 'and to Carry the said Jacobina Moir on board of a Boat which he said was waiting on him at hand, and putt her in a Ship, and Carry her to some distant Place where she should never see her Mother or any of her Friends again, unless she Complied with his Desire of being instantly Married to him'. He then sent his accomplice Syme to Jock's Lodge to get the minister.

When they returned, the minister told Jacobina to join hands with Thomas, 'and her hand being then lying upon her Lap the said Thomas Gray took hold of it; and while she was pulling and Endeavouring to take her hand from his, and was Grasping her Servant Maid with her other hand, the said Person pretending to be a Minister, Declared them to be Married Persons'. Thomas then ordered the coach to drive to Jock's Lodge. When they reached their destination he called for pen, ink and paper and wrote some lines about their being married persons, and by his threats forced her to sign the paper, which Christian Duncan and James Syme signed as witnesses.

They then grabbed hold of her 'and Endeavoured to throw her upon the Bed that was in the Room, there to have Consummated his pretended marriage'. Christian tried

> to pull the Curtains of the Bed about the said Thomas Gray and Jacobina Moir, when he was strugling to throw her into the Bed; and the said James Syme first sollic- iting, and thereafter attempting by Violence to Compell the Servant Maid to quitt the Room: But the said Jacobina Moir having Resisted this wicked attempt and preserved herself from falling upon the Bed, by keeping hold of the Curtain thereof, and Calling out for aid, the said Thomas Gray at length yielded to return into the Coach with the said Jacobina Moir, and the rest of the Company.

And then he drove her back to her mother's!

Next day her family complained to the sheriff substitute, and Thomas and his accomplices were arrested and tried by the High Court of Justiciary. On 24 July 1751 Thomas Gray, Christian Duncan, and 'Thomas Brown alias William Jamieson'[7] were sentenced to transportation to His Majesty's planta- tions in America for 14 years (Syme was fined 500 merks). Amazingly, because the High Court of Justiciary could not pronounce on the validity of a marriage, and evidence from one court was not supposed to be used in another, the commissaries allowed the imprisoned Thomas to proceed with proof. Jacobina's lawyer appealed: Thomas had been found guilty of force and compulsion, which was 'inconsistent with his present allegation that the defender was freely and voluntarily marryed to him'. Thomas did not succeed in proving a valid marriage.

In the 1755 case of John Cameron, son of Alexander Cameron of Kinnaird, the defender, Miss James Malcolm, was only twelve years old, the legal age of consent in Scotland.[8] (Although most girls named after a father of this name were called 'Jacobina', her mother insisted that her daughter was called James or Jamie, not Jacobina.) We do not know John's age, but witnesses testified that James and John were very fond of one another. A servant 'used to observe them sitting at Table next to one another and likewise observed them with their Hands joined and used to see them follow one another and go out and walk together by themselves'. But, because of her age, no one thought of it as courtship. (One witness declared that John's father offered her £100 sterling if she would swear that she knew a marriage had been agreed between the couple, but she refused the bribe.) On the day of the marriage James's mother said that when her daughter told her 'she was willing to unite to Mr Jack when he pleased,' she asked her 'if she knew what the meaning of unite

187

was and explained to her the nature of marriage,' after which James was not so keen.

James's mother eventually agreed to a marriage on the understanding that John would not bed her daughter after the ceremony but would go abroad for three years. (Mrs Malcolm told Robert Thomson, town clerk of Dysart, that John or his father was worth £500 a year, and that 'a fortune of Five Hundred pounds a year was not every day to be Catch'd.') A ceremony was carried out by a minister, who declared in court that both parents said they consented to the marriage, and that John and James audibly repeated the words he pronounced. James also signed the certificate. After that her mother found John's relatives trying to take her daughter's clothes off so that he could bed her. A furious Mrs Malcolm tore her daughter away from them and after a great row managed to extricate herself and daughter from the house.

James Malcolm was over the legal age of consent, and the commissaries found a marriage proven. On appeal, however, the Court of Session overturned this. Commenting on this case some 75 years later, James Fergusson was surprised that John had not appealed against the decision. 'His acquiescence in a decision so adverse … affords a strong presumption that the legal opinions of the Scottish bar were in favour of the judgment.' In spite of her signature on the marriage certificate, 'the extreme youth of the female party, and the surprise and precipitation employed, gave an unfavourable character to the whole transaction'.[9] (Another case involving a 12 year-old girl forms Case Study 18.)

Shades of grey appear in the case of another young girl, Isobell Steel, aged 15 when she took part in a marriage ceremony with John Meggett, shoemaker burgess of Edinburgh, in 1757.[10] She kept changing her mind and then panicked at the idea of sex. Isobell's mother's servant, Jean Kay, a reluctant witness to the ceremony, testified that when they reached the house where she was to be married Isobell told Jean that she wanted to return home, but when Jean wanted to tell John this Isobell 'stopped her, and said, No I will rather do it, rather be married, since its come this Length, But I will ask him not to Bed with me for two nights.' She then went through the ceremony in the usual way but the next day she insisted that she was not married.

A witness at the house where they went to celebrate after the ceremony declared that Isobell 'having said That she wished to be in her Bed, one of Mr Burns sons said That the Kay behoved to be milked first For that it was the Custom to milk the Kay before a young Good wife was put to Bed' – whereupon Isobell leapt up and ran downstairs calling for her maid, Jean. Presumably it was the mention of bedding that prompted this, as she expressed alarm that 'They thought her married, But that it was not so, For that it was all a joke and a mock marriage.' When John came into the room he asked her 'why she behaved so foolishly when she had come away with her own free will, and had also married him Willingly; to which she still answered That it was a mock marriage and that he had forced her and ruined her.'

Rebecca Meggett, John's sister, testified that when the minister arrived Isobell started hesitating and Rebecca told her they could either call him in or send him away and asked Isobell 'to give a direct and positive answer', which she failed to do. Rebecca told her it would be acceptable to send him away, for she 'would never be witness to a forced Marriage'. Isobell asked to speak to Jean Kay (the maid) and after doing so said that she would go through with the marriage if she did not have to go to bed with John for two nights; John agreed to this. When Rebecca testified she complained of Isobell's 'Fecklings, and said there was no possibility of keeping her one hour in one mind'.

The landlady then 'brought in a man with a White Ragged Big coat', who introduced himself as David Paterson who 'had married some of the Best in the Kingdom'. It seems to have been his appearance that put Isobell off as much as anything else, for she told Rebecca that night that 'she was afraid he was not a right minister who had married them'. And the next day, when asked by her mother and uncle if she was married, she declared that she was not. John's mother said, 'Did you say so before the minister', and she replied, 'he a minister! What the Devil made him a Minister; he had not a shirt on his Back.'

John's age is not known, so while the first impression is that he preyed upon an immature, feckless girl, it may have been a good match of (barely adult) equals. As consummation was not necessary to constitute a marriage, John's case was strong. However, it was abandoned. Either Isobell was reconciled to the marriage, or else everyone agreed to pretend it had never happened. That was not a legally recognised remedy, but (especially if money changed hands) it was a pragmatic one.

Another category of cases is that of 'He got her drunk' (Chapter 3 has already looked at the converse situation of 'He was too drunk to be wed').

In the 1801 case raised by Alexander Colston, brickmaker at Rosebank, Portobello, the woman, Margaret Meldrum, claimed to have been 'rendered totally stupid and insensible and rendered incapable of entering into any Contract of Marriage or giving Consent'.[11] Alexander responded that after the ceremony of marriage, conducted by a minister called Gordon, she went with him to his father's house where they spent two nights together, breakfasted and dined in the presence of witnesses, and then unaccountably she left him: 'All this could not be done in the Stupid and intoxicated state the Defender pretends to have been in.'

Ah, but it could. The crucial witness was Margaret's servant maid, Mary Bowie. On the morning of the ceremony Alexander sent Mary out 'for half a mutchkin of brandy'. Margaret 'appeared averse to drinking spirits but was prevailed on by the pursuer to do so who told her that if she took sugar with them, they would not hurt her'. By three in the afternoon Margaret was 'very drunk having fallen on the Carpet upon her coming in, and dropt her Gloves and a Shoe upon the stair, which the deponent picked up'. She 'was so drunk that she did not know the deponent upon coming in to the house, but asked her who she was, and what she did there'. Mary undressed her and put her to bed. Soon after that Alexander turned up and went up to Margaret's bedroom and ordered Mary 'to bring in liquor repeatedly both ale and Spirits'. Mary could not 'exactly say what quantity of liquor she brought in, but she was three or four times out for it, and brought in half a mutchkin of spirits at a time'. Alexander suggested marrying Margaret, 'who seemed like a daft body, sometimes laughing and sometimes crying'.

At that point Alexander asked Mary to bring in the neighbours and then asked a friend, Alexander Monro, to get a minister. Monro objected but Alexander insisted, 'and said a half merk minister would do'. After the ceremony Mary was sent out for more drink and said that Margaret 'appeared still insensible from drink'. The party then got into a coach and stopped at a public house, 'where more drink was called for and drunk'. From there they walked to Alexander's father's house. Margaret's clothes 'were hanging loose about her, and the witness was holding them up behind, and her hair was loose and hanging over her shoulders'. When they reached the house 'part of the Spirits purchased on the road was drunk there'. When she was put to bed Mary 'undressed her, she being unable to undress herself'.

Next morning Mary saw Margaret in bed with Alexander, 'and she had the appearance of a person not herself'. Mary saw spirits there and was told that they had partaken of some gin and sugar. She helped her mistress dress, for 'she was then unable to put on her Cloaths without assistance'. When they dined Margaret 'got more liquor, and after dinner appeared more intoxicated than she had been before'. It was only the next morning that she 'appeared more herself'. She took hold of Mary 'and cried to her, said She could never appear in Edinburgh again, and that she would drown herself'. The next day with Alexander she 'was much out of temper, threw every thing at him that was within her reach, and when she could get nothing else, she took off her shoes and threw them at him, and upon the whole used him very ill'.

The testimony established a lack of sober consent to a marriage, so Alexander conceded, and the case was dismissed.

In the 1820 case of Walter Johnstone against Mary Brown the defence of drunkenness seems less plausible, and a contrivance to evade a marriage to someone of a lower social rank (as in Case Study 17).[12] Mary Brown was over 50 and lived with her prosperous nephew, James Brown Esquire of Netherwood. Walter Johnstone, aged 22, was their gardener. One evening they went to Dumfries, about two miles away, where they called at the house of one of the town's magistrates and, in the presence of another magistrate, the procurator fiscal of the Justice of Peace court fined the couple for an irregular marriage. After that they went to Ecclefechan and found a minister to rebuke them. According to her defence, she had been drunk and insensible during all that, and after recovering her senses she escaped from him. Walter's witnesses included the magistrates, who testified in detail to the events on the night in question, and had seen no signs of drunkenness in Mary. This undermined her story that she was often so drunk as to be 'not only incapable of judging or acting with propriety in her own concerns and is consequently liable to be imposed upon by designing people but continued in a state of stupid incapacity for a considerable period after the immediate effects of the liquor may be presumed to be gone off'. However, the Defence produced plenty of witnesses (resulting in 179 pages of proof) on this point.

Mary's alcoholism became publicly known in 1815. She would behave irrationally and violently, sometimes claiming to see witches and apparitions, though she could still walk and talk. William McDowall, surgeon in Kirkcudbright, often saw her drunk and thought that the alcohol 'brought on a kind of derangement'. But even when 'she was very much Intoxicated she had a steady step'. William Maxwell, a Dumfries surgeon, testified that she consulted him once 'about herself and gave as a Cause for drinking Spirits that she was often not herself and that to relieve her she first took one Glass of Spirits and then another and another as long as the fit lasted'. She also told him that 'two days before her being in this State she described of not being quite herself she felt a straitness about her stomach and a pain in her heart which continued till her mind became confused and she then had recourse to spirits to relieve her uneasy sensations and that after leaving off the spirits she felt low and sick and languid for a few days till it wore off.'

Servants also testified to Mary's state. Elizabeth Paterson said that she had 'almost never seen a fit of intoxication continued for so short a period as one day – that she has commonly seen a fit continue for several days and on some occasions for weeks together'. Servants also testified that Mary 'was easily imposed upon both when she was drunk and when she was coming out of it', though she 'could both walk steadily and speak very plain even altho very drunk'. On the night she went off to be married Mary had been drunk for the ten preceding days, and on that day she 'drunk fully more than a Choppin of Whiskey'. (The servant who testified to this said the reason she gave Mary spirits 'was that she was so violent and raging that she was afraid she would have forced her to have given her it and that it was the Custom for the people about her to give her spirits on occasions when she was violent and raging'.)

Later Walter came to Netherwood and said to Mary, 'Now are you coming with me'. Mary refused and said 'ye ken very well Walter if I had not been in the Situation I was in I would never have gone with you'. Walter said, 'but ye cannot deny that you are my wife,' to which Mary replied, 'No I am none of your wife.' She then 'spat upon the ground with a kind of disdain and turned her back'. (Two earlier witnesses had seen Mary 'light a pipe and smoke it'.)

It was, therefore, entirely credible that such a woman could have appeared before magistrates and minister not visibly affected by alcohol, yet too drunk or disordered to render true consent. The commissaries accepted the defence, and Walter's attempt to secure himself a wife with rank and money failed.

Successful Cases

While the mere existence of male pursuers was considered subversive, the above picture of villains and rogues does to some extent conform to stereotype, as the woman was still the victim. Cases in which a woman denied a marriage which the court found valid appear to fall into a different category. However, a woman could be pressured by others beside a spouse.

William Smith, journeyman tailor in Leith, raised his 1751 action not only against Jean Nicol, but also against her parents.[13] They had 'secreted' her, he said, and denied him access to her. Their story that she had been regularly married to William Hunter, wright in Edinburgh, was a 'feint' to discourage his action. If it was true that she had gone to bed with another man after her marriage to William Smith that would be a great crime and he might sue for a divorce – but it would still be necessary for him first to establish the marriage.

And indeed a ceremony had taken place. The defence was that during this ceremony her hand had been forcibly held in his, 'and while this Farce was Carrying on she cried out and Wept bitterly and never gave any consent by Speaking or otherways but on the Contrary showd her dissaffection'. They also produced a document by Patrick Douglas stating that he had never married them – which was pointless as the minister who had done so was *Andrew* Douglas.

William produced witnesses to the marriage ceremony and Jean's willing part in it. More tellingly, they also testified to the plans for the marriage ceremony. More than a month before it was carried out Andrew Bowman was with them when they discussed getting married. William wanted to delay it until he was able to provide himself with a house, and wanted to tell her father, but Jean 'declared against this saying that her Father wanted to have her Married to a Wright Lad, but that she was resolved not to Marry him'. And Bowman's wife testified that Jean wanted to have the marriage 'done speedily, and gave for a reason that her Father wanted to have her Married to a Wright Lad whom she was determined not to Marry'. The defenders failed to bring any proof of their allegations, and the marriage was declared valid. The opposition of Jean's parents had no standing in Scottish marriage law; her own willing consent was all that mattered.

In 1769 Isobel Crawford was a widow who had borne three children (all dead), and the man she loved, Adam Morison, was a merchant and baillie in Dunfermline. Parental opposition drove her to marry in secret and deny it afterwards, so Adam raised a declarator of marriage action.[14] Adam's chief witnesses were Robert Scotland and his wife, who had seen the couple declare themselves married persons. They had married privately even before that date, but Isobel (known as 'Tibby') told Scotland that she 'wanted to have the Baillie thoroughly fixed in a Marriage as not being satisfied with what had past between themselves'. She told Scotland that she

wanted to put the thing beyond recall, as her mother and other relations were resolved to carry her off to Glasgow and put her under the care of her Uncle Baillie Spiers, And that if once she was there, she was sure she would be put under such closs confinement, that the Baillie ... could have no access to her.

That night they both came to Scotland's shop, stood up in front of the Scotlands and each solemnly declared that they took each other as their 'true and lawfull' spouse. They invited the Scotlands round to see them bedded the next night, when they repeated the same declarations. And finally they went to a magistrate and got themselves fined for an irregular marriage. Yet they still wanted to keep the marriage secret.

Isobell's line afterwards was that what happened at the Scotlands was a 'joke', a 'mock marriage', and that on the night of the alleged bedding she was thrown into the bed by Mrs Scotland. And she was not a party, she said, to Adam's going to the magistrate to be fined. She had some awkward questions to answer in court because she had written him several letters, which he produced in evidence. For example, since this 'mock marriage' was on 12 January, why was she writing before that date, begging Adam to conceal their marriage? She could only reply that he had 'put about a story of her marriage with him'. And how could she explain signing another letter written before that date 'My dearest, Yours till death; Isobel Morison'. All she could say was that he often asked her to 'to take his name, and subscribe so in a frolic or joke'. And she insisted that she often used the expression 'Yours till death' to conclude letters to various friends, though when asked to name some 'to whom she wrote in that manner', she was unable to do so.

One interesting aspect is the reaction of the residents of Dunfermline. James Alexander, a lawyer, when asked if the couple were reputed to be married persons in Dunfermline, replied that 'the people in the town of Dunfermline talked differently of the supposed marriage ... some saying, it was a good or binding marriage; and others, that it was a farce, and not binding.' And Andrew Bowie, a weaver, had heard the story of what happened from Scotland who did not refer to it as a joke, though he regretted his part in it. Bowie likewise said that public opinion in Dunfermline was divided, some believing it was a real marriage and some disagreeing, particularly because by this time Tibby was denying that she was married.

She was heavily influenced by her mother and her mother's business partner, John Eckford (who, in turn, was clearly under the thumb of Mrs Crawford). One reason for their opposition was that Tibby had been widowed only a year and all three of her children died soon after the death of her husband. John Eckford testified to seeing Tibby in company one night drinking and singing, which he thought 'indecent' after her recent losses (he threatened to inform her mother!). Before the marriage ceremony, when word of courtship had already got out (and the couple had in fact privately declared themselves married) Eckford hid himself in Tibby's house (at the behest, naturally, of her mother) and confronted Adam when he caught him in the bedroom. 'High words' passed between them, said Eckford, 'which were occasioned by this deponent's quarrelling the pursuer for coming so much about the defender's house, considering the late distresses in her family, and that she had been so short while a widow'.

When the case was being heard Eckford put pressure on Katharine Innes, a servant maid called as a witness, whom he feared would assist Adam's side. And indeed Katharine testified that a couple of nights after she saw the bedclothes rumpled and concluded that the couple had gone to bed, her mistress told her 'she was sorry for what she had done upon seeing her Mamma in such an anger about it.' Katharine 'then asked what it was she had done, to which the defender answered she was married'.

The root of Tibby's fears was that her first marriage had also been without her family's consent, and after all the anger and grief, she could not face it a second time. (According to John Eckford 'she married her first husband, Mr Veatch, upon a fortnight's acquaintance, having fallen out with her aunt, with whom she was then staying at Edinburgh, and left her house.') After the legal action commenced and she became the talk of the town, Tibby left Dunfermline to stay with an aunt in Peebles. Even this aunt advised her to cohabit with Adam 'in case the law made it a marriage, and her friends were pleased', but by this time she had convinced herself that 'she would never live with him, and that she never looked upon it as a marriage, but only as a joke'. The defence also claimed that Adam's motives were mercenary, for he had 'laid hold of her jointure by arrestment' and 'not allowed her to touch one sixpence'. But the evidence of a real marriage was overwhelming.[15]

Family opposition also arose in the 1778 case of David McKie, teacher of English and writing at Maybole, Ayrshire, against Margaret (Peggy) Ferguson.[16] David alleged that after the banns had been proclaimed they were publicly bedded and, in the presence of witnesses, declared themselves married persons. Peggy said that she did not consider this to be a marriage. She was born in 1760 and orphaned in January 1777, her parents dying within days of each other. She was 'possessed of a considerable fortune' (£500–600), and was a pupil at David's school ('to learn Writing'). Her curators alleged that David had taken advantage of her innocence, while David's side said that her relatives 'wished to keep her unmarried, and that if she were either dead or in Bedlam, that so they might share her fortune'.

David said that he was 'son of honest respectable Parents, His Father till within these few years being a weaver in Maybole, but who of late indeed followed the business of a Carrier between Maybole and Ayr, a Sedentary Life not agreeing with him'. And Peggy was 'the Daughter of a Common Country Farmer of the meanest Rank who by great penury scrap'd together a little money'. David said he probably would not have even thought of marrying Peggy if he had not received encouragement from her parents. He was 'not a Gay young man of an Enterprizing spirit in love affairs but on the Contrary a sober plain young man no ways calculated for these matters, and at same time of a person more Genteel than Common'. He was 22, while she was 'a Clever sensible Girl of Seventeen so that there is no disproportion in point of age'.

David claimed that it was Peggy who proposed going to bed, because 'this was the Day fix'd for her Mariage and that a mariage might be made without a minister at all by going to Bed and acknowledging each other as Husband and Wife and her Friends would not then have an opportunity of again inter-fering.' And whereas she had claimed that they spent only ten minutes alone in bed, he insisted that it was over an hour and that the marriage was at that time being consummated. (Witnesses disagreed about whether he had told them that he had had carnal knowledge of her or not. Neither in this case or any other was it suggested that a physical examination could settle the question of virginity.)

His witnesses were convincing. Mrs Blair said that when David pressed Peggy to tell him when she would marry him because her friends were bothering him she said that 'she did not Value her friends as they did not Value her, but her Money'. She would not give him a positive answer that night, but when he said 'that he did not chuse to linger any longer in a Vain Courtship, but held out his hand and expressed his willingness to bid her farewell and wish her well … the Tear rushed into the defenders Eye and she seemed very unwilling to give him up as a lover and said at same time to the pursuer that her love was as strong to him as ever'. Others heard Peggy say that 'her friends kept her from him', and were against her marrying him 'because they wanted a person in a higher station for her husband'. Witnesses also testified that 'Marriage Gloves' had been provided to be distributed to friends after the ceremony.

A key witness was James Wright, the minister at Maybole. He testified that Peggy came to him saying that some of David's relations thought 'that a piece of money should be taken in order to their being freed of one another but that she was uncertain whether that might be done'. The minister told her 'that he was not so much Master of the Circumstances that happened at Irving as to Judge whether there was a Marriage or not but that if there was a Marriage no bargain that they could make would have the effect to Annull it'. He thought well of David, 'a Sober Lad and Capable of discharging the office of an English teacher'. David had consulted him prior to having the banns proclaimed, because her relations were trying to thwart the marriage. The minister hesitated because Peggy was 'under Tutory' and advised him to get her relatives' consent because they might otherwise make trouble, and the minister understood that Peggy's fortune was entirely in her guardian's power. David replied 'that he was the less concerned about the Fortune if he got the Woman'.

The minister had also advised Peggy not to marry David without the consent of her guardian, 'In whose power he Understood her whole fortune was And by offending whom she would be reduced to beggary'. When the couple appeared before the kirk session David affirmed a marriage while Peggy denied it, and continued to do so. One witness asked her what she would do 'In case a process should be Commenced before a Civil Court and the Court should find what happened at Irving to be a Sufficient Marriage'. She answered that 'she would spend the last farthing of her fortune in defence of it and then beg her bread rather as live with him'. The witness then asked her 'what that would Mend her, and that if she would not do better to live with him to which she Answered that she could not live with him'. He 'said to her that she had certainly a liking to him for she had Allowed herself to be proclaimed and asked her what was now become of that liking … to which she answered that it had gone away'.

But – like it or not – the commissaries found them to be married persons.

In another 1778 case, that of James Steedman, wright and druggist in Perth, against Margaret Miller, it is not clear if the bride's change of mind was really due to influence by her relations, or because she discovered that she had been duped.[17] Margaret was also an orphan, aged sixteen, who lived in Kinross. When she was first introduced to James Steedman in Edinburgh he

> appeared in a silver or Gold trim'd waist coat with other pieces of high dress and gave out that he was a Gentleman of considerable fortune: some thing of this kind was necessary because the Pursuers personal shapes were rather against him, being of the oblique.

He proposed marriage to her, showed her around the city, and entertained her lavishly, and then, in the evening, took her to the house of Joseph Robertson, the minister encountered in Chapter 2 and elsewhere. Her story was that she 'was so struck with this unexpected event that she really lost the power of reflection and whether she went thro' the ceremony of marriage or not she does not absolutely recollect'. But when she returned home to Kinross she learned that far from being a 'man of fortune' James was in fact bankrupt, 'and this pretended marriage was no sooner noised abroad which the Pursuer did purposely to revive and Establish his Credit, than his Creditors arrested every shilling belonging to the Defender so that she at present is obliged to subsist upon the generosity of her friends'.

Joseph Robertson appeared as a witness. Naturally he had demanded a certificate of the couple's having been proclaimed, but before marrying them he noticed that 'the bridegroom was in appearance greatly older than the bride who seemed to be a Girl from Eighteen to twenty one and was very handsome.' (He 'entertained a Suspicion that she might perhaps have been got with Child' by him'.) There were also witnesses to a serious bedding ceremony. The commissaries found the marriage proven, so financially James got what he was after, but in the meantime Margaret had borne a child to a sergeant in the Edinburgh regiment.[18]

Joseph Robertson also celebrated the marriage between Thomas Gray, brother of David Gray of Broadwell, Perthshire, and Margaret Anderson in Auchtermuchty, in 1794.[19] After the marriage ceremony Thomas used to stay with her once a week, and she even bore his child, but in 1796 she denied any marriage and refused to live with him. Margaret claimed that he fooled her into crossing the Forth to Edinburgh where he asked her to marry him, but she refused, and he took her home. Nor did he ever visit her at Auchtermuchty, a mere three miles from Broadwell. She was once persuaded to spend the night at Broadwell and awoke in the morning to find Thomas in bed with her. She could 'not say' whether he had carnal knowledge of her on that occasion, but she ascribed her pregnancy to it! However, it never happened before or since.

Again, Joseph Robertson testified to marrying the couple. Margaret was unable to back up her story, and the marriage was found proven. A woman had no more right to change her mind after marrying than a man did. Although very young, Margaret appears to have acted entirely on her own volition, both in marrying Thomas and then in denying the marriage.

Another woman who changed her mind was Jean Dobie, mantua maker in Lockerbie, who denied being married to William Thane, baker, in 1812.[20] The couple had been fined for an irregular marriage by a baillie in Lochmaben, though Jean denied even being in Lochmaben on that day, and alleged that her signature on the document was a forgery. According to William, he had spent all his money improving Jean's 'subjects' (house), after which her mother, 'seeing that she had obtained her object of getting the subjects improved and put in sufficient repair and thinking that the money which the Pursuer had brought home with him from abroad having been for several years steward on board a man of war, was nearly exhausted' persuaded her daughter to disown him. The case dragged on for about four years, but William's witnesses bore out his story, while Jean could not prove hers, so they were declared to be married persons.

What conclusions can be drawn from cases in which men tried to claim unwilling women as their wives? There were instances of fraud – but only when detected can we be sure it was practised. There were shades of grey between consenting, then regretting, being swayed by family, and being deceived. At the very least, many of these women could be described as vulnerable, and the number who were orphans, or had at least lost a father, is striking.

Notes

1 CC8/6/162. Francis claimed an actual marriage ceremony but refused to divulge the name of the minister and founded on letters Maria had written to him and on witnesses' evidence of having been told by her that they were married. Francis acted dishonourably in holding on to the crucial letters after promising to give them all up, but Maria lied in denying sexual intercourse, as she had written in a letter that she was 'not in the family way'. The marriage was declared legally valid, though the case was not concluded until February 1829.
2 CC8/6/24. Her husband was Charles Spalding, a merchant in the Canongate.
3 This case was later cited as a precedent, and eventually the papers were borrowed never to be returned, for they do not appear to have survived amongst the Commissary Court records. Fortunately, on appeal to the House of Lords the key papers were printed and survive in Session Papers, Signet Library, F 29; 1 (1787).
4 CC8/6/52.
5 CC8/6/19.
6 Christian's 'false pretence' was that 'she had purchased a Parcell of Tea, and some pieces of Silks, or other prohibited or uncustomed Goods, which were lying at Leith, and that she intended to go in a coach to carry these Goods to Edinburgh, in order thereby to cover them from being Challenged and seized by the officers of the Revenue at the Port of Edinburgh, but that she was afraid of being suspected and challenged if she came up in the Coach alone, and therefor desired the said Margaret Smith, to allow her said Daughter to go with her (the said Christian Duncan) in the Coach to Leith and come up with her to Edinburgh with the run Goods.' In other words, Jacobina's mother was persuaded to allow her daughter to join a smuggling operation!
7 The name 'William Jamieson' occurs frequently as a celebrator of irregular marriages in the 1740s. See Rosalind Mitchison and Leah Leneman, *Girls in Trouble – Sexuality and Social Control in Rural Scotland 1660–1780* (Edinburgh, 1998), c.4.
8 CC8/6/20.
9 James Fergusson, *Treatise on the Present State of Consistorial Law in Scotland* (Edinburgh, 1829), 158–60.
10 CC8/6/21.
11 CC8/6/72.
12 CC8/6/123 and 135. The first case, raised in December 1818, was a declarator of freedom on her behalf. He raised a counter-process of declarator of marriage in June 1820. The final decreet was not issued until April 1823.

13 CC8/5/9.
14 CC8/6/28. All that has survived in this box is pursuer's proof (124 pages), but the defender's side was printed and can be found in Session Papers, Signet Library, 164; 14 (1770).
15 The commissaries' decreet has not survived, but her appeal to the Court of Session shows that the decision was in his favour, and there is nothing to indicate that the Court of Session reversed that decision.
16 CC8/6/38.
17 CC8/6/37.
18 James Steedman said he would divorce Margaret, but no such action has been found in the records.
19 CC8/6/62.
20 CC8/5/35.

CASE STUDY 17

FORBES V. COCHRANE: MISALLIANCE

S USAN Cochrane, Countess Dowager of Strathmore and daughter of the
4th Earl of Dundonald, must have led a lonely life. In 1728 her husband,
Charles 6th Earl of Strathmore and Kinghorne and 14th Lord Glamis, was
accidentally stabbed and died.[1] Not until 1745 did she remarry, and very
secretly, to her factor, George Forbes.

They married in April 'in her own bedroom in her dwelling house of
Castle Lyon by a person of her own procureing for that purpose who she
Called a Clergyman', and they shared a marital bed, though only her closest
companions were let into the secret. In October she discovered herself
pregnant. George had by then joined the Jacobite Army, but Susan was able to
pull some strings 'tho' not without some Difficulty' to get him out of it. He
returned to Castle Lyon and the two of them, along with her companion
Emelia Murray, embarked for Holland. They stayed mainly at Rotterdam, and
in May 1746 their daughter was born there and was given to a wetnurse. In
July Susan went back to Scotland, but it was not safe for a Jacobite supporter
to do so. It was agreed that George 'should in the Interim go to Dunkirk, and
live there as a Trader or Merchant, untill he should be at liberty to return to
this Kingdom, and she in the mean while have opportunity to Try how her
friends in Scotland could brook the Declaration of her marriage.' She
obtained credit for him at Dunkirk for £1,000 Sterling. Emelia Murray was
left behind to look after the child.

George was in Dunkirk, trading in tobacco and wine, when, in July 1747,
he received an urgent summons to Rotterdam. Hoping to see Susan he rushed
up there, only to find instead Mr Charles Crookshanks, a Perthshire
clergyman. Crookshanks offered George money to marry Emelia Murray, but
he came as a dupe, not the bearer of bribes. An appalled George told the
minister that he was already married to Susan and begged him to talk to
Emelia. After doing so Crookshanks visited the child and then told George
'that he would press his proposall no Farther'. George now had a good idea of
the reaction to his marriage; then his credit at Dunkirk was withdrawn. In
February 1749 George raised a declarator of marriage action.

Both the marriage and George's insistence on it shocked society. George,
said his lawyer, 'will at all times readily confess that the Countess Dowager of
Strathmore did him too much honour in chusing or accepting him for a
Husband, and shall admit ... that it was an unsuitable and very unequal match
apt to give offence to her noble Relations and to make herself incur Censure

in the world as for any act of high Imprudence, and by no means disposing of herself to such advantage as a Lady of her Quality and fortune and personal merit might have done upon her being minded to change her Condition'. On the other hand, she was 'not the first woman of Quality and fortune and merit who has condescended to take for her second Husband a person greatly her Inferior in point of Rank and Condition, But of whom in other Respects she must have conceived a good opinion whether justly or not'.

There had been many cases, argued the pursuer, of women resorting to this court after being abandoned and denied by the men who had fathered their children under promise of marriage, but none before 'where a Child was born by a Lady of Character, and that Child still living that the father was brought under the necessity of proving his marriage and the Childs Legitimacy and that a Defence was offered on behalf of the Lady tending to render herself infamous.' He did not, therefore, believe that she herself authorised the defence – but she had little choice if her powerful relatives preferred the scandal of a bastard child to that of such an unequal marriage.

Her lawyer said: 'As this Lady both by Birth and Marriage Is of the first Rank, and stands nearly Related to all the best Familys in Scotland, It is with the Deepest Concern she is brought under the Cruel Necessity of pleading her Defences in a Declarator of Marriage at the Instance of this pursuer lately her Menial Servant, whose highest ambition was for some time a Livery Coat, so that Abstracting from the Indignity which by this process Is offered to her personally, It is an Insult to her whole sex of any Rank and Condition.' George retorted that he was not quite so menial, or of 'such Low and Contemptible Character as the Defenders Councill Endeavours to paint him'. His father had been a merchant of good repute in Aberdeenshire, but having fought on the Jacobite side in the 1715 rebellion 'he was reduced in his Circumstances' and thereafter served as factor to the Dowager Duchess of Perth. George himself had 'been conversant in very good company (both at home and abroad) in point of Rank manners or Education'. And he had been employed as Master of Horse to 'the Pretenders son' during the late rebellion. ('It is well known', sneered the Defence, 'that the Highland Army was an Assylum for persons of all Ranks without distinction where a reasonable degree of Assurance was Likely to Obtain preferment.')

But all this was irrelevant, argued George's lawyer, 'for if he were the son of the meanest Tradesman or ploughman the Laws of this Kingdom do not render him incapable to become the husband of a Countess, and if it be true that he is … it is neither presumptuous nor daring and Insolent for him to seek the benefit of those Laws against a Defender of superiour quality to his own … for God be praised the Law has no Respect of persons, and that time is happyly over in which the High quality or great kindred of a Defender might have rendered it a Dangerous or hopeless attempt for a poor man to seek justice against him or her.' He also pointed out that no mention had been made by the Defence of the child, who would be declared illegitimate if he did not win his case.

At the time of the marriage, he said, Emelia Murray was living with the defender as her companion, as was Susan Fotheringham, whom he would be able to call as witnesses. But when the time came he found this was not so easily accomplished. Susan Fotheringham had 'been by influence on the Defender's Part induced to go furth of the Kingdom, on pretence of being a Companion to some travelling Lady'. Emelia Murray also disappeared the moment she was summoned. However, Charles Crookshanks testified to having seen her 'at Newcastle, where she passed by the name of Mrs Glass, and upon his asking her what brought her there, she answered that she did not incline to appear as a Witnes in this Cause'. It was apparent, argued George, that she had 'been influenced and induced to fly furth of your Lordships Jurisdiction, and to secret and Conceal herself furth of the Kingdom, to dissappoint me of her Evidence.' The commissaries granted commission to examine her in Newcastle if she could be found. In the meantime a number of witnesses were examined in Rotterdam.

In November 1753 it was revealed that the Countess Dowager was living in Paris and 'for a considerable time past has been altogether dissordered in her Mind'. In June 1754 she died, but this was not the end of the case, for her defence was taken over by the Duke of Hamilton and Brandon, Lady Catherine Cochrane and her spouse, Alexander Earl of Galloway. But in July 1756 the commissaries decreed that a legal marriage had existed and that Susan Janet Emilia Forbes was their lawful daughter.

Note

1   *Scots Peerage.*

CC8/6/21

CASE STUDY 18

ALLAN V. YOUNG: THE CHILD BRIDE

ANNA Young was a pupil at William Allan's school in Edinburgh. In 1772, the day after she turned twelve (the legal age of consent for marriage), William persuaded a session clerk to grant him a certificate of the proclamation of banns, on the strength of which a minister married the couple. Anna's mother took her daughter away before the marriage could be consummated, and her legal guardian then removed her from Edinburgh, whereupon William raised a declarator of marriage action.

Anna's mother had not been married to her father, John Young of Newhall (a lawyer), and Anna may have been sensitive on this issue, for she told a servant in the household that 'she thought it more honourable to go by the Name of Anna Allan than to be thought a Bastard'. When Young died he left his daughter a fortune of £2,500. Her mother remarried, and her stepfather, Mr Robertson, was also a defender in the case. But the key figure was Robert Irvine, Writer to the Signet, who acted as Anna's guardian and was a financial trustee of Mr Young's estate.

William had kept a school for five years, teaching arithmetic, bookkeeping, Latin, English and French. Anna was a pupil for two years, from the time she was ten. The Defence argued that if Anna had understood what marriage meant she would not have chosen William, who was 'remarkably ugly, and Deformed and an object of disgust rather than of Love and affection'. But William must have had charisma, and Anna's mother was by no means averse to the match, apart from her daughter's age. William produced letters from Anna, like the following: 'the only answer I can give you is this if the Lord spare me till I be Twelve years of age Nothing would give me more pleasure than to be your own wife.'

The Defence alleged that William 'tempted by her ample Fortune began to pay particular attention to her and endeavoured to gain her Childish affections by giving her money Sugar Plumbs [sic] Oranges and by continually praising her performances and using every art which a designing man could use to deceive a simple Girl'. When Anna appeared in court she declared that William gave her money and sweetmeats and showed her jewels, 'telling her at the same time that all these should be hers providing she would consent to marry him'. He also 'told her that his whole house should be at her will and that she should have a Coach to carry her out every morning'. Margaret Elder, her family's servant, testified that Anna had shown her a five and three penny piece (a quarter of a guinea) given her by William, which she said she meant 'to keep as a token' and asked Margaret to hide it in case her stepfather saw it. However, she later took it back and 'changed it and bought therewith Robinson Crusoe and some other things'. Margaret was asked if she knew that Anna 'had no Symptoms of womanhood about her' and answered that she changed Anna's bed and saw to her linens 'but never discovered any symptoms of Womanhood about her' (ie she had not begun to menstruate).

For some months Anna wrote secret notes to William and agreed to marry him as soon as she was twelve. John Aitken, a surgeon, was informed by William of his intentions. Anna was in the house at the time, and Aitken, seeing that she was very young, asked her when William was out of the room if she meant to marry him, and telling her to consider the serious step involved. Aitken could not recollect her reply but 'concluded that she understood very well what she was going about That she seemed to be perfectly satisfied and that no Constraint or Compulsion of any kind was used'. Aitken attended the marriage ceremony and told the court that he would not have gone 'had he known the trouble which he has since mett with in being obliged to attend as a witness in this Cause.'

Another witness to the marriage was William Thomson, a merchant and a church elder, who had two sons at William's school. According to Thomson, Anna was so far from showing 'any Backwardness or aversion to be married that she appeared to the deponent to be more than ordinary forward in so far as when her hand was Joined with the pursuers and Mr Brown the Minister asked her if she was now willing to be joined with this Man whom she now held by the hand the Defender Answer[ed] Yes I am Sir which appeared a little singular to the deponent for in so far as he recollects it was only usual for the Ladies to make a Curtsy into him of their Consent on such Occasions'.

According to the Defence, when she went to school on the afternoon of 1 April 1772 Anna 'found mantua makers Milliners Jewellers Hair Dressers etc waiting to attire her and when she was happy in seeing herself so fine (as any Child of her age would be) he told her she should always be as fine be her own Mistress in every thing and have and do what she pleased'. One reason for the finery was to make her look older when the minister arrived. For example, James Young, barber and wigmaker, was commissioned by William to make a 'Tupee' (toupee) for her. Being shown the wig in court James stated that it appeared 'to be full as high just now as it was when he dressed the Defender with it on the afternoon of her marriage ... her own hair was so short not reaching above halfway up the Tupee That the Tupee could receive no additional height therefrom and the witness being requested by the Pursuer to take the measure of the Tupee as it now appeared Deponed that this Tupee measured two Inches and seven eighths of an inch'. William told the wigmaker that Anna was thirteen, and he saw no reason to doubt this, adding that 'many grown up Ladies wear their Tupees of a much greater height than the present Tupee some of them at least double that height'.

James Brown, a practising minister of the gospel, was told by William that his bride-to-be was fifteen, and when the minister asked if she was big for her age, William said she was, 'Upon which the deponent replied according to the Common Scotch Proverb That if the Lady was big enough she was old enough.' This minister had married Anna's mother to Mr Robertson and was under the impression that Anna would get £400 or £500 liferented by her mother. He even said to William that 'he would get no Fortune' during her mother's lifetime. William did not put him right but said he was not marrying her for her money 'but from his personal regard to herself'. Mr Brown also asked William if Anna's mother knew of the intended marriage; William lied and said she did, and also lied and said that her tutor, Mr Irvine, had referred him to Anna's mother. The minister told the court that his recommending William to procure the consent of her mother and tutor 'did not proceed from any apprehension that the validity of the marriage might be affected by the want of it but as asking of their consent was respectfull and dutifull the deponent thought it would be an advantage to him the Pursuer in the way of his School which might be hurt by his not asking such consent'.

When Mr Brown arrived at William's house he found a group of witnesses. Disappointed not to see Anna's mother there he was told by William that 'she [was] not averse to the proposal but could not give a publick consent for fear of Embroiling herself with her husband.' Because Anna's mother was not present, Mr Brown demanded 'a private interview' with Anna, 'when he talked with her and observed what a serious and important business she was going about'. Anna told him that William 'had used no improper means to gain her affection that she really loved him That they had been resolved upon the marriage for a long time past and that she was fully fifteen years of age upon the preceeding Monday'. She appeared to the minister 'to understand perfectly well what she was going about and seemed very desirous and very willing to be married'. He did not think that her willingness to marry William 'arose from any sudden passion as she had assured the Deponent they had long been resolved to marry and had been engaged to one another for Twelve months preceeding'. Satisfied, the minister married them.

Next morning Anna's mother called on him and 'informed him that her daughter was only turned Twelve years of Age on the Monday preceeding the marriage and that she was entitled to a Fortune of Two thousand five hundred pounds'. Mrs Robertson 'did not so much Complain of any Injury having been done to her by the marriage as that she seemed surprised thereat because she had not been previously acquainted thereof'. She informed him that 'she had suspected a Courtship' and had a regard for William and 'no other objection to the marriage but her daughters age and that Mr Irvine was very angry at the marriage.' No sooner had Mrs Robertson left his house than William turned up, saying that Mr Irvine was determined to annul the marriage, and asking Mr Brown's advice. The minister 'answered he had no advice to give and added with marks of displeasure that he could not easily forget that he the pursuer had imposed upon him with respect to the Defenders fortune and age for altho he the Deponent did not Scruple to marry the pursuer to a Girl of Fifteen years of age with Five hundred pounds of fortune he would not have married him as he did to one of Twelve years of age with Five and twenty hundred pounds of Fortune'.

James Young, the wigmaker, was a witness to the marriage, and testified that Anna's mother arrived after the minister left and seemed very surprised to see her daughter dressed the way she was and to hear that she was married. As the evening wore on she seemed to accept it, but after the party Mrs Robertson said to her daughter it was time to go home. Anna was very reluctant 'and said that she thought it was now as proper she should remain with Mr Allan'. She agreed to go only when William also went along. At that stage Anna, William, and the Robertsons were all perfectly happy about what had occurred. But that was before Mr Irvine heard the news. Christian Bruce, a servant in the Robertson household, testified that after Irvine left the house Anna 'was sick with weeping'. When she asked what was the matter Anna answered, 'O! what do you think Mr Irvine says hanging is too good for Mr Allan.'

After she was removed from Edinburgh Anna was persuaded of the error of her ways. She told the young woman in whose house she stayed that 'upon her Friends disapproving and conversing upon the subject with her she had become sensible how much the pursuer had imposed upon her and how wrong she had been'. The Defence was also able to produce letters like the following to her mother: 'I am so happy of thinking I have got free of Allan that I will never do any thing of moment without your advice and consent and the punishment I feel in being absent from you I justly deserve for doing anything without your knowledge.' And: 'May I expect your forgiveness for the foolish step into which I was lead [sic] not thinking of the Consequence or that it would give you so much real distress if my youth would excuse me as I am really sorry for being lead [sic] into a marriage which I now wish to be free of my future behaviour should if possible make amends for it.' And by the time she was examined in court selective amnesia had erased the minister's explaining the importance of the ceremony, and the pressure by her stepfather or Mr Irvine to disown William as her husband.

According to the Defence, William was prepared to settle for half Anna's money, and it was only when he was unable to get a penny that he raised the declarator of marriage action. The commissaries found no legal marriage. William appealed to the Court of Session but was unsuccessful.

By a strict interpretation of the law, this should have been a lawful, indeed a regular, marriage. The girl was over the age of consent (the controversy over twelve as a suitable age of consent was irrelevant); a certificate of proclamation of banns had been procured, and witnesses to the ceremony saw both parties willingly declare themselves married. To James Fergusson, commenting many years later, Mr Brown clearly 'discharged the duties of his sacred office in this delicate matter with the utmost propriety'. But Fergusson was confident that 'an abominable fraud was defeated'.[1] The law may be the law, but it is human beings who interpret it.

Note

1   James Fergusson, *Treatise on the Present State of Consistorial Law in Scotland* (Edinburgh, 1829), 161–2.

CC8/5/13

CHAPTER 10

ABANDONED CASES

Most of the material in this book has come from cases that reached a conclusion. There are, however, things to learn from cases which were abandoned. Sometimes the person who raised the action realised that he or she really had no case. Some men fled out of reach. In some cases one can only speculate why a particular case was abandoned.

No Case

The charge laid against Lieutenant Malby Brabazon before the High Court of Justiciary in March 1753 was shocking and led to his incarceration in Inverness prison for several weeks.[1] It was alleged that he abducted Betty Duncan, aged fourteen, from her home in Forres, and when they got to Nairn at about three in the morning, the lieutenant, 'while his Acquaintances held her, went to bed to her and forcibly and violently ravished and defloured her', after which he took her to Inverness where he kept her prisoner until she was rescued by her father. However, when Malby emerged from prison he found himself no longer facing a criminal prosecution but a declarator of marriage action, on the grounds that during the journey he had publicly acknowledged Betty as his wife.

Malby (a lieutenant in the 'Old Buffs') was billeted in her father's house. She was closer to 16 than 14 and was the first to make a move. Margaret Taylor, a soldier's wife who cooked and cleaned for the lieutenant, testified that Betty asked her all about him and offered to mend his clothes herself. One day when her mother was out Betty contrived to spend a couple of hours with Malby in his bedchamber. After that Betty repeatedly asked Margaret to 'acquaint Mr Brabazon of her Inclination to be his servant'. Soon after that Betty's mother learned of her being in his room and 'beat her Daughter in a most Barbarous manner'. Margaret heard Betty's cries. Next morning Betty, 'In a most Lamentable way', told Margaret 'how she was used by her mother the night preceding, and begged of her the deponent, to tell Mr Brabazon she was Resolved to be his servant For that she could no longer put up with her mothers treatment towards her'. (She gave Margaret an apron for acting as go-between.) Betty had heard that Malby was soon to leave Forres and was determined to go with him. When Margaret spoke to the lieutenant he said he was planning to visit his colonel in Inverness and had no objection to taking Betty along.

On the night in question they stopped at Petty and at Nairn. The landlady of the house in Petty testified that 'the Young Woman or Lady who came with him, Appeared to her the deponent, to be rather his Miss, than a Lady, or married wife …. Mr Brabazon and his Miss were vastly Fond of Each other and both very Cheerfull.' They left the house 'in great Spirits,' and 'the Lady or Miss Expressed a great desire to proceed for Inverness'. Malby 'in a Jocular and Smiling manner', said to the witness that 'he was Married to the Lady who was with him, for years,' but the witness 'did not believe him As she was not Cloathed like an officers Lady, and to the deponent Appeared Young'.

As for the alleged rape, George Grant, landlord of the house in Nairn, said that 'of all the Wicked Stories ever was Invented, this is the most Extravagant and without all Foundation, for the officers Company besides the Lady, Were his own servants.' The couple took their leave next morning 'very Cheerfully ….But from her the Ladys Conduct while at the deponents house, he thought her very forward and Impudent'.

The main witness to Betty's father's 'rescue' of her in Inverness was James Geddes, who was asked by the constables to gain entry to the room where a Forres man and his daughter were with the lieutenant. When he got in he 'asked the Young Woman, If she choosed to go with her Father, or Abide by the Gentleman, meaning Mr Brabazon, To which she answered, taking hold of Mr Brabazon by the knee That she would stay with him Brabazon'. Geddes then asked Malby 'on what footing he meant to keep the Young Woman, whether as his wife, or his whore, To this Mr Brabazon Answered that he was not obliged to satisfy him in this Question'. Geddes 'asked again, if he woud Marry the Young Woman, To this Mr Brabazon Replied in some passion That he would not Marry her or any other Woman Or if he did, he woud take some time to think of it'. Geddes then said that 'He Brabazon was right in saying he woud not marry her For as there were three Evidences [witnesses] present, The Law of Scotland woud oblige him to Marry her, if he said he woud.' Malby replied that Geddes 'was Impertinent to Endeavour to Lead him in to a snare'.

Geddes then 'took hold of the Young Woman, telling her he shou'd take her either to prison or to his the deponents house, whereupon she grasp'd at Mr Brabazon takeing hold of him by the Breast'. But Malby persuaded her to go quietly with Geddes and that he would accompany her and see her safe, 'and the deponent believes unless Mr Brabazon had so requested the Young Woman, she wou'd not have gone, without being dragged or pressed, Even tho her Father, calling her often My Dear Betty, Importun'd her to go along with the deponent and him the Father.' Geddes was asked in court 'if he heard the Young Woman say That if her Father Carried her home, she wou'd the first opportunity Return to Mr Brabazon,' and he confirmed this. After Malby left, Betty 'appeared dull and melancholly, soon after fell a Crying, and Continued so untill she went to bed, and after she was in bed'.

This was a malicious prosecution by Betty's father, and it is obvious why criminal charges were not pressed. As for the allegation that Malby had acknowledged Betty as his wife, he argued that 'it would be very absurd if such a declaration as that set forth in the Lybell made to the Landlord of an Inn and which could be done with no other view earthly than as an apology for their taking the same bed should be held equivalent to a marriage.' Betty and her father then petitioned for a 'gratis warrand' (ie to cite witnesses without being charged) on the grounds of poverty but were refused. In theory this could be the reason why the case was abandoned, but really they had no hope of proving a marriage.

In 1769 Janet Thomson was granted the benefit of the poor's roll in her action against Archibald Johnston, merchant in Kelso, which meant that initially lawyers believed she did have a valid case.[2] Janet claimed that she went to bed with Archibald only after he promised her marriage at the beginning of 1766; she bore him a son in November of that year and a second one in January 1769, but he refused to acknowledge himself married to her. Archibald produced an extract of a process before the Court of Session in which she had expressly denied that she was married to him. Janet said that this was because a regular marriage had not taken place, 'tho' even at that time she was really his wife in the Eye of Law, and Entitled to have her Marriage Declared by the Judgement of the proper Court In Consequence of the Promise and Cohabitation and acknowledgement of the Husband as Lybelled'.

The commissaries allowed her to bring proof, but Janet's witnesses scuppered her claims. Elizabeth Ker, an innkeeper's wife, had asked Janet if she was married, and declared that Janet

> answered she was not married to him, and that she blessed God or was thankful that she was not for that she would have had a very indifferent life with him And added that if the defender would take the two children from her And would give her some little thing she had a pair of good hands and could do for herself.

Another witness, a confectioner's wife, never heard Archibald call Janet his wife, 'nor did she ever see or hear any thing which could lead her to think they were married, on the contrary she has been told by the pursuer herself that they were not married'. Furthermore, Janet said to her that she 'did not care for the defenders person but that she wanted some of his money'. That witness's 17 year-old daughter testified that Janet told her she expected to marry Archibald, but not that she was already married to him. After hearing such witnesses Janet's lawyer must have realised there was no point in wasting any more time on such a case.

Absconders

As we have seen elsewhere in the book, and will see again in the next chapter, women could fight a case against a man who was not in Scotland. However, if the man was out of reach it might not seem worth expending the time, money and effort necessary to prove a marriage to him. Furthermore, if she did not have money of her own she needed an opponent who would pay the expenses even if she lost.

At a very early stage in the 1769 case of Isabel Ross (daughter of the deceased Thomas Ross of Catrossie Esquire), against Thomas Forrest, lately from the East Indies, purchaser of the estate of Cluny in Fife, Isabel petitioned to have Thomas arrested as he was planning to leave the country.[3] The commissaries set his bail at £2,000, but after an appeal to the Court of Session this was lowered to £500. Isabel was 'the Daughter of a Family of old standing Character and reputation and as well connected as any in the north of Scotland'. Thomas had 'returned to this Country some time ago with the Character of having acquired a considerable Fortune in the East Indies, which in the estimation of the world placed him on a Levell with Gentlemen of superior rank [and] encouraged him to make his addresses to her for marriage to which she unhappily listened'. She accepted him as her husband, went to bed with him, and at the time of raising the action was far advanced in pregnancy. He had purchased the estate of Rothes for over £10,000, but as the bulk of his fortune 'had been vested in East India stock which he meant to dispose of and to apply part of the proceeds in payment of the price of the Estate which he had purchased', he said he did not want his marriage made public until all that was concluded. An unlikely tale, but she agreed, though naturally her friends knew all about it.

The next thing Isabel heard was that Thomas 'had disposed of the Estate he had so recently purchased and was preparing to withdraw himself from this Country' – without having communicated a word of this to Isabel. She challenged him, and he replied that he had to go to London, but as soon as his East India stock was disposed of he would return to her, only he could not say how long that would be. She insisted that he acknowledge their marriage in writing, 'and allow her to assume his name, both which he declined upon various frivolous pretences and it was this refusall which gave the first suspicion that fair things were not intended'. Heavily pregnant, and very worried, Isabel took legal advice and raised this action. She argued that he could easily afford the bail set by the commissaries. The lack of any further documents strongly suggests that Thomas jumped bail and left Scotland.

In 1770 Hanah Wickward (daughter of a linen printer at Bonington) likewise sought the arrest of the man against whom she had raised a declarator of marriage action, Lieutenant Hill Christie. His lawyer insisted that he had no intention of leaving and could give surety of this, which the commissaries agreed to, but the lack of any further documents suggests that he did indeed take the easy way out.[4]

Speculation

The 1788 case of Margaret Leslie, in Edinburgh, against John Ritchie, a mason, was raised under benefit of the poor's roll.[5] Margaret alleged that they were married in November 1785 and cohabited until July 1786 when he deserted her. John said she was 'an old decrepit widow' while he was a young man of 25. His only connection with her, he claimed, was as a lodger, and during the time he lodged there he courted a young woman whom he married in March 1786. Margaret produced two witnesses who testified that John asked them to find a minister, who proceeded to marry the couple. Another witness, Susan Blackie, a wright's wife, had known Margaret for many years and went round to visit her when she heard that her friend was married. She found her 'in company with a young Man', who 'behaved very civily'. When Margaret went to fetch some drink, Susan asked him how long he had been married to her and he replied that they were married at Halloween. She said she hoped that he would do Margaret 'Justice and not neglect her tho' an old Woman to which he answered that he meant to do for her and that he liked her as he had never seen a fault to [sic] her'. Susan did not know how old Margaret was but said she had a grown son who had left Margaret's house 'on account of the forsaid Marriage.' In view of the strength of Margaret's evidence (she also had marriage lines), and Ritchie's being married to another woman who had already borne him two children, the likeliest explanation of the case being abandoned was that some financial arrangement was made between them.

In an action raised in 1810, Mary Maur, typically, was pregnant after an alleged secret agreement to marry, which George Todd denied.[6] Mary produced letters in which he signed himself as her husband, but he said he had been only 15 when he wrote them, and that when she raised her action against him he was still under 20, 'is in no employment, neither is he capable of managing business of any kind, so as even to gain £20 a year'. And because of Mary's 'laying claim to him as her husband his father, who has a large family, has thrown him off, and will not give him any thing to support him'. Before she had thought of raising a declarator of marriage action against him Mary had had him up before the JP court 'to prevent his relations from forcing him to leave the country'. At that time he was specifically asked whether he had 'cohabited with her as his wife or Mistress' and refused to answer the question;

in other words he could not bring himself to deny that they were married. And she alleged that even since then he had repeatedly visited her 'and been admitted to an enjoyment of all a husbands rights'. She had a strong case, so perhaps her reason for abandoning it was that George's parents finally accepted the marriage.

In January 1828 Margaret McLellan in Edinburgh raised an action against John Miller, a lawyer living in Alloa, alleging a secret marriage in 1822, resulting in the birth of their daughter, Mary, in February 1823.[7] Her main evidence was a written acknowledgment from him dated 15 October 1825. Why the long delays? Margaret alleged that when he first courted her John was a clerk in an office in Edinburgh, and as he was not in a position to support her 'it was deemed adviseable to put off the marriage till he should be settled in business, which he then daily expected to be able to do'. At that time he not only visited her two or three times a day but 'he also began to assume the direction of her actions in so far as he would not even allow her to go to a party, make visits, or see any of her acquaintances without his knowledge and consent.' After he went to Alloa he generally came down 'on the Steam Boat' to visit her every two or three weeks. He insisted that his business still would not support her, and 'he thought that by remaining for some time apparently unmarried his business would increase.' However, he explained to her 'that two persons accepting of each other as husband and wife followed by copula or consummation was sufficient to constitute a marriage, and did not require farther ceremony – and he actually procured and often read quotations from Erskines Institutes on the subject of marriage to prove the Law on the subject'. He thereby persuaded her.

Then, of course, she became pregnant. Her relations were aware that John 'was considerably in debt, and as his business was apparently increasing they thought he might soon extricate himself from his difficulties – and therefore had the less hesitation in acceding to this request of still concealing the marriage for a short period.' Indeed, his finances were so bad that if Margaret were declared married to him, her own possessions might have been seized by creditors. But he continued to visit her and in October 1825, to quiet her fears, he granted her the written acknowledgment. Finally she wrote to him demanding that he either receive her as his wife or give her a separate aliment as her father thought she had been maintained by him long enough; when she got no reply she raised this action.

John's reply is rather startling: he was married to another woman who had borne him three children, the first in 1822 before Margaret's child was born. His written acknowledgment, he said, 'was looked upon by both parties as a mere blind'. Presumably, faced with evidence of an earlier marriage, Margaret saw no point in continuing.

The lack of a decision in abandoned cases renders them frustrating (like a story with the ending torn away) but, as has been seen, such cases can nevertheless add further richness to the story of disputed relationships in Scotland.

Notes

1   CC8/6/19.
2   CC8/6/27.
3   Ibid. The summons has not survived; the first document is the petition.
4   CC8/6/28.
5   CC8/6/50.
6   CC8/6/91.
7   CC8/6/158.

CHAPTER 11

UNCONTESTED CASES

A DESERTED wife who wanted to force her husband to support her had to raise an action of adherence; if the man refused to return to her he would be found liable for lifelong aliment. If she wanted to divorce him on the grounds of desertion she would also have to raise such an action in order to prove that she had done her best to get him back.[1] There was no need to seek a conclusion for declarator of marriage along with that of adherence, but some lawyers mistakenly did so, and the majority of uncontested cases fall into this category. However, some were more complex and throw further light on the story of marriage in Scotland.

Examples

The libel in the 1746 case of Katharin Carmichaell, daughter of Thomas Carmichaell of Eastend, Lanarkshire, against John Hay, eldest son of John Hay of Haystoun, told a common story.[2] In July 1744 John asked her to marry him secretly, 'Saying that tho my Father may not be brought to consent to my marrying so soon his family being then at the greatest Expence Yet that he was sure that they being once married his father would easily be reconciled to it.' He persuaded her, and in November of that year they were married by William Jamieson. Katharin had letters signed 'your Loving and affectionate husband', but John continued to put off telling his father. In April 1745 he wrote, 'Dear Catie I have not as yet spoke of our marriage to my father untill I get some money from him', and in May, 'Dear Catie … I find by conversation if agreeable to you that it will be most prudent for us not to devulge our marriage to them so soon as was agreed upon when we last spoke together if devulged I fear my present allowance will not be made any better than it is at present.' In June Katharin's brother told John's father about the marriage, who

> answered he had nothing to say against the Girle that his son was much better married than she but by his marriage at that time he had Disconcerted his Measures and put it out of his power to provide for him as he would have done his family being then at the Greatest Charge to him.

John wrote to Katharin: 'since your friends was here my father tells me he cannot affoord to give me any Addition to my allowance Therefore I do incline we should live separatly untill he can give it me.' Katharin raised a declarator of marriage action. John's lawyer said that 'to Insist on a Declarator of marriage which was never denyed nor contraverted … seems to be a little vexatious and calculat to put the Defender to unnecessary expence.' John did not deny his marriage, but as it

> was a little hastily gone into and without the advice knowledge or consent of his parents and as his haill dependance was on them so he could not live with her as man and wife as his Income was too small to support them in a married state and therefore he choosed rather that they should for some time live seperatly till he was better enabled to do her in every respect that Justice he wished hoped and ought to doe.

Her lawyer argued that for a husband and wife to live together 'for their Mutual Comfort' was 'the Grand End of marriage', but in reality Katharin was not forcing the issue of adherence; by winning her decreet she was ensuring that John could not at any future date deny a marriage.

An odder case is that of Grace Barr against George Crow of Nether Byres in 1776.[3] Grace had been George's mother's housekeeper. On 19 September 1775 they were married by a dissenting minister with her brother as a witness, marriage lines were made out and signed, and the couple slept together. Two days later he 'behaved somewhat sullenly' to her and slept alone. She 'Communicated this Change of temper in Mr Crow to some of her friends in Eyemouth', and they came round 'and expostulated with George Crow upon the impropriety and being so suddenly changed in his affections and temper'. He slept with her for two more nights, but then 'appeared more sullen and morose than formerly' and wrote to her mother asking her to remove her daughter from his house. Grace was pregnant and raised a declarator of marriage action.

William Wightman, a surgeon in Eyemouth, had wished George Crow joy when he heard of the marriage and was surprised a couple of days later when George told him 'in a Jocular manner that he did not believe he was properly married', without being able to give a satisfactory reason. Two days later George told him that he could not live happily with Grace. Wightman 'said to him it would have a very bad appearance for a Man to marry a woman one day and part with her the next', to which George 'answered that he could not help it, but was sorry for it.' Wightman testified that 'Mr Crow bore in the Country the character of a fickle and inconstant man, and when he entertained any whim which he was very apt to do – he would gratify it at any expence.' John Renton was one of Grace's friends who came to expostulate with George. He thought that George's 'lowness of spirits … proceeded from the Idea of his having married a person below his rank'.

The commissaries found them married persons, any children procreated to be lawful children 'and as such entitled to succeed to the Estate heritable and moveable of the said George Crow'. While he did not adhere to her he had to pay her £50 a year aliment until the death of his mother, and after that £90 yearly, 'being the annuity his said Mother then enjoyed', plus £25 for Grace's inlying expenses, aliment for the child, and £100 for expenses of the process and extracting the decreet.

A man who raised a declarator of marriage action against a non-adhering wife was Robert Purvis, a seaman, because Elizabeth Cairns' parents refused to allow her to cohabit with him.[4] The couple were married by Joseph Robertson in May 1786. After about three months' cohabitation Robert went on a voyage, returned and cohabited with her again, but when he returned after a second voyage (by which time Elizabeth had borne his child) her parents refused to allow him access. His action was raised in December 1787. Her lawyer argued that after her secret marriage her 'parents were both much distressed and enraged at their being thus bereaved of their only child and by a man whom they knew nothing of'. They believed his only object was to extort money from them.

Elizabeth's lawyer admitted that both parties 'were young when Married but they were on a footing as to their Rank in life'. Robert's parents were 'respectable people in the neighbourhood of Wooler who gave him an Education that qualified him for being a Ship Master', and his brother was 'Proprietor of a Farm near Dunfermline'. Grace's 'father on the other hand is tenant in a small farm in the neighbourhood of Dunfermline .... It was from mutual attachment alone the partys entered on the matrimonial state, not with any view to what they might expect from the defenders Father and Mother.' Robert did not think that Grace had 'formed any dislike to him', but she was 'absolutely prohibited from seeing him'. She was

> an only Child and being all her life under the sole charge and dominion of her father and Mother she has been uniformly taught to yield unlimited obedience to their Mandates, and from an ill founded anxiety to keep her in their own family ... they absolutely refuse to let her out of their house and while there she dare not do or say a single thing but as she is ordered – But altho' they have exerted their parental authority to a degree unknown in these days of civilization and refinement

he would rest his case on a

> single experiment Vizt that were he and the defender to meet at any other place than her fathers house and her parents not to be present, in place of returning to them she would attend him wherever he chused to go with the greatest cordiality and reckon her being extricate from her parents as a very happy release.

The commissaries had no need to try the experiment; 'in respect that the marriage lybelled is judicially admitted in the defences', proof was unnecessary and the couple were decreed married persons.

Absconders

In the previous chapter we saw that some women abandoned their actions after the man absconded. However, a wife could claim aliment from a man's estate in Scotland even if he had left the country, so it might have been worthwhile raising an action against such a man. Some uncontested cases fall into this category.

For instance, in 1768 Margaret Buchanan and Thomas Peters, son of a merchant in Virginia, both in their teens, were married in Glasgow by 'a minister or a person who gave out himself to be a minister'.[5] They went to bed together but agreed to keep the marriage a secret until Thomas went back to Virginia in the summer when he said he would tell his parents. But when he went to Virginia without publicly acknowledging a marriage, Margaret's curators (her father being dead) raised a declarator of marriage action.

Her first witness was Agnes Wylie, servant to Thomas's grandfather who testified that Thomas told her of his intention to marry in April, and when she said he was too young he told her that he would be 15 in August. Agnes said that 'it was a Scandal for such a young lad as him to marry to which he answered that there were much younger people married in the Country from which he had come viz Virginia'. When Agnes threatened to tell his relations, he said the only one who would really object was his Uncle Alexander, and sure enough Alexander was the only witness to testify that Thomas had told him that the marriage was a 'Frolick' and that he would not adhere to Margaret as his wife, so Alexander 'did advise him to take the first opportunity which then offered of going to Virginia and did assist him with money'. It is obvious why a declarator of marriage action had to be raised, and witnesses to the ceremony and bedding put the marriage beyond reasonable doubt. While he did not adhere to her Thomas had to pay her £50 a year aliment.

David Carnegie, Lord Rosehill (eldest son of the Earl of Northesk), was no longer in Scotland in 1769 when Christian Cameron (daughter of the deceased Alexander Cameron of Dungallon) raised her declarator of marriage action against him.[6] They were married by a priest in Fort William in January 1767 and subsequently acknowledged the marriage to a JP and the sheriff substitute of the county and were bedded. David was at that time an ensign in the 25th regiment of foot, and when this marriage came to light his commanding officer arrested him and then dismissed him from the regiment. He wrote Christian a couple of affectionate letters but by September he was already regretting his action and asked her to 'give up her marriage with him But which the regard she has for her honour and Charracter cannot allow her to comply with'. In his final letter to her he wrote:

I hope as you pretend to have some affection for me that you will be so kind as to think of giving up all pretensions to me and as it is impossible for you and I ever to live together it would be much better for us to part as then both of us might be happy which it is impossible for us to be if connected in the manner that we now are And I should think if I had the same affection for any person that you say you have for me I should not persist in what I knew would bring them to the grave in a few years nay perhaps months.

Christian was able to produce a number of witnesses to the marriage and bedding. Ewan Cameron younger of Fasifern was present when David acknowledged her to be his wife. He remonstrated with David about 'the impropriety of such a marriage and that his the defenders Father would certain disinherit him for so Rash a Step To which he the defender answered that it was out of his fathers Power'. The commissaries found the marriage proven and found David liable to pay Christian £50 a year while he did not adhere to her.

Another man who fled after a secret marriage (by Joseph Robertson) was Robert Rankin, who left Edinburgh for New York. The marriage with Ann Thomson took place in April 1810, and Robert told a lawyer acting for Ann that he had not acknowledged it publicly 'on account of the hostility which existed between the two families', and 'he mentioned his wish that the marriage should be still longer kept secret on account of an arrangement which he expected to take place respecting some Cash Credits in London he should obtain through the medium of his father and his friends and who he said would withdraw their promised assistance in money matters from him if they were aware that he was married to the pursuer.' He promised the lawyer that he would acknowledge the marriage a few months later and would have a house ready for her, but instead he fled the country taking about seven or eight thousand pounds. It is not clear how many years he kept her stringing along before he fled, or how long she waited after that, for her action was not raised until 1822. Perhaps she had only just discovered where he actually was, for the commissaries found him liable to her for £150 annual aliment.[7]

Denials

The majority of men who chose not to contest declarator of marriage actions raised against them were, however, still in Scotland. Such actions had to be raised because the man, after deserting the woman, denied that she was his wife, but once she took the decisive step of going to court, he conceded her rightful claim.

In 1762 Grizel Gibson, whose first husband died seven years earlier, leaving her with four children whom she 'by her own Industry Educate mantained and brought up ... in a creditable and Honest manner', was married in Edinburgh to William Anderson, a soldier retired from service after being wounded in action and receiving a pension.[8] Grizel was able to produce a marriage certificate signed by the minister, Charles Smith. But William went home to Glasgow and wrote to her in September 1763, 'I should never Countenance you in that ugly affair which happened in Edinburgh through my stupidity, so I desire you will take that line which you have and burn it ... and let us have done with all that is by past.' In October William's father wrote to her, expressing his amazement at her claim:

> *I have examined my son about it and he declairs to me there is nothing in it at all only he has been acquainted in your house some time as he says to me and he being drunk as he is very often you took half a sheet of Clean Paper and desired him to set this name to it which he did and than went and lay down beside him and then having informed some of your Neighbours who came and gott you lying Besayeds him and undoubtedly you must be a Woman that is very immodest or Else very Bad Conduct or Else could never had had the Confidence to do any such thing so I beg you will not trouble me about any such Thing.*

Furthermore, he wrote, William swore 'by the great God of Heaven and Earth ... that he will put you in the House of Correction which I dont know but you deserve it'.

The case was not contested, but Grizel still had to produce witnesses before the commissaries declared them married persons.[9]

Thomas Peterkine, excise officer, deserted Florence Grahame in November 1792, and she heard nothing further of him until October 1793 when he returned but refused to cohabit with her.[10] Agnes Wightman, their landlady in Leith, testified that Florence 'wept bitterly after she was informed that her husband had left her, and the witness lent her a gown and a cloak the pursuer having no other cloaths but a short Gown and a Petty Coat'. On the day that Thomas went away, Agnes asked Florence

> *if she had any thing in the house to eat, to which she answered that she had got some tea, but the witness upon taking off the lid of the tea pot saw there was nothing in it, and that nothing had been in it, and therefore supposing that the pursuer was ashamed to make known her necessities, The witness went to a Shop purchased an ounce of tea and a piece of Sugar which she gave to the pursuer.*

Robert Robertson, baker in Edinburgh, testified that after Thomas returned and came to see him Robertson 'asked him what was his reason for using Florence his wife so ill now, when he had formerly used her so well, that upon this he fell a cursing and damning and swore that she was not his wife and said that he could get a wife in any town'. Robertson 'thereupon told him he was a Blackguard and turned him out of his house'. Mary Walker, Robertson's wife, also saw Thomas after his return when he said that Florence 'was a bad woman, and that she was not his wife and that he would have nothing to do with her'. Mary 'observed to him that it was very improper in him now to disown the pursuer after having formerly passed her upon the witness and many other persons as his wife, to which he answered that it was only a piece of humour of his or words to that purpose'. Florence was able to produce letters signed 'your Loving and affectionate Husband to Death', and the commissaries found them married persons and Thomas liable for her aliment.

In 1794 Isobel Duncan became a servant to John Fullerton while his first wife was still alive. After her death John courted Isobel and they agreed to marry; when Isobel raised her action in February 1795, after John deserted her and denied their marriage, she was four months pregnant. John Lamond, a wright in Edinburgh who had been repairing John's house, testified that sometime after John's first wife's death Isobel 'was very finely dressed particularly had a Gold watch or one like gold', and John said to him 'Now you are to call this Lady Mrs Fullerton.' The couple 'always behaved to one another in a decent manner,' said Lamond, but after awhile John told him not to call her Mrs Fullerton any longer 'as he did not wish that to be known and repented very much of what he had rashly done or said'. Another tradesman, John Dewer, cabinet maker and upholsterer, called at the house one day when the maid servant who answered the door told him that her master 'was married to Bell Duncan his maid'. Lamond did not believe it, but 'the maid insisted it was truth and said she would carry him into Mrs Fullerton whom he would see dressed in a manner suitable to that station'. In fact, John admitted the marriage and Lamond drank to them as husband and wife. The commissaries could not force John to adhere to his wife, but he had to pay her £40 a year aliment while he did not do so.[11]

After James Watt, a Glasgow innkeeper, deserted Margaret Pollock and their child, Robert, in 1823, Margaret first of all raised an action for aliment before Glasgow Commissary Court. James declared before that court that the parties were not married, and the case was therefore dismissed until Margaret proved before a competent court (ie Edinburgh Commissary Court) that a marriage existed. When she raised a declarator of marriage action Margaret was therefore astonished that James did not dispute the conclusion for marriage and legitimacy but denied deserting her, claiming that it was she who deserted him and that therefore she was not entitled to any aliment. Margaret declared that, if necessary, she could prove that prior to raising her action she had gone to James's house, 'from which he had previously expelled her', accompanied by witnesses, and 'offered to cohabit with him as his Wife if he would receive her'. His response had been that 'he would never again admit her into his house, far less suffer her to remain in it.' Since he did not deny his marriage before this court the commissaries ordered him to adhere to her, or pay her aliment.

Battleground

Most declarator of marriage cases are mercifully free of the bickering so prevalent in divorce and separation cases, but in a few instances where the man did not deny a marriage the woman was trying to get more money out of him, and the couple used the Commissary Court as their battleground.

There was really no reason for Marion Watson to raise an action in 1785 against William Johnston, servant to Erskine of Marr, as they had been regularly married in 1770, which he did not deny, 'but nothing would content the pursuer except a process'.[13] Their story does paint an interesting picture of such a partnership in this period. They met as fellow servants of MacLeod of MacLeod, and for the first two years after marrying they rented furnished accommodation together. Then they 'took up a Grocery Shop in Nicolsons Street … the pursuer keeping the shop and the defender being all the time in service.' They moved to two different grocery shops in the years that followed, but the pattern remained the same: Marion ran the shop while William remained in service. But, according to William, Marion 'got into a habit of drinking' and when drunk she would abuse customers – and her husband. She soon ran into debt. William suggested that 'as she had formerly acted as Cook and Chamber Maid on different occasions, and that she was still a young woman' she 'should go to service or some kind of work as well as the defender did in order to pay off the said debts,' but she refused, so that he had to meet all her debts himself. He still gave her four or five pounds a year ('being all he can spare from his wages, out of which he is obliged to keep himself in Shirts, Shoes, Stockings, Boots, Breeches and Greatcoat'), but she demanded more.

William contended that he had more reason to raise a process against her than she had to raise one against him, as she had often maltreated him and locked him out of the house all night, not to mention the financial ruin she had caused. But Marion claimed that at one point he was out of work for seven or eight months and she alone supported them. It was 'exceedingly Vexatious and most Ungratefull' of him to suggest that she 'should now go into service after having been so long in the Married State born several Children to him and Suffered so many hardships since she became his wife especially too when she is now so very far advanced in years'. She insisted that his free income was at least £20 a year and asked for £10 a year aliment. William appeared in court and declared that he was

Butler and body servant to Mr Erskine of Marr That his Wages are Twelve pounds a year but his Master obliges him to find himself in Boots breeches and Great Coat, That his Master besides wages, sometime gives him particular articles of his old cloaths but this entirely in his Masters option and that he has no other Emolument than those above mentioned That he is Mantained by his Master And is not on board wages … he has no other Income than his wages from his Master.

And he declared that since they separated he had given his wife £5 a year and paid the rent for her lodgings.

In the end the commissaries decreed them to be married persons – and awarded her £4 a year aliment.

In his defences against Katharine Campbell's action against him in 1786, James Hamilton also alleged his wife was an alcoholic.[14] In this case too there had been a regular marriage – 18 years earlier – so a legal action was quite unnecessary. James claimed that at the time of his marriage to Katharine he 'had flattering prospects in life he was Factor of Islay and had several valuable farms well stocked and at easy rents', but he was ruined by the Ayr bank crash and it was not until some years later that he found work as the commander of a revenue cutter. He built a house on the Isle of Lamlash (today called 'Holy Island'), but Katharine refused to live there and – he claimed – spent all his money in 'tippling change houses'. Conscious of her bad behaviour she had agreed to a separation but then changed her mind and raised this action instead.

Katharine's version of events was very different. At the time they married he was factor to just a small part of the island of Islay with very little stock, and it was only with his wife's money that 'he acquired a very good stock and wrought himself into the Factory of all the Island of Islay but it was not long before his folly and extravagance destroyed the subject and his consequent bankruptcy lost him the Factory of Islay'. And it was not true that he lost his money through his concern in the Ayr bank as he had never paid any part of his subscription so he had forfeited his right to be a partner. His allegation of her drinking was only advanced by him 'to give some apology for his cruel behaviour to his wife', whose 'character will be attested by the Minister and elders of the parish where she resides as well as by the neighbours and that she is no drunkard but a well behaved ill-used woman'. He had 'taken every thing from her and she might have died or starved for want if it had not been for some of her friends and good neighbours who supported her'. It was true that she had agreed to a separation if he settled a reasonable amount on her, 'but that was not on account of her being sensible of any misconduct in herself but to be quit of his tyranny and abusive treatment toward her with her want of the necessaries of life'. He did not produce a contract for a legal separation 'and it is believed never had any intention to implement his promise'.

There were further arguments: the house on the island was very isolated, so she chose to live in a poorer house of his on Arran 'for the sake of having some neighbours and acquaintances to talk with and assist her'. There were innumerable petitions and arguments about what he could afford to pay her, but in the end – having declared them married persons – the commissaries ordered him to pay her £60 a year aliment.

Uncontested cases may have been successful, but that did not mean that the relationships they depicted were straightforward.

Notes

1   See Leah Leneman, *Alienated Affections – The Scottish Experience of Divorce and Separation 1684–1830* (Edinburgh, 1998), c.12.
2   CC8/5/6.
3   CC8/5/15.
4   CC8/6/50.
5   CC8/5/11.
6   CC8/5/12.
7   CC8/5/41.
8   CC8/5/11.
9   As usual in such cases, in order to ascertain the amount of aliment he would have to pay her the commissaries asked her to describe his circumstances. She declared that apart from being a Chelsea pensioner, for the past year he 'had carried on a Private distillery in the Town of Glasgow and still carried on the same', earning 16 shillings a week and that he was 'a very active strong young Man and was concerned in several other Branches of Trades and Businesses unknown to the Pursuer by which he was enabled to Live rather like a Gentleman than otherways.' The commissaries decreed that he pay her three pounds ten shillings a year.
10   CC8/5/23.
11   Ibid.
12   CC8/6/143.
13   CC8/6/45.
14   CC8/5/18.

CHAPTER 12

FREEDOM AND PUTTING TO SILENCE

M ANY of the declarator of marriage cases discussed in this book were raised as counter-processes to declarator of freedom cases, but some freedom cases are interesting in their own right.

Uncontested

In a typical case the man would assert that the woman had been falsely claiming to be his wife; the woman would not contest it, and the commissaries would decree that the woman was forbidden ever to assume the character of his wife and the man was free to marry whoever he chose. Some cases would also ask for a conclusion of 'scandal' (defamation) and for the woman to be found liable for damages. A few such cases contain additional material of interest. For example, in the 1752 case of William Reid against Margaret Simpson, Margaret's lawyer produced the following letter she had written him:

> Sir I am surprised to find that William Reid Weaver in Potterrow has Raised a Declarator of Freedom against me before the Commissarys of Edinburgh alledging that I asserted that I was his Wife, I do solemnly declare that I never did say or assert any such thing to any person whatever, I abhor the Man and never will have any concern with him in that way, he has indeed been at great pains to publish a story as if I had been Married to him, and by his Instigation I have been several times called before the Kirk Session of West Kirk and Caused me to be summoned before the presbytery and now he has raised this groundless process before the Commissarys, God forgive him for thus oppressing a poor helpless widow and two Fatherless Children, he may take as many decreets of Declarator as he please I have nothing to Object but as he Claims damnages there is not the least Ground for that on his part but I have good Reasons to Claim Damnages of him if I were able to prosecute him, my Circumstances are Such that I can scarcely maintain my two orphan Children the oldest not four year old I beg Dear Sir that you will defend me against this Malicious man, God will reward you I cannot otherways than by Prayers for your health and prosperity.[1]

The commissaries took William's word for it and decreed Margaret guilty 'of an heinous Scandall and Callumny in propagating and Reporting that she was the said pursuers Wife' – but they did not find her liable for damages.

In the 1758 case of John Lickly, minister of the gospel at Old Meldrum, against Jean Roy, his former servant, Jean had previously raised an action against him before the sheriff of Aberdeen asking for money on the grounds that he had had carnal knowledge of her under promise of marriage before marrying his present wife.[2] After John raised his action before the Commissary Court, Jean wrote to her lawyer:

> *I must inform you, That tho' I never did say, I was married to Mr Lickly or that I was his wife, yet must own I did say That he had carnal dealings with me before he was married to Mrs Barbara Wright, now his spouse and this I confess I said without any foundation for which I was the more to blame, and am heartily sorry for what I have done my strained circumstances having induced me to take this wrong method to get money from Mr Lickly and as I am much concerned at what I have done, and would willingly make Mr Lickly any Reparation in my Power, I begg Sir you will produce this letter before the Lords Commissaries, to whom I humbly submitt myself hoping their Lordships will receive this my Acknowledgment, and not inflict any punishment, as I solemnly promise, never to affirm such falsehoods of Mr Lickly.*

One has to wonder if she really would have gone to all that trouble if she had never been to bed with him, and if it was only fear of the consequences that now persuaded Jean to deny what she had earlier affirmed. John's lawyer argued that it would be absurd to let her escape punishment 'meerly because she pretended to be sorry for what she had done'. The commissaries did not find her liable for damages for scandal, though they did find her liable for the expenses of the case.

A more unusual uncontested case was that of Sir Alexander Kinloch of Gilmerton Baronet against Margaret Powell, innkeeper in Tranent, in 1809.[3] Sir Alexander was married in Newcastle in 1801 and lived with his wife and son at Gilmerton, near Haddington. But now Margaret was claiming that he had married her prior to that marriage. Witnesses testified that Margaret had borne an illegitimate child to a Captain Mackenzie eleven years earlier and then married another man, William Wilson, to whom she bore two daughters. Everyone was very surprised when she suddenly went to Gilmerton with her son, 'in a daft or mad fit', saying that the boy was Sir Alexander's. They considered her 'deranged' and testified that they 'thought she would break every thing in the house in her Madness the night before she went to Gilmerton'. After all the evidence was heard the commissaries found that she was

> *liable to temporary derangement, and that when she gave out that she had been married to the said Sir Alexander Kinloch Pursuer, she was considered by her neighbours under one of the fits of insanity.*

So, while declaring Sir Alexander free and enjoining Margaret to perpetual silence, they did not find her liable for damages. Mad or not, three years later she proceeded to claim marriage to yet another man. The case was quickly thrown out, but this time she did face damages.

Contested

Of the 89 freedom cases, 47 (53 %) were contested. Most such cases involved a counter-process of declarator of marriage and have therefore featured in earlier chapters, but some did not. In 1802 Andrew Darling, not yet 21, raised a declarator of freedom action against Agnes Purves. Agnes declared that this was the work of his relatives who were 'Displeased with the Connection' and trying to 'Quash' the marriage. There had been a long courtship and a marriage ceremony, followed by a bedding. However, rather than raising a counter-action of declarator of marriage she called on Andrew to appear in court 'to undergo a Judicial Examination, on the facts before stated'. The commissaries found his answers to her defences 'evasive and unsatisfactory' and, as he was out of Scotland, ordered him 'to answer by a writing under his own hand the pointed Allegation'. He never did so, so his action failed.[5]

However, many of the freedom cases contested without a counter-action were successful. In the 1806 case of John Veitch, tenant in Pilton, against Jean Johnston, servant at Newhails near Musselburgh, Jean said that when she became pregnant in 1797 John would have acknowledged a marriage with her had it not been for his father's disapproval, but he promised to do so once he was independent. John denied this, saying that she had freely admitted him to her embraces without any mention of marriage. When she became pregnant he told his father, and both families agreed that the child should be delivered in secret; John had maintained it ever since. All she wanted in claiming that he was her husband was to extort money from him, 'indeed her Solicitor said that she would abandon any claim in paying her Fifty pounds Sterling or thereby', but he was not giving in to such pressure. As Jean, 'with all her seeming plausability of having a good plea never has ventured to follow out the steps uniformly observed in cases of a similar nature namely to bring an action of Declarator of Marriage, Legitimacy and Adherence', the commissaries found that John was free of any marriage to her and ordered her to perpetual silence on the subject.[6]

A declarator of freedom case would obviously succeed if the woman proved to be married to another man. In an action raised in 1752 by George Hutchinson, painter in Edinburgh, against Alison Ritchie, the woman genuinely had no idea that her former husband, Elias Scott, was still alive.[7] Elias took part in the 1745 rising, and Margaret never heard a word from him again. In 1747 George showed her a newspaper report of Elias Scott's death, and he admitted in court that while he cohabited with her, and she bore him children, he too believed that Elias was dead. However, it turned out that the newspaper report referred to

another man, for Elias's father produced several letters from his son, who had
fetched up in Naples.[8] Elias had never informed his wife that he had survived
because he regretted his marriage (he even wrote that he hoped Alison was dead!),
but as Alison had clearly been married to him at the time of her putative marriage
to George, the commissaries overturned the latter marriage and found him free
to marry another woman. So Alison was abandoned again.

In a 1783 case James Trotter produced a certificate showing that Elizabeth
Muirhead, who was claiming to be his wife, was actually married to Duncan
Mackellar, travelling chapman.[9] Elizabeth alleged that she had been betrayed by
her sister 'and carried before the Minister of the Gaelic Chapell when the
ceremony of marriage had been performed', but she 'had immediately thereafter
repented so that there never was any consummation of the marriage either by
bedding or taking the name of the pretended husband in public or in private' –
and the man had since married another woman. She said she had told James all
about this, and he had assured her that if it had not been consummated it was not
a real marriage. Elizabeth and James were fined for an irregular marriage by a
JP and cohabited after that, and she argued that it would be most unjust in him

> to endeavour to annull the marriage bona fide entered into by him with the defender with
> his eyes open and by his own voluntary act such a proceeding would be allowing the
> Pursuer to avail himself of his own fraud in making the defender Believe that she was
> entering into a fair and legal marriage with him and that there was nothing in the former
> pretended marriage when in fact he intended the reverse.

James' intentions were highly suspect, but Elizabeth remained the legal wife of
another man, for the lack of consummation was irrelevant. The commissaries
therefore declared James a free man.

In the 1829 case of James Creech against Christian Yuille, it was the man rather
than the woman who was duped.[10] Christian told James that she was unmarried,
and in December 1827 they had 'what is called a Rutherglen marriage performed
by acknowledgement in presence of Witnesses before one of the Magistrates and
a Justice of Peace in the said Town, that they were married persons'. About four
months later James discovered that she was having sex with William Sheriff, spirit
dealer in Glasgow, and raised a divorce action against her.[11] He then discovered
that she had been married to William since October 1821. In the first instance the
commissaries dismissed the action on the grounds that he should have sought an
annulment of the bigamous marriage. But he argued that their mutual acknowledgment before a JP could not constitute a marriage as she had falsely claimed at
that time to be unmarried. The commissaries reversed their decision and allowed
James to bring proof. Christian Yuille and William Sheriff 'kept an irregular house
in Glasgow, the known haunt and resort of common prostitutes and others whom
they supplied with spirituous liquors and other refreshments and accommodation'.

They had a string of convictions for excise offences, always as husband and wife. The commissaries found James free of any marriage to her, put her to silence, and found her liable for the expenses of the case.

Women Initiators

Out of the 89 declarator of freedom actions only 19 were raised by women; all nineteen, whether contested or not, succeeded. In the 1782 case of Agnes Sommers against Alexander Collins, smith at Riccarton, Alexander said they had been married by 'a half merk Minister' in Linlithgow the previous year, so he was justified in claiming her as his wife. Agnes responded that 'long after this pretended marriage He solicited the pursuer and her father to have himself proclaimed and regularly married to the Pursuer without in the least hinting that he had been privately married' – and since then he had actually married another woman. The commissaries ordered Alexander to appear in court and be judicially examined; when he failed to do so they found Agnes free of any marriage and put him to silence on the subject.[12]

The 1785 action of Jean Low against Thomas Morrison, sailor at Charlestown near Dunfermline, is bizarre.[13] Thomas went so far as to raise a declarator of marriage counter-process, describing an actual ceremony – in November 1784 at Alloa – and producing a certificate. Jean appeared in court and declared that while she was staying with her brother in Alloa she saw Thomas only once, and she slept every night at her brother's until she returned home. The signature on the marriage certificate, she said, was not her handwriting. About a month after this alleged marriage, her father, John Low, was surprised one night while the family were at supper 'at hearing the trample of a horse at that hour of the night'. It was his son, who seemed 'to be in great confusion' and blurted out, '"Now father Ile tell you Morrison has spread a report that he is married to your daughter".' Jean 'having then come into the room' her father 'asked her if there was such a thing as a marriage betwixt her and Morrison to which she answered she never was married either to Morrison or to any other Man whatever'.

When Thomas appeared in court he declared that the marriage lines were written by a man named John Gray (about whom he knew nothing), who married them at Alloa. When asked 'how the lines came to be dated at Stirling' he replied that 'he believed it was to conceal where they were wrote'. He also said that after the ceremony they were bedded in the house of Peter Boyd in the presence of witnesses. He was allowed to bring proof.

John Reid, shipmaster at Charlestown, testified that he saw the couple sign marriage lines and go to bed. The man who married them was George Haig; he did 'not believe this George Haig to be a Clergyman but has heard since the adventure or meeting in Boyds house to which he has deponed that Haig has celebrated irregular marriages in the town of Falkirk'. Reid said that he himself wrote the marriage lines, which 'were dictated by George Haig who delivered them to the parties and said it was so cold a night that he could not write the lines as his fingures were benumbed'. Reid also claimed to have heard Jean say that if Thomas 'ventured ever to divulge the marriage any time before her fathers death she would deny it'.

Other witnesses were not so helpful to Thomas's cause. Elizabeth Hamilton, Peter Boyd's wife, was not sure if Jean was the woman whom she saw in bed with Thomas, as she 'was differently dressed which makes a difference in persons looks' (Elizabeth thought 'she would know the Girl that was in bed with the pursuer if she was to see her in the same dress'.) The servant, Lilias Boyd, testified that Thomas brought a woman who 'was dressed in a red Joseph or Riding coat a printed short gown a blue petticoat as she thinks and a night mutche [cap] and green ribbons', and Lilias heard after George Haig went away that there had been a marriage but knew nothing more about it. She could not say if Jean (whom she saw in court) was the woman in the house that night 'as she kept the hood of the Joseph over her face and upon her throwing off the Joseph she immediately went into bed and her back was to the deponent'.

Jean's first witness was Peter Boyd who declared that to his knowledge George Haig had not celebrated a marriage in his house on the date in question; a couple had been bedded there, but he never saw the woman's face. Jean's brother and father testified to her denial of any marriage. George Haig had originally been cited by Thomas, who then changed his mind, so he appeared for Jean instead. He testified that 'he did not see the pursuer married to the defender in the house of Peter Boyd vintner in Alloa ... or at any other time'.

The commissaries found Thomas's libel not proven and assoilzied Jean. Thomas kept appealing against this decision until the commissaries told their clerks not to accept any more petitions from him. Was the whole thing some kind of attempted con by Thomas? Or was there a genuine marriage, which Jean had doubts about even at the time? In which case, was George Haig later bribed to testify as he did? It is certainly one of the most peculiar cases in the records.

The 1804 case of Margaret Aitken against James Fergusson, tenant in Laggan of Strathyre, Perthshire, proclaimed, according to James's lawyer, 'the unhappy effects arising in this part of the Kingdom from the looseness with which marriage is still permitted or winked at'.[14] The parties 'were most improperly induced to follow up a private attachment betwixt them by the rapid mode of a declaration of marriage before a certain magistrate and in an ale house', but no sooner was this done than Margaret repented the act. Subsequently they both 'disclaimed all connection with one another, subscribing a paper to that purpose, which was deposited in the hands of a third party'.

Margaret thought that was the end of the matter, but one day James encountered Margaret and an uncle of hers in an inn when someone there 'most unjustifiably and officiously made an instant allusion to the old irregularity and, shutting the door, very impertinently proposed to bring them together'. Margaret, angry and upset, rushed out of the room, and, assuming that James had played a part in this, raised this action of freedom. James declared that he had had no such intention, and also denied calumniating her so he did not think he should be liable for damages and expenses. Margaret replied that 'having been frequently exposed to the illnatured observations of an officious invidious Neighbourhood', she had naturally assumed that James 'was privately encouraging such', especially after the meeting at the inn. However, she now accepted that he had had nothing to do with it. The commissaries found that she was not married to James and decreed that he keep silent on the subject, but they did not find him liable for damages.

Another 1804 case – that of Isabella Ramsay against James Duncan, miller at Philpstown mill (West Lothian) – was much nastier.[15] James had been going around saying that they 'had interchanged marriage lines accepting each other as husband and wife, and that the pursuer in consequence thereof had given the use of her body to him'. She was about to marry another man, but James told the minister that she was his wife. The kirk session had found no marriage proven, but to establish this legally Isabella raised an action for declarator of freedom. She said that one day when she was alone James came round and 'produced a line he had ready written and signed', asking her to sign it too. She refused and told him if he 'left any such Letter there she would put it in the fire'. He did leave it, and she burnt it. When Isabella showed herself determined to carry on the action, James started saying things like, 'if the pursuer has any regard for her reputation or her future comfortable life, She ought to have desisted from the present process'.

At James's request, Isabella was examined in court. She declared that James often came round 'and paid her particular attention, but that she discouraged his addresses'. She also declared that when James left behind the marriage line she kept it for a day or two, without showing it to anyone, and then burnt it. And she said that she and he 'never were in private room by themselves unless by accident'. The commissaries allowed her to bring proof of her allegations of slander.

James Nimmo, in whose family Isabella resided, testified that some months earlier when she was courted by Peter Kerr, he (Nimmo) was having a drink with James and his brother John. In the course of conversation John asked Nimmo if it was true that Isabella was to marry Kerr, and Nimmo replied that 'it certainly was true, for that Kerr had applied to him to put a Cot house in order for them and he supposed they would be married as soon as it was ready.' James then said, 'Damn it, this shall not be, for I have used her as my wife, and I know every part of her body as well as you do that of your wife.' It was after this that James went to the minister to thwart her proposed marriage. He also told Nimmo that Isabella had a marriage line from him. Nimmo told Isabella what James had said, 'when she denied that he had ever any carnal connection with her, and mentioned that he had left her a marriage line against her will, which she had burned'. After that James said in the presence of witnesses 'that he had often slept with her in that bed (pointing to the bed in the room)'. Isabella was present and said it was not true.

Nimmo's spouse, Henrietta Wilkie (Isabella's cousin), warned him that 'he should take care what he said as he might be called to account for using such language'. Prior to that Henrietta 'had a notion that the defender was making up to the pursuer and had a regard for her, but she knew that the pursuer had none for him.'

Perhaps they had had some kind of relationship, but they had certainly never married. The commissaries found claim of a marriage to be 'false calumnious and injurious', put him to perpetual silence, and found her free to marry as she wished. They also ruled that he had 'grossly slandered the said Isabella Ramsay pursuer by saying that in consequence of an interchange of marriage lines he had carnal knowledge of her person', so he was liable for £20 damages plus all expenses.[16] James asked to be allowed to produce proof of his allegations, but on appeal to the Court of Session his request was refused, and the commissaries reaffirmed their decision.

This discussion of cases where one party sought to disprove rather than to prove a marriage helps to round off the story, but there is one aspect of these court cases yet to be considered, and the questions raised at the beginning of the book have still to be answered.

Notes

1 CC8/5/9.
2 Ibid.
3 CC8/5/30.
4 CC8/5/31. The man was William Hardy, fisherman in Cockenzie.
5 CC8/6/70.
6 CC8/5/29/2.
7 CC8/5/9.
8 Elias Scott's adventures in Spain, France and Naples are fascinating but, alas, not relevant to the present book. I refer anyone interested to the original process papers or to my transcription on disc.
9 CC8/5/17.
10 CC8/6/166.
11 His abandoned divorce action is in CC8/6/164.
12 CC8/5/17.
13 CC8/5/18.
14 CC8/5/28.
15 Ibid.
16 On top of the damages and costs he was also liable for £3 'payable to the procurator fiscal of Court for behoof of the Charity work house of Canongate'. This is not something I encountered in any other case. It may have been a feature in some cases of scandal (defamation), a type of case I did not examine in the Commissary Court records unless it was part of an action of freedom.

CHAPTER 13

THE VERDICT

ACCORDING to law a man and woman were either married or not married; there could be no shades of grey in the verdict. Yet the commissaries did have a way of indicating whether they considered a woman had been justified in raising the legal action by the way in which they apportioned costs. In most cases, recognising the disadvantages that women laboured under, they did not find unsuccessful women pursuers liable for damages. Two examples may be given here. One is the 1776 case of Janet Lindsay against John McGirdy, both of them servants in Dunbartonshire.[1] John fathered Janet's child, and both parties satisfied church discipline by being rebuked three times before the congregation for fornication. But when the banns were proclaimed for John's marriage to another woman Janet complained to the Justice of the Peace, and when that did not avail her she raised this action. John swore in court that he had never promised her marriage, and Janet adduced no evidence, so the commissaries assoilzied him, but they refused his petition that she be made liable for expenses. The 1826 case of Euphemia Inglis against Captain Charles Barry was mentioned in Chapter 4.[2] Euphemia had been the mistress of a lieutenant in Charles's regiment before Charles 'took her into Keeping', and though he had written her fond letters she had never been acknowledged as anything other than his kept mistress. Euphemia, who bore a daughter while the case was being heard, had no proof of a different relationship, so the commissaries assoilzied Charles – but they did not find expenses due.

If the commissaries considered that both those women – and the overwhelming majority of other women – should not have to meet the cost of their claims – then in what circumstances did a woman have to do so?

In the 1768 case of Grizel McBrair against Thomas Paterson, Grizel alleged that they were married at Dumfries in 1763. Thomas produced an extract from the kirk session of Carlaverock of January 1764 when Grizel unsuccessfully tried to claim Thomas as her husband, at which time she was 'rebuked for her Impudence and Calumny with a Caution to her to be more Circumspect in her behaviour for the future'. Four years later when he was proclaimed for marriage with another woman, Grizel tried to stop the banns. After he denied everything under oath (even having ever been in a room alone with her), the commissaries assoilzied him and, despite objections by her lawyer, found her liable for expenses.[3] There was no child in this case, and she had once been told off for trying to claim Thomas as her husband without a shred of evidence, and now was at it again, so the commissaries thought it right to penalise her.

In 1787 Margaret Hardie, in Beecraigs, West Lothian, claimed that William Potter, who fathered her daughter, had courted her for marriage. But the best her witnesses could offer was that they had seen her dancing with William (but he also danced with other girls), that William had expressed great fondness for her (but never that he would take her 'to the half merk marriage'), and that he 'was endeavouring to kiss' her (but he may not even have succeeded!). The commissaries assoilzied William and found Margaret liable for expenses. She petitioned against this and even appealed to the Court of Session, but she still had to pay.[4] Margaret had wasted everyone's time.

In the 1795 case of Jean McFarlane against Thomas Downie, weaver in Fintry, Jean's only proof of a 'bedding' was witnesses' accounts of a boisterous occasion when both parties were pulled and pushed, along with one or two others, into a bed, 'the bottom of which broke down', so 'they all then came out of the bed as fast as they could'. When the action was raised Thomas had been married to another woman for the best part of a year, and had a child, so the commissaries' finding Jean liable for expenses was a strong rebuke for her frivolous and vexatious claim.[5]

In the 1818 case of Maria Stein Begrie against George Hamilton, paymaster of the Renfrewshire militia, the couple met on a steamboat on the Clyde. She subsequently wrote him a letter, and he took her to live with him as his mistress. Maria alleged that the letter she produced from George proved a marriage. The case was bitterly fought for over a year and a half, at which point George advised the court that Maria 'had lately demonstrated her own conviction of the groundlessness of her claims by a step of a very decisive and unequivocal nature … she had married a Gentleman in London – notice of that had been given in the newspapers from which the defender first learned it'. He hoped that the commissaries 'would mark their disapprobation of the conduct of the Pursuer by finding her liable in full expences'. Maria answered that soon after the commencement of the action George had 'married another lady', and, though she did not object to his being assoilzied, in view of George's letter she did not think she should be liable for expenses. The commissaries disapproved of her conduct and found her liable for the expenses, which were hefty.[6]

The commissaries were not stupid. They appreciated that the burden of proof was difficult, and that reasonable claims could fail, but they did not like being imposed upon.

We now turn back to the questions raised at the end of Chapter 1. It was noted there that some English historians perceived irregular marriage as a 'problem', with Hardwicke's Marriage Act as the solution. However, debate in England continued after its passage; repeal was suggested, the statute was modified several times, and a new Act was passed in 1836. R B Outhwaite, who believes that its passage was a necessity, has to concede that 'the Act did not put a stop to clandestinity; it simply forced it to change its forms.'[7] Eve Tavor Bannet, who takes a negative view of the legislation, comments that even at the time some women 'understood that the Marriage Act had problematised female virtue and women's sexual conduct by creating a disjunction between the morality or "troth" of sexual unions and their legality. For what had been declared null and void by the Marriage Act was not the moral validity of the promise plighted by a man and a woman as they hopped into bed – only its legal consequences.'[8]

However, the idea that irregular marriage was a 'problem', which English law had tackled but which Scottish law had not, was also prevalent in Scotland in the nineteenth century. In 1830 William Chambers wrote: 'The Scotch have fallen into the error of making the negotiation of a matrimonial union too simple and indistinct.'[9] More forceful was Lord Brougham in 1849 who considered Scottish marriage law 'the least like the law of a civilised community of any with which I am acquainted in any country'. Again, it was the 'extreme facility afforded to parties to contract that most important of all obligations' that he objected to.[10]

We consider later whether it was really so easy to contract a marriage, at least in a form the courts would uphold. But even if it had been easy, why was this so upsetting? Certainly, there have been enough examples of bigamy and fraud in the preceding chapters to demonstrate that Scottish marriage law was open to abuse, and a desire to curtail such abuses was natural. But who exactly were those commentators wishing to protect?

David Lemmings argues that Hardwicke's Act 'was passed to protect the interests of families against the powerful forces of affection between individuals'.[11] By 'families' he means, of course, the propertied. From the second half of the century onwards Scottish elite families had less control over their offspring's choice of marriage partner than their English counterparts. In 1849 the Honourable Stephen Lushington told a Select Committee that one of the principal reasons for Hardwicke's Act 'was in consequence of young men, heirs and persons in that situation, having been seduced into marriage; Lord Hardwicke's Marriage Act was rather for the protection of men than for the protection of women.' And Lord Brougham knew that many English parents would not send their sons, who were 'heirs to a fortune, or possessed of a fortune', to a Scottish university, for fear that they 'would be married in 24 hours'. In some of those families 'the second or other sons have gone to

Edinburgh, but not the eldest son'.[12] So, when commentators objected to the 'ease' of marriage in Scotland they were really expressing their fears of a man being 'entrapped' into marriage by a lower ranking woman, who had rights under Scottish law that she did not possess under English law.

A perennial cause of anxiety was the ubiquitous maidservant. In the eighteenth century moralists saw liaisons between masters or sons of masters and their servantmaids 'as the result of artful, libidinous young women corrupting naive, untutored boys'.[13] In 1830 William Chambers wrote that declarator of marriage actions were 'in almost every instance, initiated by women in the lower ranks of life, and especially house servants, against men in better circumstances', and considered 'the ease with which they generally establish their point as very injurious'.[14] He was quite wrong on both points, as we have seen from the variety of cases discussed in previous chapters. But the perception – the fear – is the giveaway.

Another objection to Scottish marriage law was its sheer messiness. Judges and administrators like things to be clear cut. Lord Brougham claimed that 'some persons have gone to the grave without declaring that to be a marriage which at any moment they might have done, but which, for some particular reason, they never did.' He also knew of at least one recent case where a man whom he knew to be validly married 'bought off' the woman and married someone else.[15] Such possibilities were anathema to a conservative elite who believed in a tightly regulated society.

However, not every nineteenth-century commentator wanted Scotland to follow England's example over marriage law. James Fergusson, one of the commissaries at the end of our period, could see 'neither the necessity nor the expediency of such a change'. As far as he was concerned the modes of constituting a marriage

have a natural foundation in equity, and accord with the best feelings of humanity when no deceit has been practised, and while the parties alone and their issue are concerned in the questions which the irregularity of the transactions may produce. Experience, too, has naturally and justly attached the people of Scotland to usages and laws which have, from time immemorial, prevailed here, without creating disorder, or evil of any magnitude .... Above all, it is extremely doubtful, whether the prevention of fraud and injustice, which doubtless must be the object in view, when any change is contemplated, would, in this kingdom, be better insured by the introduction of any unvarying preliminary forms and solemnities in the ritual of marriage which could not be made easy of observance, or acceptable to the great body of the population.[16]

Fergusson was a pragmatist. The idea that regularising marriage would abolish fraud was, as far as he was concerned, nonsensical. In 'regular' marriages public notice was rarely given, 'as being altogether unfashionable and neglected among the upper ranks, and accompanied, when it did take place, very rarely with any description which could convey knowledge of the parties who entertained the purpose of marriage'. His suggestion was that rather than attempt to change the law, a national register of marriages should be kept.[17] But this was an idea before its time.

Returning to the idea that marriage in Scotland was too easy, Edward Topham wrote in 1776 that a man in Scotland

> *can scarce be said to know when he is married or not, as his own consent is no part of the business It is sufficient that two or three people determine it without his participation. A woman who has no money nor much virtue takes it into her head that it would be a very proper thing for her to marry such a man, and she does it. She brings two people to swear that he called her his wife and that they passed the night as such together. There is not the least occasion that there should be one word of truth in all this, or that people who are unconcerned should believe it, but notwithstanding that a marriage is confirmed accordingly to the Law wisely made for that purpose.[18]*

This notion continued to prevail throughout the nineteenth century. 'It is commonly believed in England that there is a considerable risk in Scotland of being married without knowing it,' wrote a Scottish advocate in the 1890s. Indeed, Wilkie Collins based a whole novel (Man and Wife) on this misconception. However, the Scottish advocate pointed out that 'peculiar as Scotch marriage law is, the English tourist is not exposed to this risk of accidental marriage. The Court must be satisfied that the two people seriously and soberly agreed to be married.'[19]

The figures in Chapter 1, which revealed that in contested cases two-thirds of women pursuers were unsuccessful in establishing a marriage, give the lie to any notion that it was simple to trap a man into a marriage in Scotland. Again, William Chambers is illuminating. 'It is a notorious fact', he opined, 'that the law here is far too favourable to the woman, who, if she do not accomplish her purpose through the aid of lawyers who are willing to take up her case, is at least sure of putting the man to much inconvenience and expense.'[20] There is a kernel of truth here; not that the law was 'far too favourable' to women, but that it gave them a chance for self-assertion rarely afforded elsewhere. It was not just Scottish law but the attitude of the court that made this possible (and therefore a threat to men). Olwen Hufton, looking at European separation cases, observes that the judges and lawyers were all men and had not experienced unwanted pregnancies and the like, and that they started 'with an assumption of a particular God-ordained order', in which women were naturally inferior to men. But, she also realises, they saw 'themselves as guardians of moral order; and moral order is best maintained when the weak have a measure of protection'.[21]

This is a key point that has emerged in many of the cases described in earlier chapters. The commissaries were well aware of the disadvantages women laboured under, and what is striking is the extent to which they gave them every opportunity to prove their case. The only basis in reality for the fear that a young servant maid could seduce the court as easily as her master was if he really had promised her marriage, for a promise followed by sex constituted a marriage.

A study of divorce in Scotland suggested that by the early nineteenth century many couples apparently lived together without having married.[22] After the breakdown of church discipline, marriage was not policed, and if a couple behaved themselves no one enquired too closely. The material in this book bears out this contention and helps to explain it: under Scottish law if a man and a woman lived together as a married couple and needed to transact any business as man and wife then they would be legally recognised as such, but if the necessity never arose, and they decided to part, either party could marry someone else since the first relationship had never been declared a marriage. The number of cases encountered in the book in which a man or woman married someone else while the court case was still pending, and continued to cohabit with the second 'spouse' even after the first marriage was declared legal, suggests a surprisingly modern philosophy that nothing is forever, because people change and relationships change.

It may have pained some nineteenth-century commentators, but Scottish marriage law suited the majority of the populace. Marriage by declaration de praesenti and per verba de futuro remained valid in Scotland until the Marriage (Scotland) Act 1939, and Scots law still recognises irregular marriage by habit and repute.[23]

Notes

1 CC8/5/15.
2 CC8/6/150.
3 CC8/6/26.
4 CC8/5/19.
5 CC8/6/63. Jean claimed to be pregnant. Thomas said that she was 'a woman well advanced in life, And considerably past the period when women give up bearing Children.' (Thomas was 21.) He also said that she had 'been giving out for these two Years bypast that she was with Child, but to this hour has never brought forth one'.
6 CC8/5/38. George's letter to her father went as follows: 'In Several Circumstances Concurring to render my Marriage with Miss Bagray at present improper I have intended and do intend to Marry Miss Maria Stein Baigrie as soon as I find that Circumstances will permit me without injuring her and myself.' Maria's extraordinary letter to him after the

first meeting on the steamboat went like this: 'Sir Pardon the presumption of a female in making known to you the emotions which have agitated her mind since She had the pleasure of meeting you in one of the steam boats – From the time you left her she has been a stranger to happiness All her thoughts have been concentrated in you – It is from you she expects an alleviation of her grief – If disappointed elle murra pray vous Should you deign to give your proper address her name and circumstances shall follow, signed Maria Le Rue de Granot 20 Febry 1818.'

7   R B Outhwaite, *Clandestine Marriage in England 1500–1850* (London & Rio Grande, 1995), 167.

8   Eve Tavor Bannet, 'The Marriage Act of 1753: "A Most Cruel Law for the Fair Sex"', *Eighteenth-Century Studies*, Vol 30, No 3 (1997), 241. I owe this reference to Mary Prior.

9   William Chambers, *The Book of Scotland* (Edinburgh, 1830), 213. I owe this reference to Tristram Clarke.

10 Report of the Select Committee on Marriage (Scotland), PP 1849, XII, 7, 15. Lord Brougham moved from the Scottish to the English bar in 1804. When his English colleagues 'come to see what constitutes a Scotch marriage, they are always at first incredulous, they cannot believe that there is any civilised country which has such a marriage law'.

11 David Lemmings, 'Marriage and the Law in the Eighteenth Century: Hardwicke's Marriage Act of 1753', *Historical Journal*, 39, 2 (1996), 359.

12 Report of the Select Committee, 12–13, 24.

13 Paul Langford, *A Polite and Commercial People – England 1727–1783* (Oxford, 1989), 119.

14 Chambers, *The Book of Scotland*, 218.

15 Report of the Select Committee, 14.

16 James Fergusson, *Treatise on the Present State of Consistorial Law in Scotland* (Edinburgh, 1829), 123, 125, 130.

17 Ibid., 124–5, 133–6.

18 Edward Topham, *Letters from Edinburgh; written in the years 1774 and 1775: containing some observations, customs, manners, and laws, of the Scotch nation, during a six months residence in Edinburgh* (Edinburgh, 1776). Quoted in Archer v. Berrie (1804) CC8/5/28.

19 'An Advocate' (F P Walton), *Marriage Regular and Irregular* (Glasgow, 1893), 19, 38–42. Walton continued: 'There is one exception to this rule. If a man persuade a woman to go through a sufficient form of marriage of any kind with him, and she seriously intend marriage, and believe him to be in earnest, he will not be allowed to come into Court afterwards and say, "I never meant to marry her. I was only deceiving her." For it is a general rule of law that a person shall not be permitted to take advantage of his own fraud.'

20 Chambers, *The Book of Scotland*, 218.

21 Olwen Hufton, *The Prospect Before Her – A History of Women in Western Europe 1500–1800* (London, 1995), 262.

22 Leah Leneman, *Alienated Affections – The Scottish Experience of Divorce and Separation 1684–1830* (Edinburgh, 1998), 330.

23 W D H Sellar, 'Marriage, divorce and the forbidden degrees: Canon law and Scots law', in W N Osborough ed, *Explorations in Law and History – Irish Legal History Society Discourses, 1988–1994* (Dublin, 1995), 67.

BIBLIOGRAPHY

'An Advocate' (F P Walton), *Marriage Regular and Irregular* (Glasgow, 1893).

Bannet, Eve Tavor: 'The Marriage Act of 1753: "A Most Cruel Law for the Fair Sex"', *Eighteenth-Century Studies*, Vol 30, No 3 (1997).

Boulton, Jeremy: 'Clandestine marriages in London: an examination of a neglected urban variable', *Urban History*, Vol 20, No 2 (Oct 1993).

Brown, Roger Lee: 'The Rise and Fall of the Fleet Marriages', in R B Outhwaite, ed, *Marriage and Society – Studies in the Social History of Marriage* (London, 1981).

Chambers, William: *The Book of Scotland* (Edinburgh, 1830).

'Claverhouse' (Meliora C Smith), *Irregular Border Marriages* (Edinburgh, 1934)

Fergusson, James: *Treatise on the Present State of Consistorial Law in Scotland* (Edinburgh, 1829).

Forte, A D M: 'Some Aspects of the Law of Marriage in Scotland: 1500–1700' in Elizabeth Craik, ed, *Marriage and Property – Women and Marital Customs in History* (Aberdeen, 1984).

Fraser, Patrick: *Treatise on the Law of Scotland as applicable to the Personal and Domestic Relations* (Edinburgh, 1846), Vol I.

Gillis, John R: 'Conjugal Settlements: Resort to Clandestine and Common Law Marriage in England and Wales, 1650–1850', in John Bossy ed, *Disputes and Settlements – Law and Human Relations in the West* (Cambridge, 1983).

Gillis, John R: *For Better, For Worse – British Marriages 1600 to the Present* (Oxford, 1985)

Gowing, Laura *Domestic Dangers – Women, Words and Sex in Early Modern London* (Oxford, 1996).

Grant, Francis J, ed: *The Commissariat of Edinburgh: Consistorial Processes and Decreets, 1658–1800* (Edinburgh, 1909).

Gregory, Dr: *A Father's Legacy to His Daughters* (London, 1826 edn).

Head-König, Anne-Lise: 'Forced marriages and forbidden marriages in Switzerland: state control of the formation of marriage in catholic and protestant cantons in the eighteenth and nineteenth centuries', *Continuity and Change* 8 (3), 1993.

Houston, Rab, and Manon van der Heijden: 'Hands Across the Water: The Making and Breaking of Marriage Between Dutch and Scots in the Mid Eighteenth Century', *Law and History Review* 15 (1997).

Hufton, Olwen: *The Prospect Before Her – A History of Women in Western Europe 1500–1800* (London, 1995).

Ingram, Martin: 'Spousals Litigation in the English Ecclesiastical Courts c.1350–1640', in R B Outhwaite ed, *Marriage and Society – Studies in the Social History of Marriage* (London, 1981).

Langford, Paul: *A Polite and Commercial People – England 1727–1783* (Oxford, 1989).

Lemmings, David: 'Marriage and the Law in the Eighteenth Century: Hardwicke's Marriage Act of 1753', *Historical Journal*, 39, 2 (1996).

Leneman, Leah: *Alienated Affections – The Scottish Experience of Divorce and Separation 1684–1830* (Edinburgh, 1998).

Leneman, Leah, and Rosalind Mitchison: 'Clandestine Marriage in the Scottish Cities 1660–1780', *Journal of Social History* (Vol 26, No 4, 1993).

Leneman, Leah, and Rosalind Mitchison: *Sin in the City – Sexuality and Social Control in Urban Scotland 1660–1780* (Edinburgh, 1998).

Lothian, Maurice: *The Law, Practice and Style Peculiar to the Consistorial Actions Transferred to the Court of Session* (Edinburgh, 1830).

Macfarlane, Alan: *Marriage and Love in England – Modes of Reproduction 1300–1840* (Oxford, 1986).

Marshall, Rosalind K: *Virgins and Viragos – A History of Women in Scotland from 1080 to 1980* (London, 1983).

Mitchison, Rosalind, and Leah Leneman; *Girls in Trouble – Sexuality and Social Control in Rural Scotland 1660–1780* (Edinburgh, 1998).

Outhwaite, R B, ed: *Marriage and Society – Studies in the Social History of Marriage* (London, 1981).

Outhwaite, R B: *Clandestine Marriage in England 1500–1850* (London & Rio Grande, 1995).

Ovington, John: *The Duties, Advantages, Pleasures, and Sorrows, of the Marriage State* (London, 1813).

Report of the Select Committee on Marriage (Scotland), PP 1849, XII.

Sellar, W D H: 'Marriage, divorce and the forbidden degrees: Canon law and Scots law', in W N Osborough, ed, *Explorations in Law and History – Irish Legal History Society Discourses, 1988–1994* (Dublin, 1995).

Shoemaker, Robert: *Gender in English Society 1650–1850 – The Emergence of Separate Spheres?* (London, 1998).

Smout, T C: 'Scottish Marriage, Regular and Irregular 1500–1940' in R B Outhwaite ed, *Marriage and Society – Studies in the Social History of Marriage* (London, 1981).

Staves, Susan: 'British Seduced Maidens', *Eighteenth Century Studies* 14 (1980–1).

Stone, Lawrence: *Road to Divorce – England 1530–1987* (Oxford, 1992).

Stone, Lawrence: *Uncertain Unions – Marriage in England 1660–1753* (Oxford, 1992).

Symonds, Deborah: A *Weep Not for Me – Women, Ballads, and Infanticide in Early Modern Scotland* (Pennsylvania, 1997).

Watt, Jeffrey R: *The Making of Modern Marriage – Matrimonial Control and the Rise of Sentiment in Neuchâtel, 1550–1800* (Ithaca and London, 1992).